A New England Lobster Tale

Growing up with *Homarus americanus*

By Russ James

Disclaimer. All facts, circumstances, quotes, historical records, and scientific references can be found in the writings listed on page 161. Some of the following is partly a work of lifetime recollections and memories. There were no attempts to change, preclude, or hide memories by the author for any reason, although some may have faded with time. All reading is up to the reader, to determine what is fact and what may be fiction.

A New England Lobster Tale
Growing up with Homarus Americanus
1st Edition, Hardcover – published 2013

ISBN-10: 0-615-86434-1
ISBN-13: 978-0-615-86434-1

"Someday we'll share lobster in paradise, for eternity.."

__Preface__

I started writing this book in 1993. It was right around the time that I thought that I knew everything there is about lobsters. Now it's twenty years later and a lot has changed in my life since then. One thing I now realize is that you'll never know everything about a lobster, no one does. Even the most seasoned Maine lobsterman has trepidation over the season to come. I looked, saw, did things with, and read nearly everything there is to read about the American lobster. And yet, I found that there isn't enough time in 100 lifetimes to completely understand the lobster. I don't pretend to try.

It was a fascinating journey in the making of this book. One marine journal pointed to another, and that one pointed to 100 others, infinitum. Books like the Natural History of the American Lobster by Francis Herrick can certainly put you to sleep trying to understand its page after page of dry scientific jargon. While others, like the notes of renowned marine biologists Jelle Atema & Diane Cowan were wondering the same things that I was. Their simple logic made sense to me. It soon proved true, as I try to describe it to you.

Moreover, this book is written from the notes made in my journal of life. A realistic view of the American lobster as they came from relative obscurity through the heyday of today. And the possibility of what the lobster might be in the future. What I present to you is a story of the American lobster as told by me, a Connecticut Yankee.

Table of Contents

In the beginning…

A good friend once told me to look into the sea of faces. There are men and women, different ages, races, colors, and walks of life. Some are in a hurry, some walk slow, and some are in a wheelchair who don't walk at all. He said that each of these people has their own story. Stories that are as interesting and unique as the one before them, if you'll just take the time to hear it.

For many years I muddled along, running from place to place, never stopping to smell the roses. I looked, but I did not see; I breathed but I didn't smell, and I mindlessly ate, but didn't taste. God sent me a message in the form of a heart attack & later a stroke. His message was heard loud and clear. Finally, this sent home the true meaning of what life is about.

Let me tell you the story of a lobster and I…

THE AMERICAN LOBSTER

*T*o some, lobsters are stupid, oceangoing spiders that blindly crawl into sunken offshore crates. They are mindless, clumsy, brutes incapable of forethought or emotion. These filthy cockroaches on steroids are only fit for slow death in boiling hot water. To most people, lobsters only become useful after turning crimson red and being placed on a plate. The dancing red lobster figurines, place mats, and lampshade souvenirs make wonderful keepsakes from that summer vacation at the shore. In the eyes and imagination of many, this is what lobsters do at their day job. They are overly priced; iconic shoreline treats only fit for table fare and wall display. Very few look beyond the thorny exterior and grotesque outward appearance. It seems that the very young and the very old are among these few. They have the time and open mind to look beyond what meets the eye of those too busy to stop and smell the roses, as was my case for many years.

A time ago I was walking past the seafood section of a large inland urban supermarket. I love to observe people's comments and reactions as they gather around a lobster tank. The emotions run from "yummy, they taste good" to the inevitable sour-faced revulsion at the mere sight of a live lobster. On this particular day, a little girl wearing a delicate pastel sundress was standing in front of the lobster tank. The lobsters strutted and lightly danced on tiptoes in front of her. She had her little nose pressed against the glass and was completely mesmerized as the lobsters pirouetted and whirled about. Suddenly a handsome large male lobster strutted from the herd.

You can easily identify male from female New England lobsters by their claws and abdomen (tail) section. Females have much wider "tail" (abdomen) shells and smaller claws. This is to maximize egg bearing attachment surface at the expense of minimized hand-to-hand combat assets. Males have narrower "tail" (abdomen) shell widths and larger claws for sleekness and strength in battle. This big fellow with massive claws had been quietly watching the girl from his corner in the tank. He was clearly the alpha lobster and all the others scooted out of his way as he came face to face with the little girl. Less than ½ inch of Plexiglas separated these two curious beings. I knew exactly what they both were thinking, more so the lobster than the girl. You see, I've observed lobsters in the wild and in captivity for over 4 decades. This moment was really magical for me as I stood in the background. She was not afraid of the creature nearly half her size, nor was the lobster of her. The lobster did not respond with traditional defensive raised claws, he knew that he could've easily crushed the girl's arm off at the elbow if he chose to do so. They both surveyed each other for a long minute and the girl gently tapped a small finger on the glass. At that moment the big lobster tapped both his antennae against the glass where the girl's finger was tapping. The most sensitive of all human and lobster tactile sensory points joined for a moment in time. Both creatures looked at each other in the face. She quietly said; "Hello, lobster". This massive lobster, the culmination of 511 million years of evolutionary refinement, the ultimate survivor and highly adapted supreme predator of a dark world we'll never live to see, softly rubbed his antennae at the girl's fingertip. And at that moment, in a way that only the little girl and I alone could understand, this majestic creature said "Hello, human".

Just then the girl's mother hurriedly rolled a carriage past and shouted a threat to the little girl; "You better behave or I'll put that lobster in your bed tonight." The poor little girl reeled backwards in a ball of tears, completely terrified. This was one of the most despicable parental acts I've ever witnessed in my life. That little girl could've become another Diane Cowan, senior marine scientist and founder of the Lobster Conservancy, renowned champion of the New England Lobster.

And I wondered if that little girl would ever remember her once in a lifetime communion with an animal that leads such a complex and interesting life? I saw in an instant what the little girl saw in the massive creature before her. A unique being, with the forethought and inquisitiveness to step forward among the mindless rabble of those about to die, and say "hello". That moment was so special to me; I will never forget it. That big lobster came home with me and was with me for about a year. In that time he showed me things that I'd never known in my wildest dreams. He let me see some of his secrets, and all the things that I'd often wondered. When our final days came, he saluted me and said "Goodbye, human".

Accordingly, this entire book and most of my life has been dedicated to and intertwined with these amazing creatures. Do not let their thorny appearance mislead you. Large and small they are not unlike us humans. Some are smart and some are stupid. Some are strong and some are weak. But one thing is an absolute certainty. They are all inquisitive and wistful. They are also capable of learning and to remember things. To a fault they are fearless of all other beings, regardless of size or type. And finally, they are not all the same, but as unique as the human fingerprint. They are,

<u>Homarus Americanus</u>

A TASTE TO LIVE & DIE FOR

*W*hen asked, "What does lobster taste like?" you cannot give the pat answer, "It tastes like chicken." The very unique sweet, succulent, oceanic taste of lobster is often used as the gold standard of comparison to all foods. Nothing tastes like lobster, other than lobster itself. In culinary vernacular, when comparing two ultimate tasting seafood type delicacies, you often hear the best of the best described as; "It tastes as good as lobster." Rarely do you hear that "It tastes better than lobster." A steaming red lobster on a table is the accepted icon of shear elegance at a glance. It says, "I'm quite well to do and this is fine dining at its best." Have you ever seen an ad with a group of good looking young people sitting around a campfire on a sandy beach at sunset? One is strumming his acoustic guitar with his bikini-clad sweetheart nearby. The waves are gently splashing in the background. The camera for this classic TV commercial ultimately focuses on the centerpiece, a kettle full of sweet corn & clams topped with a pile of red lobsters. Most viewers' eyes go directly from the girls' bikini, the bottle of beer, and the handsome guy, to the lobsters! This traditional "clam bake" scene, topped off with huge portions of steamed lobster represents relaxation and the good life at its zenith.

Although there are many genera of lobster, only 2 are widely eaten. The first of these is *Panulirus*; also know as the "Spiny Lobster". They come in two main species types, Panulirus **argus** (the Atlantic ocean side spiny) and Panulirus **interruptus** (the Pacific ocean side spiny). These lobsters have no claws and are found in warm Florida and California waters. Often called "Rock Lobster", this is a popular item on restaurant menu lists in southern states, the Caribbean, Australia and abroad. Panulirus argus (the Florida spiny) is light colored with dark dots. An average sized argus runs between 1 ~ 2 pounds. Panulirus interruptus (the California spiny) is dark colored, often having crimson red trim around the carapace shell and tail (abdomen) joints. The interruptus varieties average size is much larger than argus, and can be found in the upper 8 ~ 10 pound range.

A few years ago I spent time with some native Floridian SCUBA divers. They were notably reluctant to talk about our mutual underwater hobby, collecting and eating lobsters.

Panulirus Argus.
The Florida Spiny Lobster

They spoke of the methods employed by Florida SCUBA divers to collect spiny lobsters. Using a "tickle stick" among other things was completely odd to me. If you poked a "tickle stick" into a New England lobster's hole, you'd pull back a broken crushed stub. Also, the concept of bathtub warm water with unlimited visibility baffled me. I was a New England diver; used to thick wetsuits to slow the onset of hypothermia in cold, murky, low visibility seawater. The daytime capture of lobsters in Speedos was completely unheard of to me.

As the evening went on and the empty beer cans piled high around the campfire, I couldn't help but ask the question that they had avoided all night. "What do spiny lobsters taste like?" This was an innocent question, as I'd never eaten one before. But, apparently these were misconstrued as fighting words and the southerners responded with considerable aplomb! In their humble opinion, not so humbly spoken that night, there was no question that the Florida spiny lobster was the best in the world. They went on and on about this, in no uncertain terms. I finally hoisted a can of beer high in the firelight, a toast to *Panulirus*, "Here's to the spiny lobster!" I made a mental note to NEVER broach the subject again with my dear friends of the coastal southern states.

More info and photos on the panulirus in the section, "New England Lobster vs Florida Spiny Lobster"

The 2nd type of lobster goes by the genus name of *Homarus americanus*. You may have also heard it called any of these nicknames, New England Lobster, Maine Lobster, or Clawed Lobster. The one name that pretty much describes this creature is *"THE AMERICAN LOBSTER"*. My distinguished southern colleagues wince whenever they hear this moniker. I invite you to go to the nearest Internet connected computer and type these words into the Google search engine: AMERICAN LOBSTER. The results and images will say it all.

My first encounter with Homarus americanus, the New England Lobster, was when I was a baby in my mother's arms. She shredded and tenderized a small piece of lobster claw meat. She dipped it in warm melted butter and put it in my mouth. I was a finicky eater as a baby and she would later tell me about that moment, when I first tasted lobster. Many years later she said that my eyes got wide as I gummed the buttery bit of lobster claw meat. My big blue eyes slowly rolled up backward behind my eyelids and closed into a dreamlike state. She said; "It was like you'd seen God for the first time."

My mother simply loved the taste of lobster, as did her best friend Lillian. As a boy growing up, we were not wealthy and the times when lobster was served took on the aura of a religious experience in our house. Newspapers were spread out covering the entire tabletop. Each of the old bluebird rimmed ceramic plates had a neatly arranged set of specific utensils on the left side: a fork, a spoon, a steak knife, a nutcracker, and a silver spike-tipped nut pick. On the right side of the plate there was a mismatched porcelain cereal bowl for the full ½ lb. of melted butter that each of us would receive during the presentation ceremony.

There are many prescribed ways to eat a lobster and countless methods of preparation and recipes (my favorite listed in "The best seafood I ever ate"). To us however, there was only one way to cook a lobster, steamed with melted butter. Any other way of preparation was unthinkable to us, and was simply sacrilegious and unholy. Once (and ONLY ONCE) the old man tried to make lobster thermidor, a creamy cheese & brandy lobster mixture, stuffed back into the shell for appearance's sake. It was nearly cause for divorce and he was reminded of that terrible waste of a cherished lobster until the day he died. To this very day I cannot hear or read the phrase "lobster thermidor" without chuckling aloud to myself and seeing the old man shaking his head in disgust at his own stupidity. To us, and all lobster aficionados like us there is only one way to cook a lobster. Boil or steam it in hot water with melted butter.

The old man would steam the lobsters on our gas stove in a heavy-duty 20-gallon aluminum naval galley kettle. He'd "liberated" it from the Naval salvage yard where he'd worked for thirty years. The lobsters were removed from the pot with a pair of big metal salad tongs (also liberated from Naval salvage). Each steaming hot lobster was laid on its back, tail uncurled, and split in half, head to tail with a big steak knife. The boiling juices were spilled out into the sink and hot lobsters piled on a large metal serving tray (with US Navy insignia on the bottom). He'd set the steaming pile of red deliciousness in the middle of the table, take his seat, and say, "Dig in". My mother would sigh and shake her head as she snatched a lobster off the top of the pile with a wild-eyed look on her face.

She'd blow on her fingers as she stretched open the piping hot lobster thorax with one hand. With the other hand she'd ladle a spoonful of melted butter along the entire split length of the lobster. If we were fortunate enough to have a lemon in the house, she'd squeeze a spray of juice atop the lobster and give it a light dusting of sea salt. She'd just stare at it for a few seconds before digging a spoon into the thorax for the green tamale and red roe (if it was a female lobster). This was first to be immersed in the vat of melted butter and eaten. It was an uncontrollable reflexive action in my mother, with the first taste of lobster, her eyes would roll back in her head and she'd make a throaty "Mmmm" sound. She did this each and every time she ate a lobster until, and including, the day she died. No spoken word could describe the ecstasy that the first taste of lobster gave my mother. This moment to her was apparently better than sex by a long stretch.

Some people simply remove and eat the tail & claws of a lobster as instructionally depicted on all Maine tourist lobster-bibs and platters. Some people go a step further and crack open the claw knuckles. Some people actually eat the tomalley and work for the small scallop sized bits of body meat at the base of the walker legs. There are however, very few people like my mother and her best friend, Lillian. They would nut-pick each and every one of the tinniest shreds of meat from the lobsters' legs and suck the juices from the hollowed out core! They would twist off the outer 2 tail flippers revealing a little known tidbit of meat torn from the tail section. They would eat the white blobs of yogurt looking substance, the lobster's blood when boiled. When encountering a "skinny" post-molted lobster with little meat in it, they would remove the carapace, scoop out the papery gills, dredge them through melted butter and eat them too. When my mother and Lillian were done eating a lobster no joint was left intact. All edible materials including juices were consumed. The only recognizable parts remaining on their plates were the lobsters' carapace, eyestalks and antennae shafts.

After I'd gotten married, my wife used to come with me SCUBA diving at night. We were both certified and licensed for the recreational taking of lobsters "by hand". This being a story that I'll cover later on. One evening we were staying at my parents' house and had returned from a late night lobster dive. Back then lobsters were largely plentiful and easy to catch underwater and we brought back nearly 50lbs. of lobsters in an old military ditty bag (liberated from Naval salvage). For laughs we let them all out on my parents' enclosed concrete patio. It was quite a sight to see, 40 or so big lobsters all walking around on the patio. My mother got up from bed and came out to see what was going on, clutching her nightgown. The next day she never got out of bed. We found that after we'd gone to sleep around 2am, she'd called her friend Lillian over. They cooked up and consumed 6 or more lobsters, EACH! They'd eaten lobsters and melted butter until dawn and were both sick for 3 days. She swore that she would never eat another lobster as long as she lived, like an alcoholic after a bender. My wife and I left a pair of 2-pounders in the crisper bin of my parent's refrigerator when we went home. The old man called a few days later and said; "Mom's back in bed, she just ate both them lobsters you left."

Many years later, my wife, my father, and I were in the hospice where my mother lay dying in bed. She was totally paralyzed from terminal brain cancer and could only slightly move her tongue and lips. Hospice staff and our priest were present to officially ask her if indeed she wanted to have her "Living Will" carried out per her previously written wishes to discontinue mechanical means of feeding at that point. She weakly nodded in the affirmative, knowing full well that this assertion meant she would die within a few days. The facility supervisor asked her, "Lorraine? Is there anything you'd like us to bring you?" She nodded in the affirmative. My father was too broken up to think or speak and the supervisor could not imagine what an elderly paralyzed patient who'd just volunteered to die could possibly have a desire for? My mother hadn't spoken for several months as the paralysis had taken over her facial muscles. She looked at me and her tongue touched the tip of her upper lip and she made the unmistakable sound of "La, lob.." Then a weak breath with tongue pressed to the roof of her mouth, sounding out an "s" sound. I said "Mom? Do you want a lobster?" She nodded in the affirmative. Her last spoken word on earth was *"lobster"*

Later that night I returned with shredded, tenderized, fresh lobster claw meat in a Tupperware dish full of melted Land-O-Lakes butter. The lobster meat was lightly dusted with sea salt and a splash of fresh squeezed lemon, her absolute favorite. I sat on her bed and put small bits of claw meat in her mouth as she'd done with me so many years ago. She could barely chew, could not swallow, and simply savored the flavor on her tongue. I heard a soft "Mmmm" sound and her eyes rolled back in her head. I truly believe that she saw God at that moment. Within the next few hours she would be eating lobster in paradise, for eternity.

Lorraine James at "the camp", July 4th 1985

LIFE IN A SMALL NEW ENGLAND TOWN

*I*n the rural area where we lived, natural foods gathered from field and stream were seasonally abundant. Wild blueberries, bullheads (catfish), quahog clams, venison, tautog (blackfish) and sweet corn were among our weekly diet. Tautog or "Togs" were a highly prized fish for eating, then and now. They have firm, pink, semi-boneless fillets that are great eating, moist, tender, and somewhat sweet tasting. They are an ugly reef dweller type fish with leathery fat lips and porcelain human-like teeth. Their unique teeth enable them to crunch shells, crabs and, unfortunately small lobsters that are a prized food source of the ***Tautoga onitis***. Togs probably eat more lobster per year than all of us humans combined.

The Blackfish aka, tautoga onitis is a great tasting New England game fish.
They are a lobster's worst nightmare, a prime predator of Homarus americanus.

Lobster was considered the cream of the crop and always cost more than any of us could readily afford. It was cause for great discussion and comment whenever anyone had a lobster dinner in town. Conversations would go something like this: "Did you hear that the McGuires had lobster the other day?" "Yup, were they full or soft-shelled?" "I heard they were packed with meat!"

Once when we were kids my friend and I were at the shore and went walking along a well-known parking area. Our families were on vacation and we'd been night fishing. I used my pocket flashlight as we walked out along the rock breakwater wall during low tide. We hopped from rock to rock with the flashlight. I spotted something moving at my feet among the kelp now exposed to the air at low tide and shined the light on it. It was a small dark shelled crustacean with little claws that resembled a lobster. The thing was about seven inches long, from head to tail and had little beady shining eyes. It looked like a big freshwater crawfish on steroids. Then I saw another one of them, about the same size. As I stepped back to widen the light beam, I saw them all over the place! There were thirty or forty of them all about 6 or 7 inches long were crawling around in the rocks at low tide.

I called my pal over to look at these bizarre little ocean-going night beetles. We had no idea what they were and carefully picked one up; pinched between thumb and forefingers from the back, like you would a small lobster. The darn things sure looked and acted like small lobsters. Up until then we'd never seen a lobster that was not over a pound in size, sold in a seafood market and had wooden pegs driven into their claws. God knows what these odd little variations were. We were sure they had to be something harmful and potentially poisonous, whatever they were.

We gathered up 8 or 10 of these snippy little night bugs, put them in a pail and brought them back to my house. We put them in the sink and examined them closely. Bigger than a crawfish and smaller than a lobster, we thought they were some sort of sea scorpion that we'd never seen before.

My pal suggested that we either kill them or boil them up for laughs before throwing them in the trash, as they may have poisonous spikes or pincers. We put them in a pot and boiled them until they turned red like a regular lobster. I put one on the counter and split the little thing open with a butter knife. The meat inside the little scorpion

These are not little sea scorpions; they are indeed "shorty" lobsters.

popped out like popcorn out of a Jiffy-Pop bag. We both dared each other to take a taste of the puffy white substance that the thing was jam packed with. Surely it had to be disgusting to the taste and/or poisonous to humans. Finally, I cut a tiny piece of the white meaty tail substance and gingerly chewed it, ready to spit it out at the faintest foul taste.

It wasn't foul at all? It was somewhat tasty and tasted just like… lobster? I melted some butter, dipped another small piece of tail meat and put the whole thing in my mouth. It was the most tender, sugar sweet, delectable lobster meat I'd ever tasted, or would ever taste in my life. We had taken, cooked, and eaten 10 juvenile "short" lobsters. My pal and I were dumbstruck. He said anything *THAT GOOD* has got to be illegal. And he was right. Had we been caught we could've honestly pled complete and utter stupidity. We'd never seen a short lobster. But, ignorance of the law is no excuse and we never did it again. However, my friend reminds me to this very day that "The taste of them short lobsters was almost worth going to prison for!"

Curiously enough, many years later my pal, Beany, became a backyard champion of the preservation of our natural environment and all living things. He went out topwater lobstering with me one day and we spoke of our experience with those tiny lobsters as kids. This particular day we found absolutely no keeper sized lobsters in my traps. We did however find a pair of lobsters with big claws, both under legal carapace size by less than 1/16th of an inch! Actually, by legal definition of "snug fit" the lobsters were probably keepable. We were looking forward to a fresh lobster dinner back at the cabin, and I tested his stalwartness in character. I asked him, "You wanna' throw these two in the bilge and call it quits?" (Something I have never and will never do). He said, "I'd rather eat the feces out of that rotting menhaden you use for bait than to keep these two lobsters!" Back ashore at the cabin we ended up eating grilled chicken that night. We laughed like hell at our poor luck lobstering and the vision of him eating menhaden poo.

Beany with a fat-clawed short lobster

Back to my story, one day word got around town that a new restaurant had opened, featuring a buffet of "All you can eat Lobster". It was located in nearby North Kingston Rhode Island and called "Custy's". Every adult in our town ended up going to Custy's at one time or another when able to set aside the entry fee. At that time the price of admission was around $15 per person, nearly one-third of my weekly paycheck back then. I recall my first trip to Custy's with several of my teenaged hoodlum pals. We paid cash at the door and walked into what can only be described as a veritable Shangri La of food. There were 50-foot white satin covered tables in every direction. The tables were piled high with beautifully eye appealing and exquisite delicacies of all kinds.

There was a desert table with every sort of pastry, cake, pie, candy, crème filled crepe, and fruity sweetness under the sun. There were 5 carving chefs standing at the ready in their crisp white uniforms with tall stovepipe cooking hats. They waited to carve piping hot meats onto your dish. There were fillet mignon, prime-ribs, lamb, pork, and veal, all delicately seasoned and fresh off the rotisseries and grills. The scent in the room was deliciously indescribable.

And then we saw the seafood table. It was fifty feet of heaven on earth. Piled high, they had every sort of fish under the sun, cooked in every possible configuration including grilled swordfish and pan seared Chilean sea bass. At mid-table sat a row of whole pineapples. They were covered with jumbo shrimp that were skewered onto the pineapples like shimmering waterfalls. Steamed bluecrabs, Louisiana crawfish, and broiled jumbo sea scallops were next in line. We finally saw the pot of gold at the end of the rainbow, a small mountain of steaming red lobsters. They were all neatly arranged with claws forward as if bowing to the customer. The huge lobster-filled stainless steel pan had green chicory lettuce garnishing the edges for eye appeal. The table had its own integrated butter warmer and lemon dispenser. One of the most breathtaking sights any of us had ever seen.

All of this was at your behest. You could eat whatever you wanted, as much as you wanted, for as long as you could stand or sit without passing out or vomiting. Bulimia was unheard of back then, but I know for a fact that some of my friends certainly became selectively restroom bulimic during binge eating sessions at Custy's. We were all hell-bent to get the most bang for our $15 bucks. My all-time record for eating lobsters at Custy's was 13, just over a dozen. My uncle, a large dairy farmer who also loved lobsters nearly as much as my mother, held the Custy's record for many years. He ate 28 lobsters in one all-day sitting. I once saw him eat a lobster at a family picnic. His fingers were the size of large sausage links. He'd scrape two fingers down the entire length of a split lobster, tearing out the papery lungs, leg sockets and brain sack. He'd dunk the entire drooling mess into a butter bowl and jam it all in his mouth. Even my mother found this to be disgusting. I was told, and local legend has it, that my uncle's record at Custy's later fell to a fellow who was on tour of the eastern seaboards' professional wrestling circuit. His name was Andre Roussimoff. He stood 7' 4" tall and weighed over 500 lbs. His stage name was Andre the Giant and he is said to have eaten 40 lobsters at Custy's in one sitting. I was told that no accurate count was recorded because he ate them 3 or 4 at a time, so quickly that counting was impossible. When he'd finished off a full crate of lobsters, it's said that he then consumed a full steamship round of beef before wiping out the entire French pastry table. There are no written accounts of this legend, as it has been passed down orally through the Swamp Yankee network for many years. And a young lady weighing 98 pounds later bested this record by eating 44 lobsters in 12 minutes! This will be covered later on in the tale.

As in all things desirable, the cost of lobsters rose, as did the entry fee at Custy's. It soon reached a breaking point of $79.95 a person. At that point it was more economical to buy as many lobsters as you could possibly stuff down. Custy's closed in 2010, but I'll always remember it. Regardless, costs for either method was beyond the means of the working class in our area. We all had to make due with eating lobster on the rare occasions when discretionary funds were available. Those times were far and few between.

The lust for lobster knew no boundaries back then and it even had a tangible effect on local dating preferences, believe it or not. In addition to the normal facets of human natural selection and desirability in our dating rituals, a girl's preference for eating lobster weighed heavily. For instance, a very pretty, well-endowed female who liked to eat lobster was not as sought after as an ordinary looking girl who did NOT eat lobster. Odd as it may sound, the trade-off of lobster for looks was the unspoken rule among some of my friends. Eventually this fact became evident as the lobster loving beauties sat home night after night, while the lobster-phobic plain-Janes enjoyed unbridled popularity.

Unfortunately, all the nubile stock in our area caught on to this ploy. All claimed to hate lobster and refused to eat it on a date. These highly adaptive females, not unlike lobster females during selective mate choosing, threw all the males for a loop with this tactic. Many of my friends eventually married these wolves in sheep's clothing and the wedding vow of these girls usually went something like this, "I do, and I want a pair of baked stuffed lobsters at the reception!" Not only did they eat as many lobsters as their struggling husbands could afford, they also blessed them with several offspring, all of whom craved lobster like a pack of hungry striped bass.

Baked lobster with crabmeat stuffing & drawn butter.
A girls' best friend..

WALKING AMONG LOBSTERS

*Y*ears later I came by a well used, dinged up SCUBA tank and regulator. The regulator was an old, fat, double-hose kind that Mike Nelson used in the black & white TV series "Sea Hunt". The tank was the old J-valve type where you had to pull a rod to release a small amount of reserve air in emergency outages. There were no octopus spare regulators or auto inflatable buoyancy compensators back then. There definitely were no fancy submersible pressure gauges (SPG) to constantly monitor your tank air fill state. When you were running low on air in the tank the inhaling got hard, you pulled the reserve pressure rod, and came up. You swam to shore or back to the boat and the dive was over, plain and simple. It was dangerous as hell, but very simple science.

I played with the rig in waist deep water on our lake and got comfortable using it. I had no intention of using it for anything more than an extended mask and snorkeling platform, capable of short, shallow water submersions for watching bluegills and perch at our cabin. Of course, you can drown in a tablespoon of water and/or explode your lungs in an improper ascent from only 3 feet. But, such incidentals are nonsense to bored young men of that age.

One afternoon I was rummaging through the shed. The old man was a true Yankee pack rat and there were literally tons of discarded scraps in that shed. Among the piles and heaps that lined the walls were tons of naval salvage discards. Nothing with any true intrinsic value, just junk. I found a curious looking orange colored metal canister in the mess. It had a thick glass face plate surrounded by a heavy metal grating screen. I pushed the rubberized throw-switch on the top and it shot a dim shaft of light across the shed. The old man later told me that it was a US Navy "Battle Lantern" taken from a decommissioned USN destroyer.

I jerry-rigged a modern lantern battery to fit in the water-sealed canister. The intensity of the light beam got slightly brighter and lasted for about 20 minutes with each new battery. One night a series of thoughts and recollections lined up in my head and struck me like a ball-peen hammer between the eyes. The small lobsters we'd found one night on the breakwater and the SCUBA rig that extended my time underwater? The last part of the puzzle being the old man's water resistant battle lantern? This could actually work.

My pal Beany and I drove to the breakwater where we'd vacationed so many years ago. We sat in the parking lot drinking beer until the sun set, then dragged all the heavy stuff to the beach. Having no wetsuit I put the SCUBA rig on over my clothes. The cold ocean water instantly wiped away the slightest beer buzz and the total darkness underwater was frightening at first. I stood up in chest deep water and looked back at Beany standing in the darkness with a Narragansett beer pressed to his chest. He made a palm-up motion with his other hand as if to ask, "Well?"

I ducked back underwater sucking air rapidly and clicked the battle lantern on. Finally a small spot of visuality appeared in the cold inky blackness all around me. The lantern's beam was further diffused underwater but after a while it became my only reassuring link to the world, as I knew it. I slowly crawled along the sand seafloor. Being overly weighted-out with the steel tank, battle lantern and deflated snorkel vest I was negatively buoyant, a deadly combination for an uncertified first time night diver. I pushed myself over to the bottom edge of the breakwater and became comfortable underwater, my breathing slowed to a normal pace. The exhaust bubbles on that old single stage regulator were deafening underwater as it blasted out the ports near my ears.

I started to see all manner of underwater sea creatures along the sandy edge of the breakwater. I saw blackfish, cunners, crabs, and snakelike eels hanging out of rocky pockets. They ignored me and the light shining in their faces for some reason. Was it because I was invisible to them? I became part of their environment, just another member of the reef community. I was only 5 feet under the surface but yet, in another incredible world far from the air-breathing world of humans. It was absolutely amazing and intoxicating. Then, something very large pushed up against my legs. The force spun my entire body underwater. At first I thought my friend had waded out and kicked me. I turned to put the light beam on whatever it was. All I saw was a swirl of sand where a huge tail had just propelled some big fish away into the jet-black ocean. The diver's knife on my ankle shrunk to the size of a toothpick for any possible means of defense from God only knows what had just banged into me.

Then I saw him. He was briskly walking along the sand directly in front of me towards the kelpy rocks. A big, dark-shelled lobster, with claws swaying boldly from side to side as he strutted along. It was a moment of epiphany for me. The big lobster walked directly into the kelp and disappeared. It took me a few seconds to appreciate what I'd just seen and forget about the great white shark (in my mind) that'd just bumped my legs a moment before.

I dolphin kicked my way over to where the lobster had gone and frantically rummaged through the moss and kelp. Certainly he couldn't have gone that far? I arrived at lobster diver's rule #1 being that; when a lobster moves to kelp or moss, it is gone, PERIOD! They are true masters of camouflage in their murky underwater realm. A few seconds later another lobster, not as big as the first, came strolling out of the kelp, marching urgently across the sandy portion of the seafloor. His silhouette made him clearly visible and easy to approach. I carefully snuck up beside him but he paid the lantern light and me no heed. It was incredibly simple to grab him from the rear by his carapace like a lobster in the house sink. His claws snapped up and reached around farther than I'd ever seen a lobster do so before, almost double-jointly. He grabbed two claws full of my ungloved forearm and clamped down, HARD! I refused to let go of this, my very first *free* lobster, regardless of the painful fleshy avulsion that SOB was administering to me. At that moment, the lantern battery died. My world turned black, except for the yellow pain-stars in my eyes from the enraged lobster shredding my forearm. I made a mental note of Lobster diver's rule #2. Being, in a semi-weightless underwater state, lobsters are far more agile than when they are out of water. To this day I wear a painful reminder of what happens if you break rule #2.

I managed to plant my feet on the bottom, stand up, and stick my head and arms out of the water. When the pain in my arm stopped I knew that the little fellow had cut me severely enough for the pain sensors to turn off. No longer holding the battle lantern, I pulled him off with my opposite hand. After wading to shore like a drunken sailor I held up the prize of all prizes. My pal looked at it in the moonlight and all he could say was "you gotta' be f%&*# kidding me!" I held out a big, dark, hard-shelled lobster. Its tail wildly flapped as he reached out for more human flesh. For nearly an hour, we sat speechless on the sand and watched it crawl around, a real live lobster. My bloody forearm paled to insignificance in comparison to this gift from Poseidon, a *FREE LOBSTER!*

We brought it home and boiled it in seawater from the beach. That lobster caught fresh from the Connecticut shoreline tasted better than any lobster I'd eaten in my life, including the tender juvenile short lobsters that we ate as stupid kids. The next day we returned to the beach. I snorkeled around for an hour trying to find the battle lantern, but it was gone. The ocean had taken it in payment for the free lobster dinner.

The recollection of what I'd done and seen that night intrigued me for several weeks. I did some research and found that it is actually legal to "take lobsters by hand or SCUBA diving" if you purchase a license costing about $15 back then. I also found that I could no longer refill my steel SCUBA tank without a proper certification card. I got a lobster license and took a PADI SCUBA certification course, which was definitely eye opening. I should've died many times while using the antiquated SCUBA rig, which was later discarded. I slowly amassed modern SCUBA equipment, as funds became available. The new aluminum 80cc tanks were light and offered more bottom time. The new 2-stage regulators had thin hoses and were relatively quiet when exhaust bubbles were blown out. The thing I liked most was having a genuine wetsuit! It kept you toasty warm in cold New England waters, and scar free when crawling through razor sharp barnacle covered reef rocks. And, the heavy sponge gloves added a layer of safety when grabbing angry creatures with hydraulic scissor-cutters for hands. They could still mash a finger to the bone, but at least it would stay on your hand within the diver's glove until you got to the hospital for reattachment.

Night diving became my only interest, hobby, and pastime. To me, there was nothing of interest to see or do in a daytime underwater environment. At night, all types of odd nocturnal sea creatures would come out. You could swim right up to them and actually touch them as they were largely in a mild state of suspended animation at night. I purchased a handheld underwater light. It was bright as hell by 1970's standards, but nothing compared to today's million candlepower triple LED diver's lights.

Being the only SCUBA diver in town, I had no partner or buddy to dive with. This is a prime no-no in the SCUBA handbook. But I was young, strong, capable, and indestructible (in my own mind). The best my pals could offer was moral support while watching my diver's light flickering up through the boiling surf as I swam past the beach break. In retrospect, although absurdly dangerous, I preferred it this way. To conduct a properly coordinated 2-man buddy/buddy night dive, you spend half of your efforts keeping sight and contact with your partner in the murky blackness. If he or she jinks left or right you are obliged to cling to his/her swim path even though you want to swim and search elsewhere. If his/her equipment fails, tangles, or screws up, you are obliged to escort them back to the dive platform or shore. Ergo, your dive is aborted although your gear is in perfect working order and through no fault of your own. And I can tell you for certain, that sucks!

Once underwater, on my own, I became part of the reef environment. I rigged my weight-belt so as to have slight negative buoyancy and would hunker myself down into rocky reef pockets. The tide and wave action would send kelp and sea weed into a rhythmic sway, back and forth, back and forth. One night this dizzying sway made me sick to my stomach and I vomited into the mouthpiece. It was scary at first to settle your body into this black abyss of grayish motion in which you are totally enveloped. But, after a while you become as warm and comfortable down there as in your own bed.

Many nights I'd spend half of the dive time and air supply simply observing lobsters. Watching them on their home turf was intriguing. I saw little ones climbing up strands of upright kelp, searching for bits of food. The little bugs would boldly threaten me with tiny claws. The sheer audacity of these creatures has always amazed me. Most times I'd merely swim away from the little ones clinging to the upright kelp. Other times I could not resist showing the little bugger who is the boss. I'd pin my middle finger against my thumb and flick the bold little fellow off his lofty perch, *PING!* It'd fly away in circles, and instantly disappear into the mossy seabed.

This little girl got a ride back home sitting on a lobster trap

I saw big ones lumbering along like armored battle tanks. They'd become too heavy for upright kelp climbing and abrupt vertical movement. Their movements were confined to horizontal ramblings. They'd push things out of their path with big claws, like gorillas moving through bamboo. Although I now have a fairly good idea where they were going and why, it mostly remains somewhat of a mystery to this very day. I do know that large lobsters have recall capability. Several times I shadowed a big boy as he made his way along a straight line of march. Believe it or not, they make mental notes of potential burrows, holes, and rocky hideouts as they are walking along. Time after time when I'd make a misguided attempt to grab a large lobster, it would tail flap its way backwards, disappearing into a nearby hole or crevice. The lobster body would not touch the sides of the jagged crevice. They flew backwards into the hole, dead nuts, and bullseye center, ZIP, GONE! This is impossible to do without having some sort of memorized geographical recall.

I saw lobsters, only minutes out of molt, lying on their sides with shells as thin and flimsy as a sheet of wax paper. They looked to be dead, weakly struggling to stand on legs with the tensile strength of Jell-O. You could not pick one up, even delicately, without crushing the life out of it. Its own body weight in your open hand would just about squash it in two. I recall passing by many large "shedders" laying listless in rocky crevices. I felt sorry for the poor things, being that vulnerable in such a deadly environment. But, I suppose this is what lobsters "do"; its their job. Lobsters spend an entire lifetime in some stage of molt. Only when the few lucky ones reach mammoth size do they stop shedding their exoskeletons with any regularity.

I observed lobsters in most of the acts of their natural life facets. This includes eating and doing things for the fun of it. One evening I saw a lobster corralling a green crab in a small culvert at the bottom edge of a reef. The little crab was obviously terrified as the lobster, easily 20 times his size, bullwhipped him with antennae and blocked his escape from the culvert at every turn. The crab finally resigned himself to one last-ditch defense in the center of the deadly pocket, by raising its tiny pinchers. The lobster could've easily crushed and ate the crab with little or no effort. Instead, he closed on the tiny crab. He raised his massive crusher claw over the crab and slowly lowered the bottom flat edge onto the crab's head, ka-bonk, like a scene out of the 3-Stooges. The lobster backed off a few inches to look at the crab, now slightly embedded in the sand due to that bonk on the head. It scurried to get back on its feet, and the lobster walked up and DID IT AGAIN, ka-bonk! The crab finally regained his feet, and sidestepped his way, slowly but surely past the towering giant. I could imagine the crab whistling a little tune as he gingerly tiptoed past the monster, out of sight. The lobster slowly turned to watch the crab walk away. The crab had to literally walk OVER the lobster's legs while whistling a little tune as if to say; "I'm just minding my own business here, bye bye". The lobster then walked away, no big deal. If this was not an act of "play", or sheer "for the fun of it", then nothing is.

One night I even saw what I thought to be a pair of lobsters eating each other but turned out to be something completely opposite. It was during a period of what we call "slack tide", when the ocean tidal current is neither coming nor going. The ever-swaying kelp and sea grass would lay flat, without the normal dizzying, hypnotic effect. Range of visibility was maximized and any slight movement in the diver's light beam stuck out immediately. I saw puffs of sand belching out of a rocky crevice above me, at the middle of a large harbor breakwater wall. I slightly inflated my BC (buoyancy compensator) to quietly ascend to the depth where the action was taking place. Shining my beam into the hole, I saw a pair of lobsters in there. One was on its back with claws stretched out. The other, being much larger, was on top and holding the bottom lobster tightly with its walker legs. The top lobster was shaking the bottom one vigorously and the burrow was enveloped in puffs of sand that obscured my view. My first thought was; "Them rotten CANNIBALS!" I hand fanned the dusty water away and moved my mask face-plate right up to the burrow hole, with dive light under my chin for a closer inspection. When the smoke cleared I saw 2 pair of lobster eyes looking back at me. The smaller bottom lobster was now upright. The larger one was still on top and gently holding the smaller one with his walker legs. His big claws were raised in a threatening defensive position. I feigned a one-finger jab at the big boy to see what he'd do. He snapped viciously at my hand, and then moved even further back into the rocky retreat. He lifted the smaller lobster softly and brought it with him deeper in the burrow. The smaller lobster was apparently alive, but in a soft-shelled state of post-molt as its legs was rubbery at best. I surmised that the larger lobster had found the smaller, vulnerable post-molt lobster and had dragged it back to his murky lair for a cannibalistic meal. This disgusted me beyond description. Luckily for him, I didn't have my sling-spear with me that night or I'd have speared that horrible creature into shreds within its hole. Unknown to me until nearly 30 years later, I'd witnessed something rarely if ever seen by human eyes, a pair of impassioned New England lobsters, Homarus americanus, mating in the wild.

Many years later I started reading about a Scandinavian marine biologist named Jelle Atema. This man is considered to be the leading authority on all aspects of Homarus americanus, especially its mating process and associated rituals. Through decades of research at the Woods Hole Institute in Massachusetts and Boston University Jelle Atema has literally "written the book" on New England lobsters. In a basement laboratory at Woods Hole he set up a large lobster observation aquarium. For years he managed to record pairs of lobsters mating in this controlled environment and make scientific sense of it all. His findings basically went like this; when a female lobster wants to mate, she selects the alpha male (biggest and badest) lobster among the smaller males. In that big male lobsters love to crush and eat all smaller lobster, she seduces her vicious would-be mate. After several nights of being beaten up by her big boyfriend, she eventually follows him to his burrow. She secretes a powerful pheromone and fans it into his burrow with her fluttering under-abdomen swimmerets. The big boy becomes totally enamored with the little girl and she simply sachets into his den without getting killed and eaten. The couple will spend quality time together for several days and the female ejects her shell in a mating molt ritual. They both dine on her discarded exoskeleton shell like a human couple out for a romantic dinner. As her new shell begins to harden, the male gently cradles the female in his walker legs, carefully rotates her upside down, and they copulate in the missionary position. She stores the males' sperm in an inner-body receptacle for future uses (another story all in itself). The couple lives happily together for a few days as the female's shell fully hardens. After her shell is hard, she walks away, never to see her boyfriend again. I can honestly say that I'm probably one of only a handful of human beings that has ever seen a pair of New England lobsters having sex in the wild. Would this be considered having "wild sex"?

In 2007 I set up a large marine aquarium / seafloor environment at my home. For several years I was able to make close observations of lobsters going about their daily business (to be discussed later on). I was fortunate enough to witness a very rare "inter-molt" mating. It happened exactly as Jelle Atema described it, in front of my very eyes. I called my son downstairs to witness this incredible event, which was performed and done within only 2 or 3 minutes. I wanted to be sure that someone else saw what I thought I was seeing to be absolutely sure.

"Well hello there!"
Lobsters are solitary grouchy animals except when mating.

HUNTING LOBSTERS

*N*ight after night we'd drive to far-flung entry points along the rocky Connecticut coastline. Sometimes I had to march hundreds of yards, dragging my gear in the dark through thicket to get to the sea. Other times we'd find secluded parking and easy beach entry. Either way, I did not go home until I'd found prime hunting grounds. My pal Beany would stay with the car while I disappeared into the darkness. He knew that it'd be worth the wait.

As with most things, if you do anything long enough, you eventually become good at it. You find shortcuts and devise more efficient methods and techniques to accomplish the tasks at hand. And so it was, when I departed the world of humans and slipped into the inky darkness of the nighttime ocean. My equipment had long since been refined from the days of the battle lantern and single-stage regulator. Now, I was armed with a pair of brilliant underwater lights that could light up a section of reef like daytime. I carried a Hawaiian sling spear to add large tautog, fluke and scup to the catch bag. My BC vest contained every single implement, some bought and some handcrafted to maximize underwater catch and kill operations. Approaching an underwater reef or breakwater in the dead of night I was a lobster's worst nightmare. I became the apex predator of the sea.

Lobsters are nocturnal and have peculiar yet regular patterns of movement. They can burrow into sand or hard packed rock like small post-hole augers. They are masters of camouflage and evasion and can squeeze into crevices 1/3 their overall size. Rarely did I go chasing after a lobster that was in full retreat. It was a waste of precious bottom-time and dangerous. Firstly, they can swim backward faster than you can go forward. When they do swim backwards, it's in concentric, wildly erratic circles, very much like a party balloon with a pinhole in it. They always land tail end first into a rocky crevice or disappear in the weeds.

When lobsters seem scarce, you can always spend some time hunting the hunter species; such as the two tautogs I shot using my Hawaiian sling. In a way, you're helping the lobster stock by this. I cannot imagine how many baby lobsters were killed & eaten by the brute I'm holding on the right.

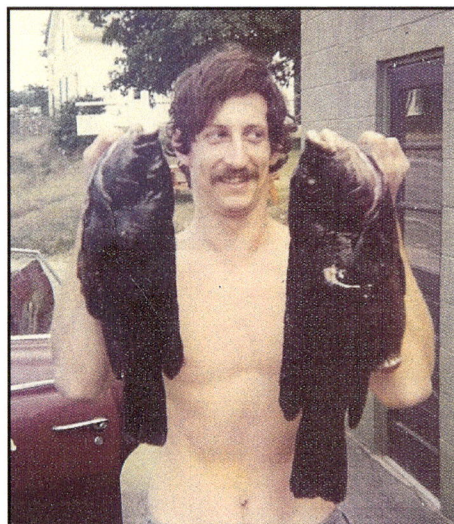

As with all new SCUBA divers hunting lobsters at night, you eventually see a whopping big pair of claws hanging out of a rocky prominence or under a ledge. And, as all new lobster hunters must do, you try to figure out how to retrieve this big goody from its hideout. You won't see the antennae that are tightly tucked back along the lobster's carapace. The big business end of this beast, its claws, are yawning wide and better judgment is telling you to pass this one by. But, the little devil on your other shoulder is saying; "Grab him you SISSY!" You poke him a bit with the dive light trying to dislodge it, but the big claws just snap the light, and the body moves even deeper in the crevice. Now you've committed to this effort and you say to yourself, "ah, what ta' hell, I'm wearing a thick divers glove" and you reach in there. You'll make a valiant attempt at it, and besides, what's the worst that can happen? Depending on the size of the lobster, it's a matter of what size garbage disposal that you're reaching into, in order to pull out a spoon. Small, normal sized, or the large industrial size garbage disposal, like the one at left.

A painful temptation

One of several things is going to happen, all of which are bad. You only have one working hand, as the other is committed to holding the divers light. If you grab one of the lobster's wrists (the big knuckle joint below the claw) then his other claw will get you, period. In this case you'll either get bit and bloodied, or pull out a big lobster claw, broken off from the body. Or you end up with a finger or thumb so badly crushed that it requires hospitalization. Either way, you *DO NOT GET THE LOBSTER!* If you happen to have a dive partner shining his/her light into the hole, then you can drop your dive light and make a 2-handed grab on both of the lobster's wrists. In 9 of 10 tries, the lobster will perform an act of self-preservation called *AUTOTONOMY* and "auto-eject" (self-amputate) both claws. The body will remain tightly wedged in the crevice. In that it is illegal to bring lobster "parts" ashore you've only managed to de-claw and mutilate a perfectly good specimen that you may have caught intact later on. And lastly on the macho scale, it's not a matter of "if" you'll get bit; it's a matter of "how badly". Ergo, lobstering rule #3: *NEVER PUT YOUR HAND IN THE HOLE.* Pass them by immediately. I'm snickering right now, knowing that many young divers reading this, will have to do as I did so many years ago when I saw those huge claws: Put your hand in the hole. Good luck!

The best way to find a lobster while SCUBA diving is to cruise slowly on your hunt. A lobster's mottled top coloration makes it literally disappear into the background like a scene from the movie "Predator". If you quickly cruise over the top of a reef, scanning the light from side to side, you have no idea how many lobsters you have just passed by. Stop at regular intervals and keep the light focused on one broad area. Eventually as the kelp sways from one side to the other, you see the brownish shape of a lobster take form in your perception. He was there all the time, but your eyes could not discern him from the background. After you see the first of these visual trickeries, they become easier and easier to spot.

From this stationary hunting position you'll eventually see lobsters appear and disappear. The kelp will sway to the right and expose a lobster sitting on a rock. A second later it will sway to the left. When the kelp sways back to the right, the lobster has disappeared. The trick is to time your grab perfectly, at the exact instant the kelp is moving from one side to the other. Sometimes you come up with a handful of enraged lobster and sometimes you come up with a handful of nothing.

The easiest place to spot lobsters is over sandy beach type bottom. My favorite area to hunt was over the sand, where structure such as a reef, large rock piles, or breakwater walls would meet the sandy bottom. When lobsters or fish momentarily move out of the dark reef onto or over the sand, they stick out like sore thumbs. They were easy to see and easier to pick off.

Lobsters often make long distance marches from one reef to another. Sometimes lobsters will make a mass pilgrimage across the sand. They march in a single line column like a little wagon train. If you're fortunate enough to intercept one of these crossings, you must act quickly. Circle to the rear of the column and start picking them off from the last lobster in the column and work your way forward. If you grab the leader or anywhere in the middle, they'll immediately scatter. As tempting as it may be to slam onto a large lobster in mid-column, do not do it. Lobster diving rule #4: **START AT THE BACK OF A LOBSTER COLUMN & YOU'LL GET'M ALL!**

A captured marching column of lobsters

One night I went out on a boat with several certified SCUBA divers. We paired off according to experience and I, having the most night-diving hours of the group, was partnered up with one of the new guys. Jerry was a huge man. He was a weightlifting body builder and a very likeable guy. He had a big smile and good sense of humor. The 80cc aluminum air tank looked like a tiny knapsack on his thick, wide back. I prepped him as to what we'd be doing and what he should expect to see. For some reason the mechanics of SCUBA diving in the pitch darkness did not seem to concern him as much as the particulars of how to handle a lobster. I'd handled lobsters all my life and it didn't occur to me that some folks might not have ever done so? This should've been a red flag, as the handling of lobsters was to me, the very least of things that could go wrong underwater at night on a deepwater reef. After we'd all done complete and thorough buddy-checks of our equipment, Jerry continued to fumble with his stuff. All the other teams splashed in, while Jerry was still patting his equipment and pacing the deck in floppy dive-fins. I'm more at ease in water than on land and did a backward "tumble" entry. I floated near the boat waiting for Jerry who finally, did an awkward scissor-kick entry. I knew that this was not going to be one of my banner lobster dives by any means. Although I was not a dive instructor, you could see the stark fear in Jerry's face and I coached him along, sticking to him like glue, as would a dive instructor. We did a slow easy feet-first descent to the bottom, holding each other's BC vests, face to face. I continuously gave him the traditional SCUBA diver's signal of circled thumb and forefinger, asking and stating, "OK?"

On the bottom, about 80' underwater, we transitioned into the horizontal swim plane and started to move along the reef edge, where the sand met the dark reef. Jerry had a one-hand death grip on the edge of my BC as we slowly traversed the seafloor. There was little or no tidal pull and the water was exceptionally clear that night. It was an excellent night for a new diver to experience the beauty of the after-dark underwater world. The first lobster we encountered was a little guy, probably a 1-pounder. It boldly stood out on a rock about 5 feet off the bottom. Maneuvering underwater had become totally natural for me. When I saw a lobster, the approach was reflexive and instantaneous. Once on target, hovering slightly above the little lobster, I pointed to it in the dive light and looked at Jerry's dive mask. His eyes were literally as big as teacup saucers! His arm holding my BC stiffened and he pushed his entire body as far away from the lobster as he could without letting go of me.

Here was this huge muscle bound fellow that could've crushed me with one arm, now petrified at the sight of a tiny lobster. I was shocked, but did not want to embarrass Jerry, then or back aboard ship. Giving him the signal to "watch me", I reached out with my little finger and teased the lobster. Our diver's lights illuminated the rock top like a theater stage. The little lobster stood his ground at center stage! One thing that I'd explained to Jerry when topside was the tenacity of lobsters. Lobsters do not immediately back off or take flight when under attack like other normal animals. They stand their ground and counter-attack the intruder, regardless of size differential.

In the amazing 2001 video story called "The Realm of the Lobster", there is a scene where a half-ton Beluga white whale encounters a 5 lb. American Lobster. This incredible video footage shows the playful young Beluga whale approaching the grumpy lobster walking along the sandy ocean floor. The agile ½ ton whale put its big white nose down onto the unsuspecting lobster's back. The lobster, having the relative size of a mosquito, spun and instantly threw his claws up! He did not try to escape, cower, or hide. Quite the contrary, the lobster advanced on the behemoth white whale, jumping off the seafloor trying to claw-grab the retreating monster by the nose. The grouchy stalwart lobster had ruined the playful Beluga's fun. The whale swam away seeking play elsewhere. In another documented instance, a renowned marine biologist was allowed to explore a deep section of the Atlantic Ocean aboard a US Navy nuclear submarine. This particular submarine had an external viewing system and highly sophisticated forward-looking sonar. A bottom "contact" came into view on the deep open seafloor. The biologist saw a massive American Lobster estimated to be around 4 or 5 feet long. It reared back in a defensive posture and snapped its claws up at the 20,000 ton nuclear submarine passing overhead. *That,* is big cajones!

As I'd expected, the little lobster turned to face my black-gloved finger, antennae tightly paired and whipping at my glove. He grabbed hold of my fingertip in a quick pinch and release. The gutsy little fellow was telling me to "beat it or I'll get serious next time". Jerry relaxed his grip a tad and the terrified look left his face. We both laughed into our regulator mouthpieces at the sheer nerve of that plucky little lobster. To show Jerry that we divers are the masters of that underwater domain, I curled up my finger and dramatically flicked the lobster on the nose spike. Lobsters hate having that done to them and he flew away like the bug that he was. I gave Jerry the thumb and index finger circle sign, "OK?" Trying to tell him "See? It's easy, fun stuff."

Jerry completely let go of me after that and we swam abreast for a while, both scanning the seafloor like seasoned night divers. Eventually I spotted a large lobster moving along the sand below us. I tapped Jerry's arm and pointed down to the unmistakable silhouette of an American Lobster, six or eight feet under us. I gently pushed his tank downward to get him started in the right direction, and his eyes got wide. Wanting to afford him the privilege of catching his very first lobster, I moved aside to give him full access to the big bug now within arms reach. Jerry didn't know what to do at that point, but he knew he had to do something. His hands were shaking and his face went ashen. With all the courage he could muster, he reached a gloved hand for the lobster's shiny black carapace. He touched the tip of the lobster's rearward waving antennae; (lobster no-no Rule #5) and all hell broke loose. The lobster spun around, grabbed Jerry by the wrist and he lost all control. He dropped his divers light and flailed his big arms as if fighting with the devil himself.

The lobster had long since released and flew away as I stood by, watching my partner wrestling with his personal demons at hand. Thankfully, he remembered the #1 rule of SCUBA diving 101. The easiest and most painful way to die is by an uncontrolled rocket ascent to the surface when scared to death, as Jerry now was. I would not have allowed this to happen and would've had to try and restrain him, which would've been ugly at best. He finally calmed down and we managed to recover his divers light on the seafloor. We sat on the sand for a while, and I gave him the middle finger to break the tension. He smiled, took a deep breath of compressed air, and we continued. I'd given up on trying to catch lobsters and had written off the dive as a purely scenic training expedition. As we slowly cruised along, my hand now on his tank pack to keep him close, I started random scans of the deep-water horizon opposite the reef rocks. This is a good way to spot and target game fish for spearing. The bright divers' light would only light up the nearby sea area and diffuse into the dark infinity of the underwater horizon. As I was doing one such scan, shining the beam under Jerry into infinity, I saw a pair of tiny glowing dots way far off in the darkened horizon. I'd never seen this before in countless night dives and I halted our travel. I tapped Jerry and gave him the one-finger-in-the-air signal; "Hold on a second. Let's wait here"

I scanned into the deep dark infinity again. The glowing dots had gotten larger and farther apart! Jerry saw the dots for the first time and froze kneeling on the bottom with me. Now we kept both diver's lights shining into the open ocean and watched the glowing dots grow in size and get even further apart. They eventually started making a serpentine, side-to-side motion as they approached. It finally entered the total illumination of our diver's light beams like an actor enters the stage. In countless hours of after-dark underwater operations this was the first time I'd ever seen a shark. It was a blue shark about 6 feet long. Underwater, the mask's faceplate magnification made the shark appear to be 20 feet long. It was casually cruising the seafloor, and coming directly at us. It did not appear to be on the attack as its head swung side to side in a slow glide-swim. The shark *DID* however want to swim under us in the small space between the seafloor and us. And *that*, I would *not* allow to happen. Jerry was literally frozen, as the big top-fin was about to bump him. In retrospect you always say, "I should've done this" or "I should've done that." But when you have 2 seconds to react to a six-foot shark coming directly toward your stomach, you do whatever comes to mind. I reared back with my heavy diver's light and bashed the damn thing squarely on the nose, right between the eyes. Then the lights went out, figuratively and literally speaking.

The slow moving shark went ballistic. It instantly thrashed up a blinding cloud of sand and banged us with its tail. I tried to hold onto Jerry's tank yoke to make sure he wouldn't make a deadly rocket ascent. He squinted his eyes shut so as not to see what was happening, but it didn't matter. His divers light was torn from his wrist thong by the thrashing of the sharks tail. We were close enough to the bottom to have a sand storm whipped up with us. I lost hold of his tank and grabbed Jerry's BC vest in tight, ready for a ride to the surface in the dark. But to his ultimate credit, he did not rocket to the surface, when stronger men certainly would have done so in a similar situation. Jerry later told me that the photos shown in his diving class, of divers suffering **Barotrauma** was worse (in his mind) than a shark bite.

After the smoke cleared he looked at me with weary eyes and pointed a limp finger up towards the surface. Poor Jerry had had quite enough night diving for a very long time. We ascended arm in arm and as we broke the surface, the boat tender shouted to us. "Hey? What happened down there? Some kinda' huge fish just flew out of the water and went crazy, skipping off towards Block Island!"

As we climbed aboard I tried to explain that we'd encountered a little blue shark, no big deal. The boat tender, a seasoned diver himself, simply grabbed our gear without another word spoken. Jerry was catatonic and didn't say a word. He tried to make himself small and unnoticed by scuttling to the corner. I went to help him get off his gear. He could say nothing, but kept shaking his head as if by a nervous tick. I guess it was the response of whether he wanted to go on a 2nd dive that night?

A little 6-foot Mako shark, about the size of the one
Jerry encountered during a night dive. It could definitely ruin your swim.

After an hour's respite aboard ship, we realized that Jerry's expensive diver's light had been left on the bottom. It was abandoned during what we later called "a shocking (sharking) experience." All the other divers had come aboard and the busy ocean was calm. Jerry was done with SCUBA diving as I went back down to recover the light. It was easy to locate as it shined upwards into the water like a homing beacon. I sat there on the bottom for a while thinking about all that'd happened.

As I started a slow ascent back to the boat, the other divers were aboard and measuring their catch. It is next to impossible to measure and properly check a lobster (for egg bearing and V-notch females) while in the water at time of capture. Imagine if you will, holding a diver's light, your only link to the visual underwater world, in one hand. And now imagine holding a fully enraged, snapping lobster in the other hand. The act of simply unclipping your catch bag, stuffing said enraged lobster into it, and re-clipping the bag is a huge feat all unto itself. Now, imagine having to also flip the lobster over to check for sex organs, then trying to jam a metallic measuring device into the lobster's eye-socket and rear carapace joint? This however, is *the law*. I did not understand why such a law, putting almost impossible demands on SCUBA divers was in effect. Before I came to the surface with Jerry's dive light, I found out, up close and personal, why such a law was written.

About 20-feet from the surface I started to see lobsters flicking their way back to the bottom. They were large-clawed short lobsters, gauged and thrown overboard by the dive teams above. A few seconds later I was surrounded by a school of striped bass and bluefish. The bass snatched up the lobsters in a feeding frenzy. They literally inhaled the lobsters as they tried to tail flip their way back to the bottom. Gangs of marauding bluefish instantly ran down the few short lobsters that managed to get to the bottom. I doubt that any of the short lobsters survived this wanton slaughter. Another unique and awesome sight that I'd never before witnessed. The reasoning behind the law stating that "A SCUBA diver shall check a lobster for all regulations *immediately upon capture* and before removing it from its underwater hiding place or environment" became crystal clear to me.

I fully complied with the law from that moment on. I would not be party to the wasteful slaughter of undersized or egg-bearing female lobster. Further, I often described what I'd seen that evening and made it a challenge among my diving cadre to do it "the hard way". We had fun designing specialized equipment to accomplish this, such as size-gauges mounted on our lights. Ultimately, it resulted in more fun and much safer dives requiring practiced teamwork to land only pre-gauged, keeper lobsters. Lobster diving rule #6: *FULLY CHECK YOUR LOBSTER BEFORE YOU PUT IT IN THE BAG!* There are many seemingly superfluous laws in lobstering. This rule is not among them. Fully comply with this rule not only because it's the law, do it because it's the right thing to do out of respect for these amazing creatures.

Lobster gauge mounted on SCUBA diver's light

Lobster traps are always another bone of contention when night diving for lobsters. You cannot avoid them when diving in any rocky areas. The old threat was that a lobsterman had the legal right to shoot anyone tampering with his or her traps, no questions asked. Of course this is nonsense, but it was always in the back of your mind when slipping past a string of submerged lobster crates on the ocean floor. I didn't want my exhaust bubbles rising to the top and seen anywhere near a lobster buoy if at all possible. Many times however, simply out of observational curiosity, I'd hover to the side of a lobster trap and watch what was happening around it. I saw many curious things that lobsters do when encountering a trap.

Years later these observations would become invaluable when I became a "topwater lobsterman" using traps. As a SCUBA diver however, it was apparent that lobsters seemed to find more joy in walking on top of the traps than into them. I never touched an underwater trap and always felt sorry for the hardworking topwater lobstermen. There were always dozens of lobsters scurrying around, easy pickings for the night diver, but only a rare few near or inside the traps. Lobster diving rule #7: *STAY AWAY FROM LOBSTER TRAPS!*

People often ask, "What was the biggest lobster you ever caught while SCUBA diving?" I can tell you for a fact that the biggest American lobster ever caught was captured in 1977 off Nova Scotia, Canada. It weighed 44 & ½ pounds. The average size of Fishers Island Sound inshore lobsters caught while SCUBA diving was 1 ½ to 3 pounders in the late 1970's.

One night my dive instructor made arrangements with a tugboat operator to bring us out into New Haven harbor. We were to dive on a reef near the commercial freighter shipping lanes. The wind kicked up that night to around 35 knots and the water was rougher than hell. The deck was pitching and heaving as we donned our gear, equipment slipping and sliding all around. Splashing down and going under the boiling surface waves, the world became quiet, calm. The turbid water was absolutely FILTHY! The seawater in these shipping lanes had a slight smell and taste of diesel fuel. Visibility was the very worse I've ever seen. You could not see your hand at the end of an extended arm. Brown bits of what looked like rust particle clouded the water, like a brown snowstorm. The diver light beam became extremely defused and it was like being immersed in sludgy crankcase oil. In order to find which way was down, I had to track in the opposite direction of where my exhaust bubbles were going. This was the very first time that I had concern about my well-being in an underwater night dive. I decided to simply find the bottom and hunker down for a half-hour or so, just to say I did. In this way I could falsely preserve a macho appearance and impress the salty old dive instructors back aboard ship. I felt the bottom coming with outstretched hand, before I could actually see it in the cloudy water. I rigged my BC for extreme negative buoyancy to belly down onto the bottom. After a few minutes I noticed a pair of big eyes in front of me, something else was also bellied down on the dusty seafloor. It was the biggest fluke (large summer flounder) that I'd ever seen in my life. It sat there in perfect camouflaged colors. It was as thick as a house doormat, all 10 to 12 pounds of it. I thought to myself, "Now that's something you don't see everyday down here."

Author holding 10-lb. fluke, similar to the one he speared
during night dive in New Haven Harbor

I blindly pulled out my big diver's knife and stabbed the thing just behind the top gill slits, pinning it to the seafloor. It went wild and flapped up a blinding dust storm that reduced the visibility to zero. I managed to get control of the big fish by feel after it simmered down a bit. It had to be folded over in order to squash it into my large hinge-mouthed catch bag. I surfaced with the lunker fluke and slung it up to the waiting topwater dive attendant. Later that week we ate delicious fillet of sole dinners, with guests for the next month; sole Florentine, crab stuffed sole, batter dipped fish & chips, flounder bouillabaisse soup, baked lemon sole, etc, etc.

By now the tugboat was really rolling in heavy seas, as I took the emptied catch-bag and headed back down through the murk. This time, quite by accident I bottomed out directly onto the reef and began to slowly prowl around. With visibility less than 2 feet, I started bumping into more lobsters than I'd ever seen in any of my very best night dives. All were big lobsters, no shorts or juveniles like you normally see elsewhere. They were all covered in chunky, brown silt-like soot, from the stuff suspended in the filthy water. It looked like they were wearing tattered winter coats as they marched along. Before long I had a catch-bag nearly full of 2 ~ 3 pound lobsters with an occasional 5 pound giant in the mix! Moments before surfacing with more lobsters than I had ever caught at one time, I saw a big one rumbling along. It was covered in soot and looked more like a furry dog than a lobster.

Slightly sooty large lobster nestled in reef rocks, similar to the ones found in New Haven harbor in the late 1970's.

It barely fit in the opening of my catch-bag. Landing this sack full of lobsters nearly cost me my life. When we all surfaced, the topside conditions were now that of a small midnight hurricane. The big steel landing-platform was flying up and down at the tugboat's stern. One of the dive masters was the first to try and board with the help of 2 boat attendants hanging on for dear life. He handed all his gear in and then timed the downward drop of the platform, grabbed it with both hands, and it pulled him up out of the water, and threw him tumbling inboard like a puppet. I handed in most of my gear but could not get the heavy bag full of lobsters up out of the water. I misjudged the platform's downward fall and it bashed me on the head.

The weight of the 30-ton tugboat pushed me 5 feet back under the black water. I saw stars, but somehow managed to hold onto the lobsters and get back aboard ship that night. Back at the dock the big lobster I'd caught weighed slightly over 7lbs. A few days later we cooked and ate some of those New Haven harbor lobsters. They tasted like lobster, but had a distinct after-taste of diesel fuel. We heavily dunked them in melted butter and hoped that the diesel fuel taste would go away, but it didn't.

Although having the biggest concentration of lobsters I'd ever seen I would never return to this area for lobstering ever again. But, I always wondered why in hell lobsters would be attracted to, and mass in this particularly filthy, polluted stretch of ocean? The probable answer came to me years later by an old Maine lobstering myth. It was said that you could attract more lobsters to your trap if you weighted it with bricks that had been soaked in kerosene. Of course this is ecologically unsound and environmentally illegal at the very least. Interestingly enough, Jelle Atema and his Woods Hole Institute team put this ridiculous sounding postulate to a scientific test, like Mythbusters. Their findings were troubling.

Lobsters depend on their sense of scent for just about all facets of life and survival. They find food, keep track of peer group rivals, and conduct mating rituals solely through the scent in the water around them. It was found that some chemicals, specifically hydrocarbons in fuel-based products are perceived by male lobsters to be the strongly intoxicating mating pheromone secreted by female lobsters looking to mate. Once scientifically proven, the issue became a huge topic of concern. It became the main agenda of discussion at high-level conferences and meetings among top marine biologists around the world. Suddenly apparent, the impact of oil spills took on yet another devastating and incalculable consequence: the destruction of countless and entire biomass groups of lobsters. Mass extinction scenarios loomed and are subject of discussion even now, years after the Woods Hole revelation. Sadly, I'm unhappy to say that I witnessed this horrible ecological anomaly first hand, up close and personal, on one terrible evening on the bottom of the New Haven harbor.

The very largest lobster (per se) that I've ever caught was during my honeymoon on the British Virgin Island of Tortola. We were with a group of advanced SCUBA diving tourists going on a submerged wreck dive. We dove on the RMS Rhone, a 310-foot ship that sank in a hurricane back in 1867. Interestingly enough, this wreck was featured in the 1977 movie "The Deep" starring Jacqueline Bisset and Nick Nolte. The underwater wreck site is an official sanctuary where no artifacts or wildlife can be taken or disturbed.

Being used to the frigid murky waters of New England, the unlimited crystal blue visibility and bathtub warm Caribbean water was awesome. We were all meandering around the huge sunken steamer when I swam over to look at the big metal propeller. It was the size of a small house, lying on its side. As I flipped weightlessly over one of the three big propeller blades, I spotted a pair of long tubular shadows on the bone white seafloor. The shadows moved, and I had to descend to the seafloor to see what it was. The source of the shadows was a pair of large stalk-like pipes sticking out from under the big propeller blade. The brownish stalks were solid, like a pair of boat oars. I held the top edge of the sunken propeller blade and looked over the edge to the seafloor. There, in the shadow stood a Caribbean spiny lobster. It was a panulirus and it was *HUGE!* I'd never seen one before, only in pictures, and I had no idea if it was dangerous or how to handle a monster like this one. I recalled a magazine cover photo at our beachside hotel with a fisherman holding a small Caribbean lobster by the antennae. The antennae were solid as opposed to our New England lobsters' soft whip-like antennae. By now the dive group had moved on, but I could still see their bubbles in the distance. I gingerly grabbed the lobster by both its antennae. It felt like holding a pair of baseball bat handles. The lobster at first slightly resisted then allowed me to lift it out of the shadowy den. It was a giant panulirus "Argus" nearly 4 feet long from nose-spike to tail tip. By the thickness of its carapace the darn thing was at least in the 15 pound range. Its big legs moved in search of bottom footing but it did not make any violent movements or real attempts to get away from me. I swam as fast as I could to the dive group, dragging this monster under me, hoping that someone would take a photo. Finally one older diver with underwater camera spotted me. He clanked his tank to attract the groups' collective underwater attention. They all gathered around looking at me holding a spiny lobster easily half my length. As the photographer lifted his camera, that big lobster decided that he didn't want to be held any longer. He went ballistic! His huge tail snapped crazily and he flew away like a MK-48 Torpedo. The only picture that remains is in my mind.

As we ended the dive tour, the thought of that monstrous spiny lobster played over and over in my mind. While we were securing the dive gear I looked out over the crystal clear Caribbean water at a 40-foot sailboat that was anchored on the periphery of the underwater park. It was a rented pleasure craft from a port in Florida. A pair of SCUBA diver heads popped up at the stern. One of the men heaved his fins up and inboard before climbing up the rear swim platform. He quickly offloaded his tank and bent over with outstretched arms to help his buddy, still floating in the water. The man in the water lifted his arms and handed his pal a huge spiny lobster! The lobster, another monstrous panulirus argus, wildly flapped its tail as the man on the swim platform grabbed it by the antennae stalks and dragged in into the boat. I initially thought that the lobster might have been the one I'd held underwater. After a second look I could see that it was not. The two divers had taken a much larger one than the one I'd held.

The sailboat captain came on deck with a heavy aluminum garbage can. He scooped some seawater into it and set it down in the fantail onto what I assumed was some sort of propane heater as I saw a slight trail of smoke wafting up. As our dive group was motoring away I watched the sailboat anchored up for an overnight stay against the backdrop of a bone white desolate beach lined with a jungle of palm trees. It looked like a scene from the movie "Castaway". I knew that the lobster they were cooking was taken illegally, something I will never condone. But, just for a second, I wished that I were on that sailboat for the night with some ice-cold beer and a pound of Land-O-Lakes melted butter.

If you want to see the largest panulirus argus spiny lobsters on earth in their natural wild habitat, do the following. Get an advanced recreational SCUBA certification from your local dive shop and climb aboard the quickest flight to the British Virgin Islands. Shuttle out to the desolate island of Tortola where you could climb palm trees to crack open and eat fresh coconuts. Charter any of the local SCUBA dive tours for a 3-tank full-day dive. Tell the tour operator that you want to dive on the Rhone. You won't regret it.

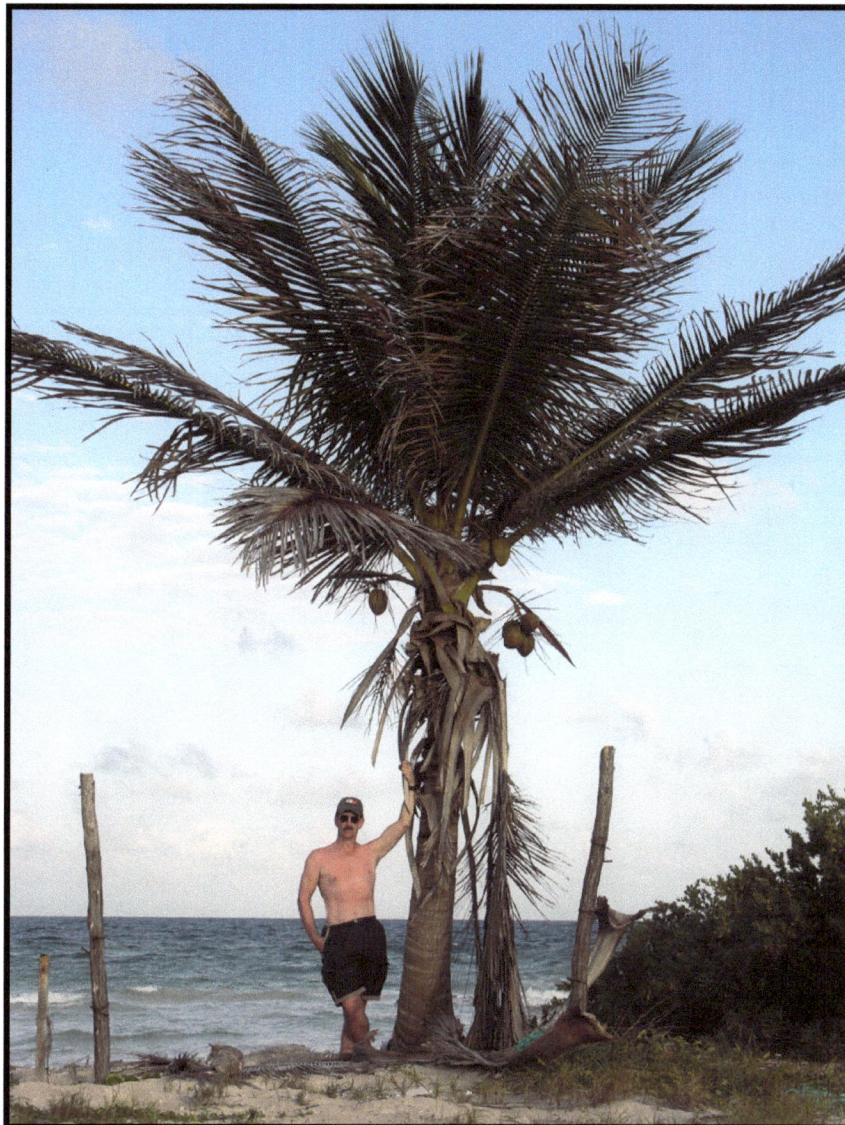

British Virgin Island of Tortola, home of the largest spiny lobsters on earth.

A PRICELESS GIFT & CHANGING TIMES

*B*efore acquiring a boat, after-dark shoreline lobster diving became a nightly obsession. It was rewarding as well as challenging both mentally and physically. The reward in this case was having an unlimited supply of free lobsters to eat, every single day of the week. We had lobsters for nearly every meal in some configuration or another. At one point during the early lobster hunting years (one of the very few times in my life), I got tired of eating lobster. We often had lobsters in every refrigerated space, bin, and drawer of the house. None, not one, ever went to waste. And I can honestly say that from the very first free lobster that I'd caught, until the last, I've never sold a single lobster. I've had countless offers to purchase them during times of abundance, and payment to provide them for parties. This is something that I could not do in clear conscience, out of utmost respect for these special creatures. Eating a lobster was then, and still is today, more than a mere act of consumption. It is something that I do with veneration. I would rather return every lobster I'd ever caught back to the sea, than to cheapen these wonderful natural gifts by selling so much as one single lobster for a mere handful of rice. This being said, some find it quite a conundrum and hard to understand why I continued to hunt lobsters with such passion? Passion is in itself the answer. After spending so much time with these animals, seeing their most intimate triumphs and defeats, knowing their strengths and weaknesses, you develop a deep appreciation for them. After mastering the nighttime underwater world you became highly selective in capturing prey. It became more rewarding to simply observe and tease a large lobster and let it pass, than to capture and eat it.

In the mid-70's my wife and I, both certified SCUBA divers and night diving enthusiasts, inherited a boat. My uncle's 24-foot Grady White cabin cruiser was old but solid. We kept it on a floating mooring ball at a small marina on Long Island Sound. Once or twice a week we'd head out to sea, as the sun was setting and anchor-up on one of the many reefs in the area. The two hours just before sunset on the ocean was magical for us. We sat in open topped wetsuits as the boat swayed back and forth on the anchor line. The winds diminished, the waves subsided, and the sun melted into the blue water horizon. The gulls would finally shut up and float quietly on the water and the boat traffic disappeared. The world got quiet except for the "hoot-buoys" tooting out their monotone song all night long. When you could clearly hear these buoys echoing across the water, all the daytime background noises were gone and it was time to go diving. We often thought of the diurnal sea life going to their time clocks and punching out after a long day's work. The lobsters, fresh from an all-day sleep were punching in for a long night's shift.

We zipped up our wetsuits, performed a thorough buddy/buddy equipment check, and splashed overboard. My wife was a great SCUBA diver and nighttime lobster hunter. We'd patrol the reefs in a perfectly spaced tandem pair. Keeping a peripheral glance on each other's light beam, we moved in concert as one. Since there was at that time an overabundance of lobsters and we'd been eating them at every meal, we became highly selective. We eventually passed up more lobsters than we collected. For instance, when grabbing a large new shedder, you can feel your fingers bend into the still soft lobster carapace shell. The outward appearance, the big new shell, belies the actual small amount of meat inside this lobster. New shedders and totally soft-shelled lobsters were immediately released, as were all female lobsters, regardless of size, allowing them to fulfill their destinies. There was no longer a need to gauge (measure in size) our lobsters.

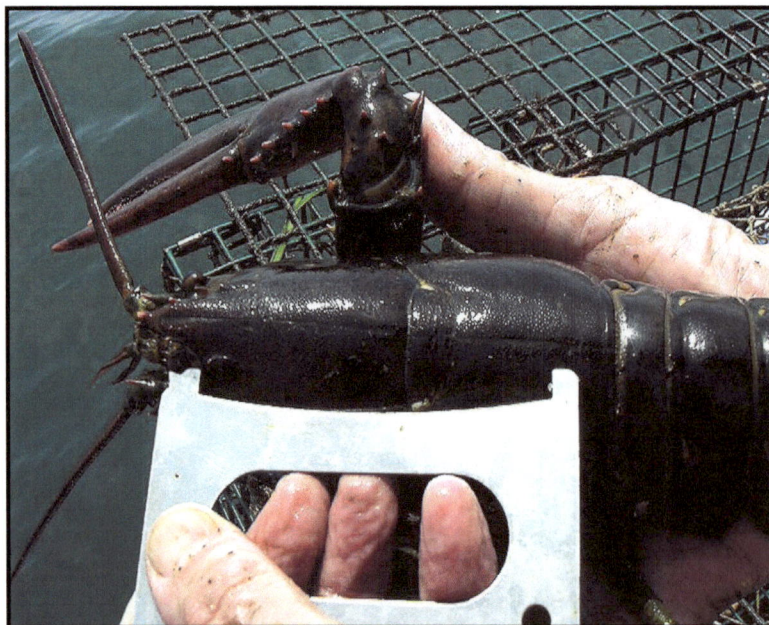

Lobster gauge, measuring rear of eye-socket to end of the carapace. It's a keeper!

On sight alone, we knew which lobsters were too small to keep, which really had no bearing at that time. After countless dives where we filled army duffel bags with over fifty pounds of lobsters on a single tank, we now only took a single pair of large male lobsters for dinner. We passed up all the rest. Our motto as far as marine fishing and lobstering was this: "You only need enough for dinner. All the rest is just for showing off back at the dock." We use this motto as our guide even now, some 40 years later.

My wife & best lobster diving buddy, the morning after a dive.

SCUBA diving was not a popular pastime back then and night diving was pretty much unheard of. One evening in the late 70's my wife and I were anchored up on a far-flung ocean reef. We sat on the fantail looking at the stars until well after dark. As we began the pre-dive prep that we'd done countless times, something banged into the side of our boat. It hit the boat with enough force to slightly rock the cabin cruiser. We both leaned over the edge and looked down into the darkness. The water sparkled and was lit up from the flashing bright beams of 14 or more diver lights. Another pair of SCUBA tank yokes banged into the bottom of our boat. The careless new SCUBA students stared straight down, paying no attention to their depth, direction or surface obstructions. The large pod of new SCUBA trainees passed under the boat, looking like an underwater circus. This was the very first time we'd ever seen another night diver in the area. We were flabbergasted at the sight and splashed down after the light show disappeared. They left a trail of lost and discarded diving equipment, from mask & snorkels to mini spear guns and expensive diver knives. They also left a wide path of total destruction. They took *EVERYTHING*. Clams, mussel clusters, and periwinkles (scungilli) were all dug up and gone. Blackfish of all sizes were gone. Wedged in a rock, we actually found a spear gun with a small dying blackfish still quivering on the roped spear tip. After traversing the entire reef for about an hour one thing became eerily evident. No lobsters, not so much as one of the countless juvenile short lobsters could be seen, anywhere. The once flourishing reef had become a baron wasteland.

A friend, the first time she'd touched a live lobster. Lobster says; "Ta'daa"

When we exited the water and climbed back aboard ship we were absolutely speechless. After securing our gear for the long ride back to port, my wife made one comment to me. We were both sick to our stomachs as she said; "All good things must come to an end."

And so it was with the lobster population, as we had known it. Greedy teams of unscrupulous divers ravaged our favorite reefs and breakwater walls, night after night. We called an end to our SCUBA diving and lobstering operations after a wonderful 15-year run. Armed with advanced modern equipment and easy to launch Zodiac boats, the crowds of new SCUBA divers would eventually decimate underwater ecosystems, as I knew them. This was too much to bear. We moved away from the sea, but carried vivid memories of times when natural reef-life flourished like scenes from the Mystic Aquarium.

Fast forward 25 years in time, my wife & I decided to take recertification classes in modern SCUBA diving. As in the distant past our ultimate desire was to once again become part of the after-dark underwater reef environment in order to see what things were the same and what things had changed. I was asked to write a short article about our first ocean night-dive for a local sportsmen's association. Some of the members had been considering sport SCUBA diving and wanted an insight into "what's it like?" The following is a reprint of that article:

I hadn't been SCUBA diving in 25+ yrs. My wife and I used to go night diving, 3 or 4 times a week using the old "Mike Nelson" double hose systems. Octopus rigs were just starting to come in way back then. Our buoyancy vests were flat "snorkel vests", not the cool looking BCD's used today.

Last winter we took the time and training to get re-certified and put many hours in, learning to use the new "stuff" of modern SCUBA diving. I'd forgotten what a HUGELY equipment intensive sport SCUBA diving is. Packing, putting on, taking off, unpacking, and washing down of all the "stuff" is a workout in itself. This was times 2 in our case.

This photo on the right contains a few of the items needed for 2 people to SCUBA dive, not including a pair of modern BC's with integrated tank/hose/buoyancy vests full of clips, snaps, weight-pockets, air-hoses, etc. And a pair of heavy 7mm "exposure suits", no longer called wetsuits.

We practiced, practiced, and practiced some more with all this stuff in a local pool, some deepwater lakes, and a few low visibility ocean dives (daytime). With your eyes closed, if you can't kneel on the bottom, and swap regulators, clear your mask, unsnap a catch-bag, take out and put back your knife, and easily locate (by feel) every doo-dad on your BC, then you have no business night-diving, period.

200-lbs. of SCUBA equipment

I'd been topwater lobstering for several seasons, and had a burning curiosity to once again "see" how the little buggers are at night. So, we scheduled a night dive with a great gang of experienced dive nuts. Got there at sunset, did a pre-dive brief, handed out and attached cyalume glow-sticks (attached to tank yokes) and flashing mini-strobes to SCUBA flags. (A cool way to keep track of everyone underwater at night)

We paired up according to experience, and hit the dark surf. Within minutes, things went awry. One guy's 2nd stage regulator free-flowed. Another guy's dive light (and his spare!) went dead. My wife's BC gave her trouble. She couldn't maintain negative buoyancy and went up like a cork. Another guy had forgotten to "weight himself out" for saltwater (you use less weight in freshwater).

And, when things go wrong on a night-dive, in the middle of the ocean, it's a showstopper. Pull the cork, surface, and swim in, you're all done for the night. Within 15 mins, only two divers remained on station under the water. Just my dive partner (a dive master) and I made it to the reef. And the stuff we saw was absolutely amazing!

Big fat, tasty blue crabs were here n' there n' everywhere! Why don't they run from the light? So, I grabbed one from the rear, top n' bottom with thumb and forefinger. He reached between his legs, and pinched my finger like a set of diagonal cutters. WOW THAT HURT!

OK, for the next blue crab, I had a better idea. I'd made an integrated dive-light/lobster gauge attachment and used it to pin the little SOB to the sand. It worked like a charm. I held him by the back flippers (side to side) and put him in the catch bag. As I tried to put a second blue crab in there the first one flew out like a bat out of hell, literally! Lesson learned? You have to hand-sweep them to the bottom of bag before opening it up each time or POOF~ away they go.

Then we started to see fluke, a highly sought after edible New England flatfish. We saw a lot of them. Going slow, cruising the bottom at night, you see so many cool things. Unlike daytime, the sea life is somewhat dormant. Why do they all disregard you and the bright light, like you're no threat to them?

I saw fluke (toothy summer flounder) no bigger around than a silver dollar, and winter flounder the size of a postage stamp. Both were perfectly formed miniature specimens. Then, I saw a pair of doormats (large fluke). Just lying there, eyes open, gills puffing sandy breaths in and out. They let me drift right on top of them. I finally had to touch one with the light. POOF! Both were gone in a twinkling.

Scup (Porgy) of all sizes seemed to be sleeping. They weren't hunting; they just propped themselves on the bottom with dorsal fins, not moving? Beady-eyed one-foot long eels known as "striper candy" were peeking out from under little tufts of seaweed. They definitely saw the dive lights, and didn't like it a bit. After a while they came curling out, and slowly snaked their way along the bottom. It's no wonder that striped bass love eels so much. They are such little teasers.

Jellyfish are BAD STUFF! Like underwater cayenne pepper mines, they are destructive and unavoidable. The tentacles are thin as white hair. These toxic strands drift back 6 feet or so from the big red & purple jellyfish. The New England ocean visibility is normally only 4 or 5 feet. Thus, you don't realize that you're swimming into one, until your exposed lips are burning like you'd been razor cut and splashed with battery acid. It HURTS!

Squid appeared and it's very cool to watch them up close. Big fat multi-colored, puffy ones. They were singles, not schooled, and seemed to be busy sifting up puffs of sand on the bottom. Un-molested, they move along slowly, "backwards"? They swim towards the tentacle end, not the head end. They kiss at the top of kelp strands, and flicker along. I finally had to poke at a squid and it took off like a bullet, head end first.

We navigated from the deep sand to shallower rock and kelp bed. Then I saw my first underwater lobster in 20 years, a little one, about 5 inches long. It marched along the sandy edge of a rock, proud as punch. It had absolutely no fear. Then, 2 larger ones, just under keeper size, walking along urgently. It was kind of funny; they look so serious and busy marching along. Definitely not loitering, as if they had somewhere important to go, and a drop-dead timeline to get there! Not scared, or put off by the light or me. My 200,000-candlepower dive light had to be blinding them. They went on with their busy pace undisturbed, as if I wasn't even there. This absolutely fascinated me.

Of course, you can't just watch forever, and I had to go and give one of the little guys a poke with the lobster gauge attached to the light. I figured he'd fly away instantly like the squid. No sir-ree! That little pip-squeak halted his march and turned about. He flared his legs, gripped the bottom, arched his carapace up, and brandished his little claws at me, like he was going to KILL ME! The nerve of this little fellow was absolutely hilarious. I poked the light at him a bit and the little SOB would not back off an inch. As a matter of fact, he kept coming forward at me. He clipped & snapped at the metal lobster gauge, until I gave up. I laughed exhaust bubbles out the regulator and saluted the little devil as I swam away. I'd long forgotten what truly amazing creatures they are.

I looked down at my SPG (air pressure gauge) and it was approaching red line. What seemed like 5 minutes had actually been 1 hour and 15 minutes, and it was time to quit. Enroute to shore I passed a steep kelp covered rock wall. The kelp swayed and I saw a glint of shiny brown movement. It swayed again, and there they were, a pair of big lobsters. Both moving along the vertical, marching with purpose to somewhere, like 2 big cockroaches. They totally ignored me as I approached. This was a moment of decision? Grab for the biggest one in front and chance loosing both? Or the trailing one and hope it's a keeper? I went for the sure thing. He let me reach right up to him and didn't flinch until I was pulling him out of the kelp. I thought to myself that it just doesn't seem fair somehow.

I prefer slightly negative buoyancy, which allowed me and the lobster to sink down into the rock bottom. He was reaching back, and if this guy got my finger, it'd be all gone (my finger). I easily one-handedly gauged him with the light-attachment invention of mine. He was way over keeper size, about 1 1/2 lbs. I checked for berries (eggs stuck to the tail) and for a V-notch. It had neither of these, which would've made the lobster releasable.

I opened the catch bag; forgetting to hand-sweep it down and all the blue crabs flew out. I cursed into the regulator. Lesson #2 on the evening, putting lobsters in a catch bag; Put them in TAIL FIRST! If you try to put them in head first, the nose-spike catches on the mesh, the wildly snapping claws grab the bag rim and it is literally impossible to shove the lobster in.

I'm absolutely positive that had I extended the dive through a 2nd tank, I'd have gotten several more keeper sized lobsters. But, as with fishing, my motto is that you only need enough for one meal and the rest are just for showing off back at the dock.

My partner said that he had a real hankering for lobster thermidore. I told him in no uncertain terms "The only way you'll get this lobster from me, is to chew through my wrist!" And he promptly attempted to do so as seen below. My light mounted lobster gauge also made a dandy little self-defense device when used to ward of a lobster crazed dive master.

This is a cool little thing I dreamed up to one-handedly gauge lobsters underwater. It is also good for pinning blue crabs to the bottom and a dozen other oddball things underwater. It's made from aircraft aluminum solid rivets and a hose clamp.

All in all it was wonderful to see the underwater world of the New England shores after dark once more. The effort to do this is immense, as is getting a pilot's license. But the experiences are simply exhilarating. At one point in my flight training I was about to quit after 5 long years of study and practice. My CFI, one of the finest flight instructors in the business, saw the despair in my face and said; "Stop crying! There's no crying in aviation! If it was easy, everyone would be doing it!" And so it goes with nighttime SCUBA diving in cold murky New England seawater.

Lobster Bite!

THE COMMODITY OF LOBSTER

*D*uring our years away from the sea, the addicting taste for lobster would return, strongly at times. Seeing the photo of a big red lobster while leafing through the Sunday newspaper back then, and even today, stops me dead in my tracks every time. I just have got to see what the PPP (price per pound) is. To me, lobster is a commodity very much like pork bellies or gold. During our time living far inland and having long since abandoned our SCUBA gear, a market "Special" on lobsters always brought urgent phone calls from friends. Being relatively well off at that time, I could afford lobster regardless of the cost anytime at all. But, there was something about the pricing that actually tainted the taste in my mind and palate. To pay nearly $12 per pound during the "dry times" was just not going to happen. Likewise, when the price dropped to $3.99 for one-armed cull lobsters, I simply have to purchase and eat them continuously until the sale ends, whether I really want them or not.

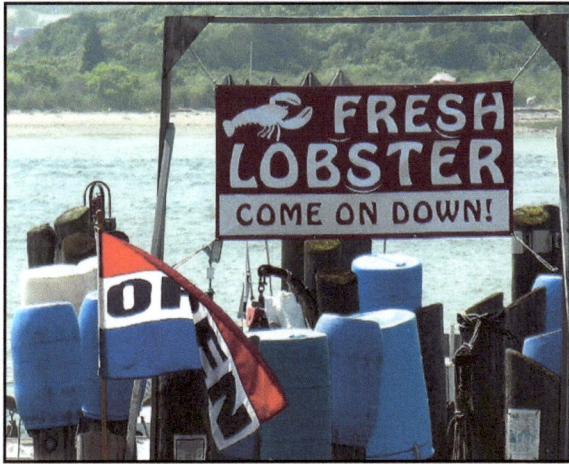

Point Judith at Galilee RI

Day trips to the shore with friends or family inevitably turn into a search for lobsters. Strolling along the boardwalk at Watch Hill, Rhode Island or Ogunquit, Maine, the ladies are magnetically drawn into each and every souvenir shop and nick-knack store. My eyes constantly scan for placards pointing to back-alley lobster pounds and sidewalk vendors. I squint hard to find each and every one of the smallest cardboard posters with the word "LOBSTER" written on it. Signs like the ones on the docks at Galilee, Rhode Island are irresistible to me

Most show the PPP (price per pound); some leave it a mystery. To the neophyte lobster lover, finding the PPP is simply a matter of walking up to the vendor and asking outright: "*How much are your lobsters?*"

The seasoned and wary lobster buff however, like my mother, does not use this kind of gauche frontal assault. She would poke around the lobster tanks and totes until the attendant approached her (not the other way around). The first question was not PPP; it was "So? When did you catch these?" This opening volley immediately put the vendor on alert to the fact that a) this lady knows her lobster and b) I may have to temporarily lower the PPP to get this haggler, the hell out of here!

One of the very best dockside open markets for "Fresh off the boat" lobsters is Point Judith at Galilee in Narragansett, Rhode Island. On any summer day you can walk along the fishing docks among the countless commercial lobster boats. For a solid mile the sidewalks and docks are literally lined with "LOBSTER FOR SALE" placards, flags, and banners. Lobstermen from the crusty old salt to teen-aged girls all hawking their fresh catch with promises of "lowest PPP anywhere!" The truth is that lobster vendors all working in that close proximity, pretty much all have the same PPP. They all know the current inland PPP rates and exactly what other nearby vendors are asking. Some dockside "off-the-boat" lobster vendors get creative. They offer a PPL (price-per-lobster) type scheme such as "$6 per each chick lobster, $8 per each 1½ lb. lobster" etc. It sounds good, but if you do the math, it will always come out to about the same PPP offered by the next vendor down the line. My mother and her lobster-loving friend Lillian knew the best way to spend the day at Point Judith, Rhode Island. It went something like this.

Avoid the $10 in-town parking rates by parking out in the vast charter fishing boat parking lot for free. Then take a slow stroll down the length of the charter docks and lobster vendor's "row". The burly charter captains always got a kick out of the two handbag-toting little old ladies walking down to the lobster boats. They thought differently after dealing with these women over the price of lobster. These old ladies were like a pair of surly Arabian horse traders when it came to purchasing lobsters. They knew lobsters inside and out and made the fact known early on in negotiations. Unlike most tourists afraid to touch a living lobster, my mother demanded to hold and examine each lobster in question. She squeezed the carapace sides for signs of soft post-molt conditions. She examined the underside to determine the lobster's gender, as she preferred tail meat to claw meat. Female lobsters, her favorite, have larger tails for egg bearing. Lillian on the other hand preferred claw meat. Thus she would always select a male lobster because they have compact tails and larger claws for fighting. My mother went so far as to squeeze the tail tips in order to test the lobster for fecal emission! This was the ultimate test of freshness in her book. A lobster that's been in a tank for any period of time without feeding would have little or no fecal emission.

The old ladies left in their wake a long line of pissed off lobster vendors. They had no intention of making a purchase until the very end of the day. After a few trips, I could not walk with them on their opening pass down lobster vendor's row. The burly boat captains were fit to be tied and would be more likely to beat *ME* up, than the two old ladies. I'd simply wait for my mother at the edge of town near the tourist attractions.

After a leisurely luncheon of clam cakes and chowder at "Aunt Carrie's" at senior citizen rates, my mother and Lillian returned to the lobster docks in earnest. They knew precisely which lobster vendor had the freshest catch, the very best PPP, and they made a beeline to that particular boat. The lobster vendor winced at the approach of the two women. After another half-hour of dickering, the vendor gave my mother a one-time, lowest PPP on the dock just to get her to go away. As the deal was sealed, Lillian would get the frustrated captain to throw in some fresh kelp, a styrofoam cooler full of seawater, and have his young first mate carry all of it to the car.

The old ladies made a beeline back to our cabin on the lake. My aunt Eva was waiting there for their arrival. She was an age-old Swamp Yankee with a big handbag full of government surplus butter and cheese blocks issued to the elderly back then. She also brought fresh garden vegetables, herbs, spices and a gallon demijohn of my uncle Milt's homemade wine. It was as potent as any fine French Cognac in the world! My hoodlum pals and I got into a croc of his home brew one day, and we later wished that we hadn't.

By nightfall these old ladies would get silly as schoolgirls. Around midnight they were too drunk to drive and my father would deliver them all safely to their homes. He and I would sneak back to the cabin and polish off the lobster, condiments, and fresh salads that were leftover. We'd all enjoyed a lobster feast fit for royalty for only a few dollars. The lobsters were the freshest, the highest quality by personal selection and were purchased at the very lowest prices available.

These are a few simple ways that you too can select the best lobsters from available stock. Obviously the freshest selections are found at the shoreline. More specifically, near shoreline areas where commercial lobster boats are found.

Look for chalkboard price signs & placards in conspicuous places. This shows that the prices often change with current stock, and indeed the lobsters often come and go quickly to assure freshness. Stores or lobster pounds with static roof signs with the word "LOBSTERS" written on them, usually maintain their lobster inventory for long periods of time in holding tanks. This then becomes a crapshoot whether or not the one pulled and purchased by you is fresh from the ocean or a long surviving captive. If you can find a chalkboard placard like the one at the left, you have hit the jackpot! Note the prices on ALL LOBSTERS; from 1 lb. chix up to 6 lb. jumbos are set at $5 lb. across the board. And all culls "cracked, bumped & bruised" lobsters of all sizes are only $3.99 per lb. The vendor wrote the word "WOW!!!" Which is absolutely correct.

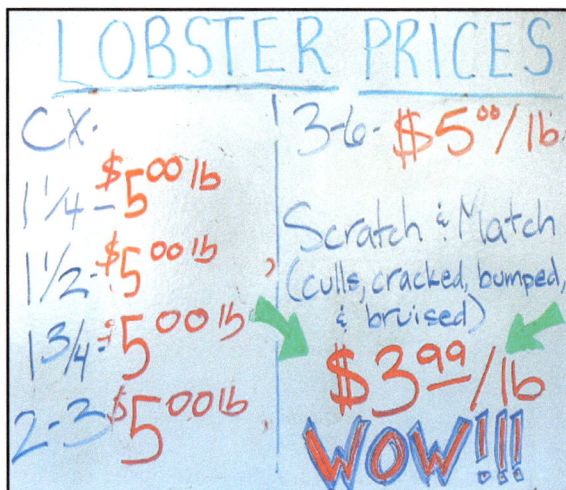

Best ever pound-per-lobster sign!

Now that you've located the best prices, it's time to start selecting the best lobsters, physically speaking. You can use these techniques whether you're dickering with dockside lobstermen or the part-time high-school seafood clerk at the local grocery store. More times than not you'll be looking into the glass lobster tank at the local market. Watch it for a while and you'll eventually see the alpha lobster(s) parading around on top of the pile. Look for a lobster with a long perfect pair of antennae whipping around ahead of it. It has not yet lost in many battles both at sea or here in captivity. These are the strongest and possibly freshest lobsters in the tank. They will last longest in your refrigerator and have the highest odds of being "full" with meat. When the clerk removes a lobster from the water, look to see if the claws flex upwards in a menacing defensive motion and the walker leg are frantically trying to get hold of something. Look at the swimmerets (pleopods) under the tail (abdomen). Are they flipping wildly spraying water rearwards all over the clerk? If so, this is a healthy, fresh, lively lobster well worth the final inspection technique, being the old carapace squeeze technique.

Most seafood clerks are proud of their lobsters. They love showing off the fact that they know how to handle lobsters and have some small modicum of knowledge about this high-priced crustacean. Don't be shy to ask if you can "see" the lobster before purchase. There is no need for a complete anal exam as my mother used to do, but it does make very good sense to give the carapace a quick 3-finger squeeze to check the hardness. The carapace is the main top body-shell where the eyes and antennae pop up. If you ask "may I touch him?" 9 out of 10 times the clerk will be delighted to allow you, an eager neophyte in his/her mind, the unique privilege of touching a live lobster.

Gently reach your thumb, index & middle finger over the top carapace, just behind the eyes, like you were going to pick up a bowling ball. The lobster is banded so no need to fear getting bit. Place your fingertips down low on the carapace, near where the small walker-legs protrude, and give a firm squeeze (Fig #4 below). If the shell dents inward easily, like squeezing an empty paper-towel tube, this is a "shedder". This lobster has recently shed its shell in the growth cycle. We could leave it at that, but I'm sure you want to know EXACTLY why this shedder is not a wise purchase. You may want to clearly explain why this lobster is unacceptable to the seafood clerk now staring at you, with mouth agape.

Lobsters molt and shed their exoskeletons several times a year in order to grow larger and larger. This amazing process has the scientific name of **ECDYSIS**. It's pronounced: eck-diss-sis, in case you want to quote it to the grocery clerk. During this process the lobster forms a perfect match of his outer shell, inside the old shell to be discarded. The old shell cracks open at the seam where the top of the tail meets the carapace back. The lobster struggles to pull his new body out of the old one, and usually pops free after an hour or so. These are dangerous moments for the lobster. This process often results in death due to over exertion and/or the lobster getting stuck in the old shell. In order to survive the squeeze, a lobster's muscles (the meat) must atrophy and shrink as much as possible. They are like helpless jellyfish on the ocean bottom for several hours after the molt. Slowly but surely the new, larger shell starts to harden. The interior fills with seawater to give the new shell shape and a small semblance of rigidity. Eventually, after a few weeks, the new shell fully hardens and the interior muscle (meat) regains its natural fullness and firmness.

Now, let's return to the carapace squeeze that you just performed. The shell felt like squeezing a cardboard paper-towel tube. Although the lobster appears big and healthy and has a shiny new shell, you now know that it's in a post-molt stage of ecdysis, aka shedder. There's a better than average chance that the muscle (meat) is somewhat shrunken and the body cavity and most interior tissue are filled with saltwater. You'll be paying for the scale-weight of saltwater, and water soaked meat. All will boil away to nothing when cooked. Ask the clerk to select another lobster for you and feel free to become touchy-feely with the carapace again. This time, the lobster's outer shell is shiny and as hard as a stiff double-thick metal cup. It has a perfect pair of antennae tucked back along its shoulders, the claws are lifting high over its head, and the swimmerets are flickering wildly. This is the lobster you've been looking for!

Since you've driven the seafood clerk to distraction thus far, why not go all the way with a final maddening request. Tell him that you have a preference for claw meat (or tail meat). Explain that you want to be gender specific in your final selection due to the nature of your lobster meat preference. If you like claw meat then request a male lobster. Request a female lobster is you prefer tail meat. Reason being that female lobsters have wider tails and smaller claws than males. If you look closely you can tell a male from a female lobster as they are walking along in the tank. Look for the lobsters with big rounded crusher claws, narrow angular tails, usually marching around tapping other lobsters with its antennae. This is a classic male lobster. Knowing this, you can pick your own lobster specifically and spare the seafood clerk the aggravation.

If however, you want to be absolutely sure of a lobster's gender, there is one proof positive way to tell. Most seafood clerks already know what to look for in lobster genitalia recognition, some don't. And, since you've probably already pressed the clerk too far, he may be tempted to try and pull one over on you by giving you the wrong gender of lobster than that which you'd requested. After you've done several carapace squeeze tests and have a final group of possible final selections, ask the sour-faced seafood clerk to turn the lobster over, bottoms up!

Look at the swimmerets, or pleopods, the little feathery fins lining both sides of the lobster's tail (abdomen) bottom. The very forward-most pair of these indicates the lobster's gender. If the forward-most swimmerets are a stiff, fingernail-hard pair of pointy sticks, it is a male lobster. (Fig #1) If the forward-most swimmerets appear to be just another soft feathery pair of swimmerets, then the lobster is a female. (Fig #2)

Fig 1: Male lobster sex organs

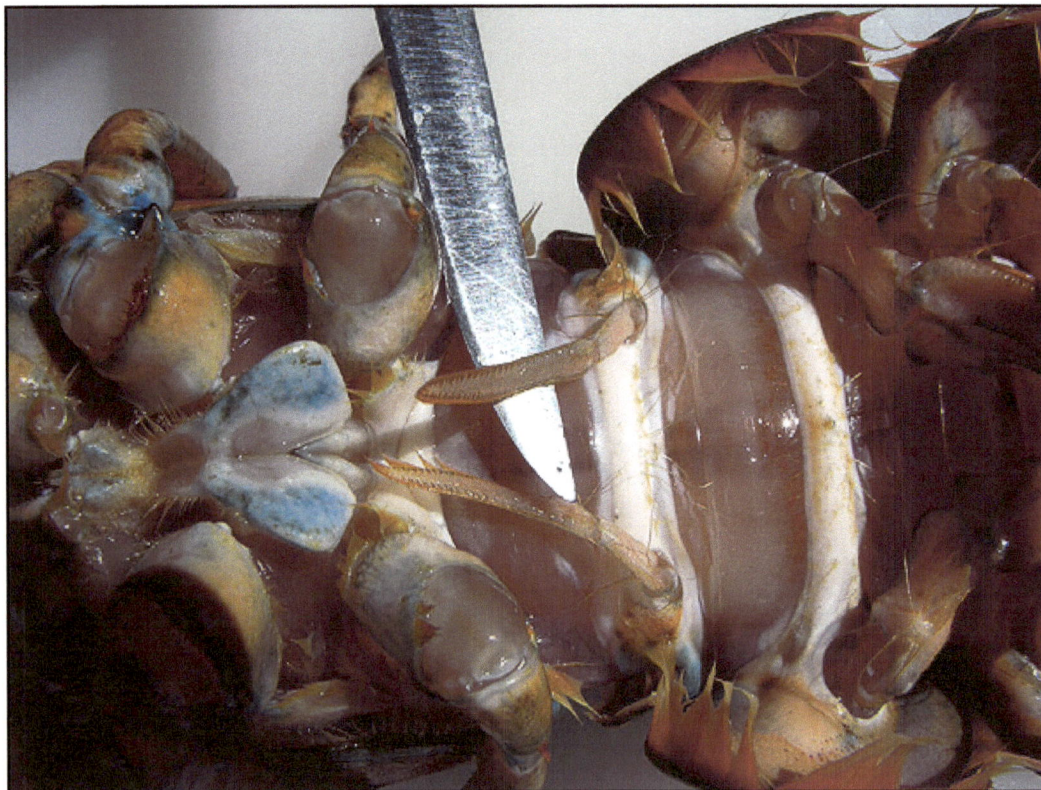

Fig 2: Female lobster sex organs

This is a rare one, containing both male & female sex organs. It is a true hermaphroditic species of lobster. It cannot reproduce; therefore it can only be produced as one of a kind. It has one stiff sex organ and one feathery sex organ as seen below.

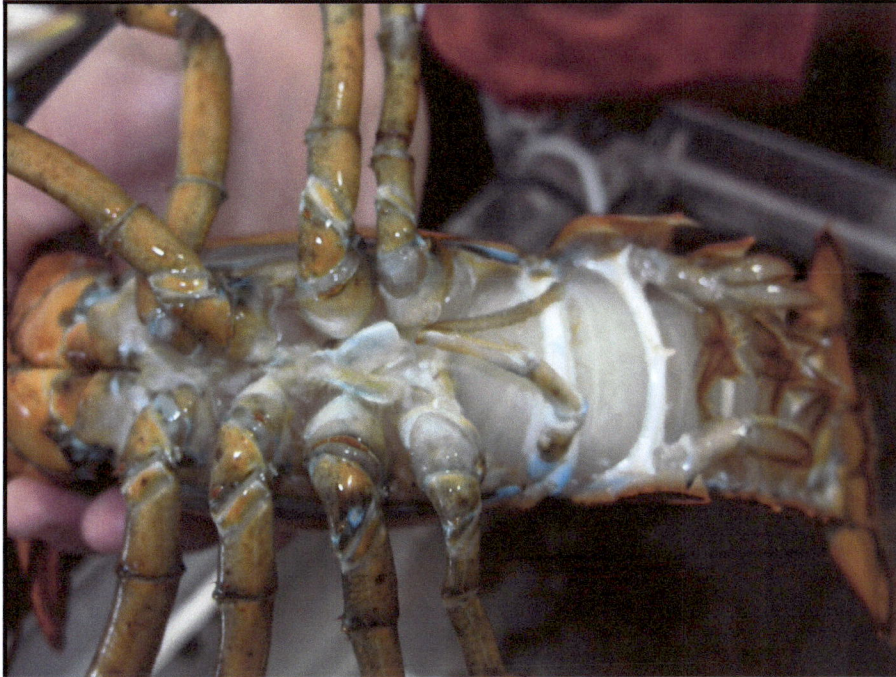

If tail meat is your passion then look for a lobster sitting in the corner on its wide, rounded, semi-curled tail with head and claws laid flat in front of it. The bottom pointy edges of the tail shell will flare outwards. This is the classic look of a female American lobster tail (Fig #3).

Fig 3: Classic, wide female lobster tail

There are a couple things that you do not want to see in choosing a fresh lobster aside from a soft carapace shell. The first thing is drooping claws and walker legs when being picked up out of the tank. If the lobster appears to be unconscious, he/she probably is, or shall be very soon. This lobster is at its maximum stress threshold. It has been badly handled previously, banged around or dropped. Or it has been in captivity without natural sustenance too darn long. One thing that you absolutely do not want to see is the skin showing through, from a large gap between the rear carapace and the forward-most tail shell joint, like the one in figure #3 above. Living lobsters have a tight attachment of carapace & tail at this strong body joint. This muscle only relaxes and separates in a post mortem state. In other words, look at the female lobster above in figure #3. It was dead for about 3 hours.

Now that you've made your selection, the lobster is removed from the water and bagged. Imagine yourself on the old game show "Beat the clock". The countdown to lobster mortality starts immediately. Lobsters can live for days out of water, given the right conditions. They will die within minutes if kept in any environment that is warm and dry. Keeping them in a cool place is extremely important. Always plan ahead when purchasing lobsters that will spend more than 2 hours before being cooked. Bring a cooler with some ice in it with you to the store. Place the bagged lobsters in the cooler, *IN THE BAG!* Do not take the lobsters out of the bag and lay them directly on ice, like the lobster on page #6. Fresh water is deadly poison to lobsters and melting ice will kill them quickly. When buying lobsters near the shore, the absolute best way to transport them is in a cooler full of freshly scooped saltwater. For long overland trips on warm days use a cheapo battery powered minnow aerator in the saltwater filled cooler. With this relatively inexpensive arrangement you can extend the life of a lobster to several months!

In the short run, store your lobsters in the refrigerator. Put them in the lowest vegetable crisper bin, loosely covered in the bag they came in. The bottom drawer always has the coldest air. I've had lobsters live for up to 2 weeks in a refrigerator crisper bin. How long after death can you eat a lobster? This depends on environmental conditions at and after death. For instance, a lobster dying in the trunk of a car on a hot summer day will turn rancid within a half hour. The meat will become toxic with each passing minute and inedible within 15 minutes or so after death. On the other hand, a lobster passing away while in a cold saltwater aquarium, that is quickly placed in the lower crisper bin of a refrigerator (like I did to the one above in figure #3) can retain its chilled post mortem edibility for up to 3 days and possibly longer.

This lobster was cooked after 3 days, which changes the entire chemistry of the thing and further extends the edibility period. At the time of this lobster's death, we had just come off a full 10 days of eating delicious New England lobster in every imaginable configuration. After being cooked, this dead lobster was put back in the crisper bin and eaten 3 full days later. It tasted as good as any freshly caught & cooked lobster that I'd ever had, nearly a full week after its death. This, of course, is not something that you want to plan on like the ageing of a prime rib roast. The rule is to eat seafood as fresh-from-the-water as possible.

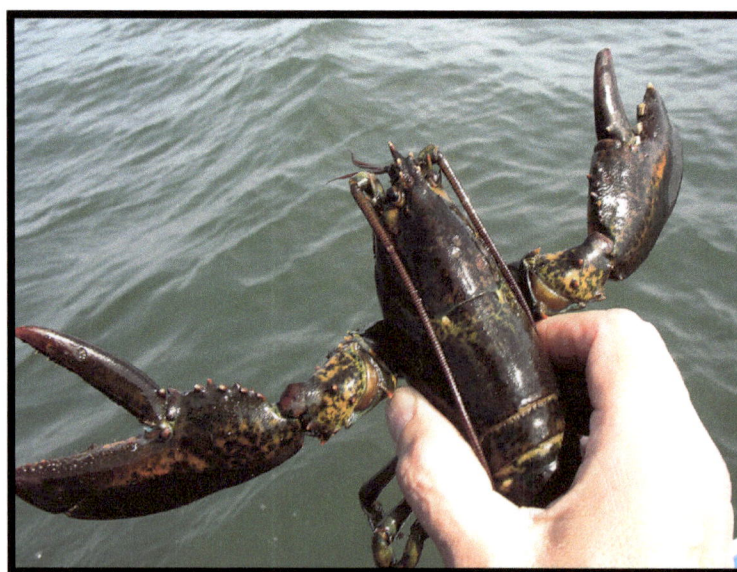

Fig 4: "Shedder" squeeze-tested

CATCHING LOBSTERS THE OLD FASHIONED WAY

*S*ome 20 years after our last night dive, I opened an old steamer trunk in the attic containing all of our SCUBA stuff. Except for the thick rubberized "US NAVY DIVERS" mask and fins, all else was dry-rotted and completely ruined from 2 decades of neglect. The tanks were out of code and hydrostatically useless. The regulator diaphragms were fused together and our wetsuits crumbled like dry cork. I simply closed the trunk lid and walked away. It was a distant memory from youthful days, long gone.

Now at the tail end of our working careers, we had more time to do some things that we'd always wanted to try. My wife took up golf, and as with most things she's done, became very good at it. I spent a year or two refurbishing a small runabout boat that had been left to rot at our cabin near the shore. It was an interesting project that panned out quite well. It was a 16' Starcraft with dual consoles and a 70hp Evinrude "Hustler" outboard motor. We retrofitted and rebuilt that boat from the bare metal hull up. I reinforced the side gunwales with stainless steel diamond plating to permanently fit a pair of downrigger fishing brackets. As I surveyed the completed project, one of the downrigger brackets caught my eye. It was made of super rugged plastic with a rounded forward edge groove. A length of anchor line was lying across the bracket top and slipped neatly into the groove and onto the garage floor. Standing in the boat I pulled on the anchor line and it slid back and forth in the downrigger receptacle groove with ease. The thought struck me that a lobster trap on the end of that line may not be a bad idea.

I'd never even touched a lobster trap in my life to this point, and I certainly have had worse ideas. I replaced the oversized foldout helm seat with a new pedestal single swivel seat. This made plenty of rear "working" deck space to manipulate lobster traps in the small 16' footer on the right. A pair of transom mounted cutting boards and utility holder-board for tools completed the project. From this point, all that I needed to get started is a lobster trap. Afterall, how hard can lobster trapping be?

16' boat retrofitted for lobstering

I found a local lobstering supply vendor near my old shoreline stomping grounds and paid him a visit. He was a genuine crusty "old-salt" and ran a one-man operation out of his oversized basement garage. I was somewhat skeptical of the place until I stepped over the big sleeping dog at the entrance door and walked inside. He had every single thing that you could possibly imagine for all types of fishing and shell fishing from claming to lobsters to offshore tuna fishing. The shop was neatly arranged into specific areas of marine needs, including boat supplies. He had clam rakes of all sizes and types, netting, and charter fishing gear from fillet knives to offshore outrigger repair kits. In a side room overlooking the rocky coast where his home was located, he had a full compliment of lobstering supplies.

I followed him as he meandered through isles of lobstering "stuff" that I had no idea existed nor how to use. I did recognize the plastic coated wire lobster traps stacked in the corner. The old man was rather tight lipped and wrongly assumed that I knew what I was doing. He stood near the counter waiting for me to gather the goods I'd need to be an honest to goodness lobsterman. His arms were folded and he wore a sour scowl.

I finally had to laugh out loud and confessed to the old man that I had never trapped lobsters before and asked, "Can you show me how all this lobster *pot* stuff works?" Once my ignorance was clearly admitted, the man became extremely helpful and gave me a full hours instruction on "lobster trapping 101". He cracked a smile and grabbed a big, brand new, blue lobster trap off the top of the stack. Setting it down on a clam basket he began a show n' tell that was more informative than most Department of Environmental Protection seminars I'd been to. He spoke clearly, with a classic New Englander's accent. He did not talk down to me and made sure that I understood all the things he was teaching before he went on to the next. After describing each item and technique used in lobster trapping, he'd look me in the eyes and say "yeah?" as if asking, "you got that?"

"This heya's a lobst'ah **TRAP**. It is not a lobst'ah **POT,** yeah? A lobster **POT** is what'cha cook 'em in." On this point he was angrily emphatic. I could only imagine how many thousands of blithering tourists walked into his shop and asked about lobster "pots". The square rectangular box lying at the bottom of the ocean into which lobsters walk is a TRAP. It looks like a big varmint type trap. It operates on the same principals of bait and catch retention as a trap? It opens and closes like a trap. So why does everyone call it a lobster "pot"? Some years later I found the answer to this strange conundrum. In the later 1700's, back in the days of yore, fisherman used a netlike mesh bag to catch lobsters. The bag was given structure by using strips of hemlock or pine to hold it open. The entryway extended out away from the main bag. It consisted of another wooden strip bent into a circle and sewn onto a hole in the bag. The entire contraption looked like a huge bizarre teapot sitting on its side. And thus we have it, lobster pot!

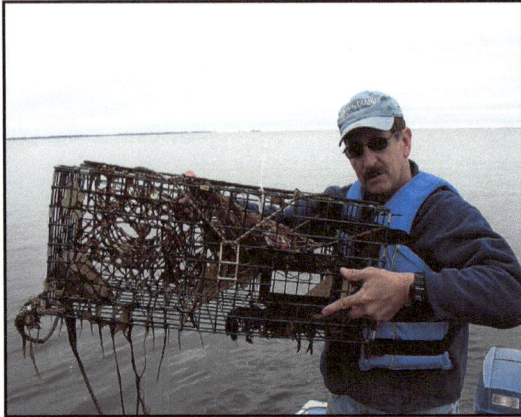

This heya' is a lobster trap, not a POT!

Attracted to a chunk of rotting mackerel, lobsters would climb up the side of the pot and jump down to the bottom. Some were unable to quickly escape as the pot was hoisted back aboard ship. As time went on, good old American ingenuity kicked in and many adaptations to the lobster pot were made.

Eventually the big mesh bag contained more structural wooden strips then netting. The flimsy bag became a rigid wooden box with separate compartments and tricky one-way internal netting traps and pitfalls. These lobster boxes could be set for longer periods of time and were easy to attend with top loading hinged doors. It became infinitely harder for lobsters to simply walk out of the box. This lobster catching device was no longer a pot, it was for all intents and purposes a *TRAP!*

Wooden lobster trap "making" became an art and trade all unto itself in the mid to late 1800s. Many backwoods hackers tried their hand at making lobster traps. Some were marginally successful, creating odd-looking facsimiles of the masterfully built, wooden round-top Maine lobster trap as seen in the stack below.

Most hacker traps would fail within the first few weeks of use. Wooden traps eventually became square in shape for ease in stacking and storage aboard ship in rough weather. They were weighted with stones, cast iron rods, and pairs of discarded red building bricks. In areas of strong tidal current or deep water it was often necessary to use 3, 4, or in rare cases 5 bricks. The term "bricker" was often used among lobstermen when commenting on a man's virility or stamina at sea. For instance a tireless stern-man was referred to as a "4 bricker". He could pull up the heavier 4-brick traps all day long. This of was course, before mechanical motorized pulley systems became popular.

As technology progressed, lobster traps were made of heavy gauge metal wire, coated with hardened plastic. This was a quantum leap in lobstering technology and remains the standard used today. Wire traps weigh much less and are twice as strong as the old wooden traps. The biggest advantage of metal wire traps is that it will not rot within 2 or 3 seasons; the metal traps can last forever.

Of course these new metal "last forever" traps posed one big ecological drawback that the old wooden traps did not. Since the beginning, lobstermen have experienced "lost traps". Lost traps can happen by any of myriad causes, such as tidal pull, boat propellers severing buoys or oceangoing vandalism know as getting "cut off". Being "cut off" happens during turf wars among rival lobstermen in disputed marine fishing areas. One lobster fisherman will cut the buoy off another lobsterman's trap line. The buoy floats away, the trap line sinks to the bottom and the trap becomes lost forever. Financially this is not a good way for lobstermen to conduct their squabbles and it rarely happens nowadays. A lost "ghost trap" can however, become ecologically devastating. Wooden ghost traps lasted only a short time on the sea bottom before rotting into pieces.

The new metal wire traps can last under saltwater an estimated 20 years before degrading to the point of failure. This type of ghost trap continues to fish, trap and kill lobsters, without bait, for 20 years. As lobsters continue to explore and use the ghost trap as an underwater hiding place, they become trapped one after another. As one dies in the trap, its body becomes bait for others, on and on into infinity. The metal wire ghost traps became unending black-hole killing machines for lobsters. Laws were enacted to prevent this from happening. Strict regulations now exist on the size, shape, and materials that can legally be used in construction of lobster traps. A biodegradable metallic substance was designed for specific use in lobster traps. These large metallic staple-like clips often referred to as "hog rings", are now the main joining component of all lobster traps throughout the world. The hog ring is designed to slowly corrode when immersed in saltwater. Lobstermen always have their hog ring kits at the ready, prepared to replace corroded trap joins here and there as needed. Regulations also list certain types of internal netting material to be legal or illegal. Basically, all internal netting used in a lobster trap must be of the common cotton twine type. This twine rapidly decays in saltwater and you'll often see twine knitting needles aboard all commercial lobster boats for onsite repairs. The simplest and fastest way to repair internal trap netting is to use plastic wire-ties. However, wire-ties are not biodegradable and therefore illegal to use in certain areas of lobster trap repairs.

To further protect juvenile and undersized lobsters, all traps must have what is called an "Escape Vent". This is a plastic plate with a hole cut-out in it. The plate is cleverly wedge-fitted into the trap wiring as seen on the previous page, between my left thumb and forefinger.

Law mandates escape vent sizes. The dimensions of the hole size changes sporadically due to federal and state shellfishery management calculations. Recent trends indicate that the dimensions of escape vents will increase with the minimum carapace size limits (how big a lobster must be in order to be a "keeper"). A recent vent size change in Connecticut raised the vertical size of rectangular vents (they come in circular vents also) from 1 & 15/16th of an inch to 2 inches. That's an increase of a paltry 1/16th of an inch. Put your thumb and forefinger as close together as possible without touching and look at the sliver of light between them. THAT is 1/16th of an inch.

Lobster trap escape vent flap

An old Andrew Dice Clay comedy shtick went like this; "The teacher asked me, so? what's the difference between 1 & 15/16ths of an inch and 2 inches? I told her, damn right teach. What's the freakn' DIFFERENCE! It don't matter!" Let's put the difference into another perspective. Imagine being a small lobster having the time of your life one evening. You find a tasty bag full of yummy rotting fish to pick away at, and fall backwards into the cramped parlor compartment of lobsterman Joe's trap. You turn to see a huge, enraged female lobster towering over you with claws twice the size of your body. Only one avenue of escape (vent) available and you head for the door! Your body compresses to the max and squeezes into that life-giving vent hole but you get stuck halfway to freedom. The very bottom edging of your carapace wedges into the vent door because of a measly 1/16th of an inch! The big, hungry, egg-bearing female lobster has been trapped in the parlor compartment for the last 6 days without any food. She slowly tears the little lobster to bits, back to front, and eats him alive. 1/16th of an inch may not matter to Dice Clay, but it sure as hell matters to that little lobster.

Escape vents are snap-fitting replaceable units. They free-clip into the top of the trap's vent cut-out hole, and are solidly attached at the bottom via biodegradable metal rings. These rings are made of a special substance that will quickly rust and disintegrate with water and time. Once dissolved, the vent flaps fully open and falls away. Lobsters of any size can easily walk out the uncovered trap hole. Always check vent rings. The one seen on right is stainless steel. It was erroneously placed on a new trap, factory built. You should check and replace biodegradable vent rings yearly. Do it not only because it's the law. Do it because it's the right thing to do.

Illegal stainless steel hog ring on vent

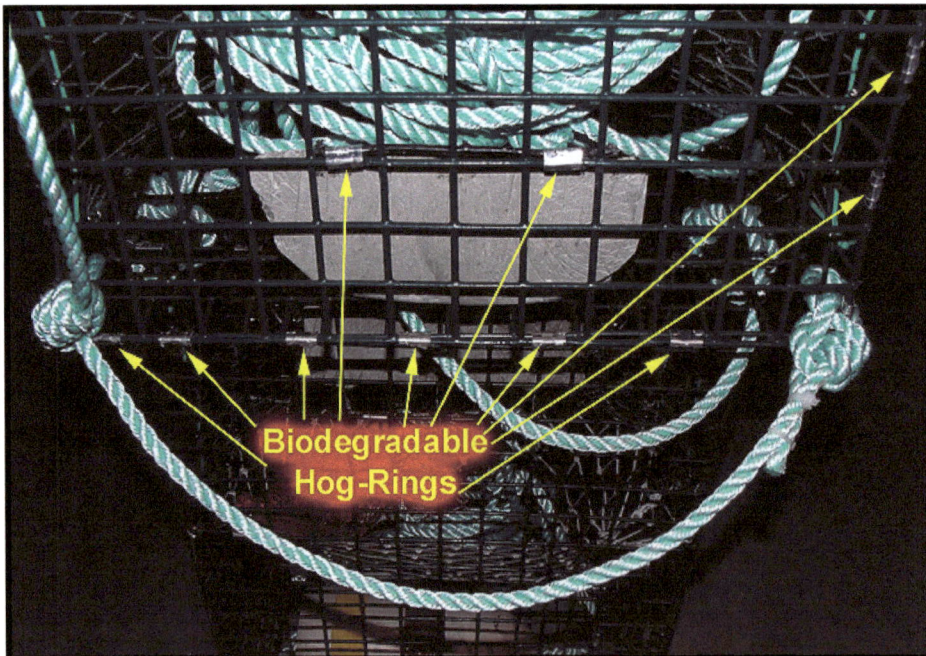

Wire lobster trap with biodegradable assembly

At the end of the day, all ghost traps are now rigged by design to fully implode and collapse flat, as the hog rings corrode and fail underwater. The internal netting disintegrates, the tide washes the pieces into the seafloor and ghost traps fade into oblivion. This is a good thing for the environment and lobstermen alike. The old man pointed to two circular metal rings that hold the entrance netting open at either side of the trap. The rings are about 6 inches in diameter. It seems incredible that a full sized lobster, with two fat claws, could actually squeeze through the rings.

I pressed my luck and asked; "How do the big ones fit in there?" He answered with a bit of sarcasm; "First off, there ain't no big ones in the sound (Long Island Sound) and next off, ya' can't keep the big ones even if'n you caught one!" I made a mental note not to ask another question until his entire demo was concluded. I later learned that indeed lobsters with carapace measurement lengths exceeding 5 ½ inches must be released.

"This orange plastic mesh stuff is bait-baggin' material." It's a rugged fluorescent plastic mesh tubing that comes in one continuous role and is sold by the foot. You cut off one-foot lengths per trap. One end is permanently strapped shut using a plastic wire-tie. The other end must be woven with heavy string so as to act like the mouth of a purse or cinch sack. The lobster bait is jammed into the expandable mesh bag. Then the bag mouth cinched shut, and tied up in the center of the trap top.

The salty old salesman went on to describe the concept of exactly how lobsters become trapped in the box. "They walk in heyah..." he put his arm in through the entry ring. "Then they tear at the bait bag until another one comes in and pisses off the first one..." He made a fighting fist with his other hand. "The smallest one runs away and ends up in heyah, yeah?" He stuck his arm into the back compartment of the trap.

The whole concept seemed ludicrous to me. And at the cost of pissing the old man off again I just had to ask him: "Let me get this straight. A lobster smells the bait hanging in the "kitchen" compartment. He squeezes his claws and body into this entry ring to get at the bait. While he's ripping at the heavy plastic bait bag, a second lobster comes in. Lobsters hate being close to each other and they have a shoving match and fist fight, right there in the cramped kitchen compartment. Then the loser, usually the smaller lobster, does an emergency retreat, going backwards into the funnel shaped parlor entryway netting? He drops off into the parlor compartment and that's where I'll find 'em when I pull the trap up?" The old man's answer was short and sweet: "You got it."

I stared at the lobster trap with more questions than I dared ask. Chief among them was a presupposition that any single lobster could come in and feed at his leisure and leave when he wants without getting pushed into the inextricable parlor chamber. Therefore, for every one lobster in the parlor compartment, at least one other lobster was in the trap and had escaped. Also a statement made by the old man that, "If you leave 'em in there too long, they'll get bored and walk right out again," simply defied all odds as I saw them in front of me.

If you're ever at the shore and have the chance to inspect a modern lobster trap, be sure to look at the funnel netting that leads to the parlor compartment. The netting is tightly woven, pulled drum-skin tight and almost impossible to pull your hand out once pushed in past the funnel mouth. How in the world could a lobster so much as even find the backside of the closed-lipped funnel opening, let alone squeeze his prickly spine covered body out through it? Some months later all of these unbelievable assertions proved to be fact. And for those of you who can't wait to read the answer later on, I'll tell you for certain: *YES!* Lobsters do get bored quickly and will squeeze their way out of any entrapment made by man.

Once the old man had covered all the nuances of lobster trap mechanics, he explained the use of "warp". Warp is a term used for the lines or cords employed in lobstering. He made it crystal clear that the weighted, sinkable polyester core "warp" in his hands was definitely not called ROPE! "Rope is what your wife hangs the dirty laundra' on!" If you're going out pleasure boating it's called "line", not rope. If you're going out lobstering, it's called warp. Warp lines are somewhat more expensive than the standard polyester rope for sale at Home Depot. Warp line is somewhat more tightly woven and has a dense core material running through its length. Warp line will not float due to the heavy core material that causes it to sink in water. Boat propellers become entangled, and trap lines are cut from buoys when lines float on the surface. This is a bad thing for lobstermen and pleasure boaters alike. The old man explained that all thrifty lobstermen, simply use a 10-foot leader of the expensive sinkable warp line running from surface buoy to a length of cheap standard polyester clothes line going down to the trap itself. The frugal old Yankee ways run deep in New England lobstermen.

He showed me how to tie a bridle loop-handle on the trap for ease in lifting them aboard at sea and explained how much warp line is needed to set up a trap. If you drop your trap in deeper water than you have line attached to it, the buoy disappears under the waves and your equipment is gone. If you tie 100-feet of line to the trap and drop it in 12-feet of water, the excess line either coils around underwater boulders and/or is snagged in boat anchors and fishing lines. All of which are conducive to a lost trap.

"You use the rule of fifty plus ten," said the old man. In other words, you decide the water depth that you are going to drop the trap in, add 50% of that depth number to the total. Then, add 10 to get the total number of feet of warp line needed on any given trap. You add the final 10 feet for the line needed to tie the bridle-handle loop. So, if you were to set up a trap to be dropped in 60-feet of water, the calculation would go like this: 60' + 30' (50% of 60) + 10' = total of 100' of warp line.

The buoy is the last component used in lobster trapping. It's a bullet shaped styrofoam float with a hole running through the middle of it. There are several clever ways to tie it to the warp line end.

Some of these methods include having a wooden broomstick handle stick up out the top for easy grabbing in rough seas or tying a pair of buoys together in tandem. The old man showed me the simplest and most efficient way to tie it off to the warp line. He doubled over a couple feet of the line, fed the doubled loop up through the buoy center-hole, and tied it off in a box knot at the top and base. A very clever, solid loop-handle stuck out the top end of the buoy, with the bullet end pointing down into the water. "Ya want to have the bullet-end pointin' down into the water to minimize tide pull." This guy knew EVERYTHING!

Buoy with loop handle

Since I intended on starting off with 10 lobster traps, I asked him for 10 buoys. He said, "You'll be needin' 11 of 'em." According to regulations, you must prominently display a buoy with your own unique color pattern on the boat where you pull and set the traps from. "I'll take 11 buoys; thank you very much."

Ten recreational size lobster traps do not fit in a Chevrolet Blazer regardless of how you stack them, so it takes 2 trips to and from the shellfish shack. You must come up with a unique paint scheme for your buoys, something that will be easy to spot in the open choppy seas. I used a honeybee color pattern, bright yellow ring top, white ring center and red ring bottom. You use a hot-tip soldering iron to melt inscriptions in each of the styrofoam buoys, including your shellfishing plate number, and buoy number. Next you decide what depth you intend to fish, cut and attach the warp lines in lengths accordingly. Coil up the warp with attached buoy, squeeze it into the parlor compartment of the trap, throw in a length of bait bag and close the trap top. Voila ~ One trap is ready to go to sea. Repeat this process (takes about 1 or 2 hours per trap) on ten traps and you're all set. Commercial lobster trappers have to repeat this process on 500 to 1,000 traps each year, definitely not fun.

We are not to be discouraged in our quest to catch a wild American lobster by our own doing in a way that has become world renown as a true New England tradition. Only a few things now stand in our path to becoming part of a rich American heritage and lore. Our licenses and traps are now all in order and we move on to the next major obstacle, namely, knowing *WHERE TO PUT THE DARN TRAPS?*

**Lobster traps prepped & ready
for new season.**

LOCATION, LOCATION, LOCATION!

*O*nce you understand the biology, likes & dislikes of lobsters, how to rig a lobster trap and the logistics of acquiring bait, you now face the most important task of deciding exactly *WHERE* to place your traps. In this decision, lay the ultimate outcome of your lobstering efforts, either success or failure. The effects of failure in trap placement will far exceed the mere lack of lobsters to eat. It can put an end to your entire operation, sometimes on a grand scale, as we will now discuss.

There are many important factors to be considered when making the final decision on placement. Obviously, the prime consideration is taking a wild guess as to where the darn lobsters are, and where they are not. They come and go regularly depending on myriad environmental factors. They have definite species-specific likes, dislikes, and general biological requirements too numerous to list. After five or six lobstering seasons a pattern of nuances will become evident and have clear meaning in your mind. Armed with this understanding and several seasons under your belt, you'll be able to lay your traps in places more likely to produce higher results. But, until then, trap placement is a confusing set of meaningless hints as to where lobsters are, and are not. Knowing this, I strongly suggest that the rookie lobster trapper simply sit back, relax and use the KISS approach: Keep-It-Simple-Stupid! You often catch as many lobsters by dumb luck as by intuitive reasoning and meticulous trap placement schemes.

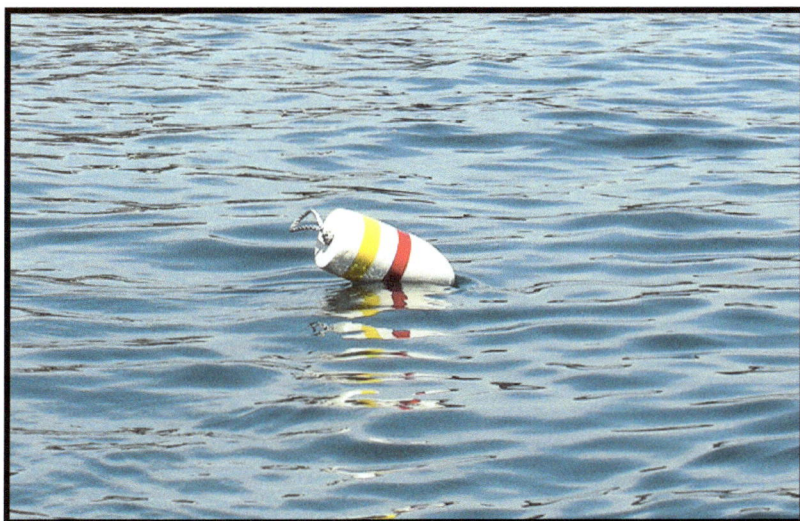

Lobster trap buoy

The first basic fact that you should know is that lobsters live in and around rocks. This is their cradle, safe haven, and general home turf. They are born as tiny bug-like nymphs free-floating on the ocean waves. They are no more than mosquito sized krill, consumed en masse by filter feeder fish such as the majestic baleen whale and the lowly menhaden. Only one in every 10,000-lobster larva survives long enough to grow to the size of a large house fly and sink to the seafloor. Finally having some control over their tiny destiny, they literally hit the ground running. They wiggle into the nearest crevice, overhang or kelp leaf and hide out for as long as their little empty stomachs will allow.

After growing to the size of a small human thumb, they instinctively know that they are now at the very bottom of the food chain. They know that just about every living thing on the ocean floor is actively hunting them and will eat them instantly on sight. Looking up from tiny holes in the murk at daytime, they see large shadows passing overhead. Some expose themselves briefly for a clearer look. These unfortunate few are instantly sucked up, crushed, and eaten by daytime predators such as cod, tautog, porgies and cunners.

The wise survivors learn to instantly react to passing shadows, and will reflexively go into defensive posture even when later grown into large alpha lobsters. Daytime movement for these tiny juveniles is far too dangerous. They learn to take full advantage of the natural gifts they'd obtained through years of evolution. Having little need for eyesight, they only come out at night. Their sense of smell and touch exceeds that of any underwater creature in their realm. With these senses, they can clearly detect food, mates, and enemies from hundreds of feet away. They can discreetly "see" through sense of touch, their immediate surroundings, remote seascape structure, and escape routes in murky darkness. They have a sense of recall and can remember things in an ever-changing underwater environment. The very few who live beyond thumb size, become battle hardened survivalists. They have seen and done things that we humans cannot begin to imagine. Of the many survival techniques hard learned by these few, the single most important is to *STAY IN THE ROCKS!*

So now we know where they are for sure. We check our nautical charts and watch our onboard SONAR chartplotters for underwater rocks, humps, and lumps. With your partner at the helm calling out the drop "NOW!" you heave the traps overboard like precision depth charges on an enemy submarine. And, likely as not, most of them do in fact land directly atop a rock or pile of rocks, the home address of Mr. & Mrs. Homarus americanus. Sometimes our cleaver understanding of where lobsters live pays off. But sometimes, it does not. Sometimes the greatest underwater rock pile in the area provides nothing except what we call "Long Island Opilio Crabs." These are those disgusting, bait-robbing, inedible, hairy looking spider crabs. Even the seagulls are reluctant to touch them!

This is a huge Long Island "Opilio". Jokingly named after the Alaskan crab

A few weeks of feeding expensive bait to Long Island Opilios can get depressing after a while. Where did the lobsters go? They live in rocks right? Yes they do, but God gave them eight legs and a tail for a reason: So they can move around. They may be sleeping right under your trap all day, but heading out for food somewhere else all night long.

One evening in the early 70's, we did a lobster dive around a small circular rock island in the middle of the ocean. It was a boulder-strewn island about 50 yards end to end, covered in nesting seagulls. We anchored in the deeper water off the rock pile and did a sweep of the deep submerged rocks all around the island. It was uncanny that we spotted only a few juvenile lobsters in this outstanding stretch of rocky terrain. Out of boredom I swam to the shallow beach-break near the island, and stood up in hip deep water. The bottom was literally covered in broken clamshells. The seagulls had spent a full summer season dropping clams on the rocks to crack them open. As I bent over to clear the fog from my diver's mask I looked under the water at my fins. The bottom was covered in lobsters, big ones. I floated along in 3 feet of water using only my snorkel to gather a bag full of lobsters in a few minutes. They were sifting through the broken shells like beggars at a town dump in thigh deep water.

This rock pile in the middle of nowhere had one of the biggest concentrations of lobsters that I'd ever seen. However, there were only a mere handful of lobster buoys in the area. Reason being that the "keepers" (legally keepable sized lobsters) all went ashore every night for dinner. The topwater lobstermen gave up on the reef surrounding the island where a huge biomass of lobsters slept everyday. Had one of them waded ashore and heaved a few traps in the puddle deep water, they'd been jammed with lobsters!

Lobsters have been known to travel over 3 miles in a 24-hour period. Where they go, when and why they go there is a matter of countless variables and conditions. Theories among veteran lobstermen range from scientific fact, to mythological beliefs, to astrological nonsense. The fact remains that lobsters travel great distances every day. They are largely nomadic. However, there are great numbers of semi-permanent settlers that will inhabit an area for extended periods of time. When conditions so move them, they will quickly kick heels for another place to live.

When they do decide to move from one rock pile to another, it often takes the form of mass exodus. Someone cries "westward ho!" and it looks like a lobster wagon train heading out from one reef across the sand to another. This mass exodus can be caused by any of several conditions, from molt cycle to water salinity changes. It can be maddening trying to understand why your favorite lobster-producing reef suddenly goes completely dry. You wonder if all the lobsters have been caught and move all but one trap to another area. For three weeks that one trap comes up spotlessly empty. Why is it that the fourth week a lobster trap comes up chock full of lobsters?

The one thing that's easiest for us humans to monitor is water temperature. In my humble opinion, this is the single most calculable factor in the lobster equation. Seasonal changes are probably the second most calculable factor. Both, in combination, play yet another role in the movement of New England lobsters. For instance, the water temps go up and down all year. Lobsters move and react to temperature changes independent of seasonal changes. As seasons change, days get longer or shorter which triggers movement and biological functions pre-programmed in a lobster's nature. Together, water temps and seasonal changes create a separate and unique pattern of movement and actions. For instance, in the case of an extremely warm winter turning into spring. Or, conversely, an extremely cold summer turning into fall. Now consider the dozens of incalculables, such as the effects of acid rain or total snowfall, salinity levels or riverine contaminant run-offs. As you can see, it's impossible to accurately figure out why lobsters move from place to place. Once again it is best to use the KISS method, knowing that seasonal and water temperature plotting will suffice nicely.

Beany catches a huge King Salmon using temp probe

Water temps in large bodies of water are usually stratified to some extent. The temperature at the top of the water is rarely the same as at the bottom. Also, there is often several strata, or bands of differing water temps anywhere in between. Great Lakes salmon fishermen like Beany on the left, uses a submersible temperature gauge to locate the depth at which the band of water holds a specific temperature. Trout and salmon are most comfortable and often feed within water temp rages of 42 ~ 52 deg f. That specific band of water is found, for instance, between 80 and 95 feet of water in a spot where the bottom depth is 200 feet.

Thus, downriggers are set to troll lures at the 85-foot level, in between the perfect temp range strata. Most lobstermen monitor the season and the topwater temps observed on standard SONAR chartplotter units. In deeper offshore waters this will suffice as bottom temps in hundreds of feet of water seldom change. In the "short-water" inshore areas however, it's best to take a lesson from the Great Lakes fishermen. Unlike those who search for the right depth level, the inshore lobsterman need only worry about temperature at the very bottom.

Here are a few things to consider in finding the right place with the right temp range to set your lobster traps. Lobsters can live in water with temps ranging from 1 degree above freezing up to 70 degrees f. Big bucks grocery store lobster display tanks are set to chill the water to around 42 degrees for longevity. It has been reported that lobsters do not actively feed in extremely cold waters. Also that lobsters make a traditional end of the summer pilgrimage out to deeper waters to spend the winter. In my personal observations, some of these are true and some are not. After watching captive lobsters in large seawater aquaria I can assure you that they will start dying in water temps exceeding 70 degrees f. They will eat when they are hungry in nearly all temperature ranges in all seasons. They do however, seem to eat more aggressively in temperature ranges of between 48 & 62 degrees f. I can honestly say that the theory of offshore winter pilgrimages is true to a small extent.

During cold-water winter night SCUBA diving trips near Connecticut shores I saw and collected lobsters. They were not as active or in as great numbers as during the warm summer dives, but they were certainly present. Did some of their masses exit to deeper water or were the majority of them simply hunkered down in place? I don't know. Do the remaining inshore lobsters go into some mild form of dormancy and slow down their eating habits, therefore limiting the trapping catch in the dead of winter? NO! I've personally witnessed several seasons of inshore winter lobstering and inshore lobsters in captivity in bitter cold tank water. The winter trap catch in water temps near 34-deg f were often times better than some mid-summer periods. Captive inshore specimens in tank water having 38-deg f temps acted as lively and hungry as any time previous in warmer waters.

As an interesting aside, I did observe a large 8lb. male lobster from the deep Canadian maritime waters off Nova Scotia. In the same tank with the inshore lobster, the Canadian deepwater specimen did, very obviously, seem to go into a mild state of hibernation when the water temps dipped to around 38-deg f. He hunkered himself down on the bottom in between large rocks and would only move to snatch up his food (dropped every 4th day). This lobster can be seen below in mild state of hibernation.

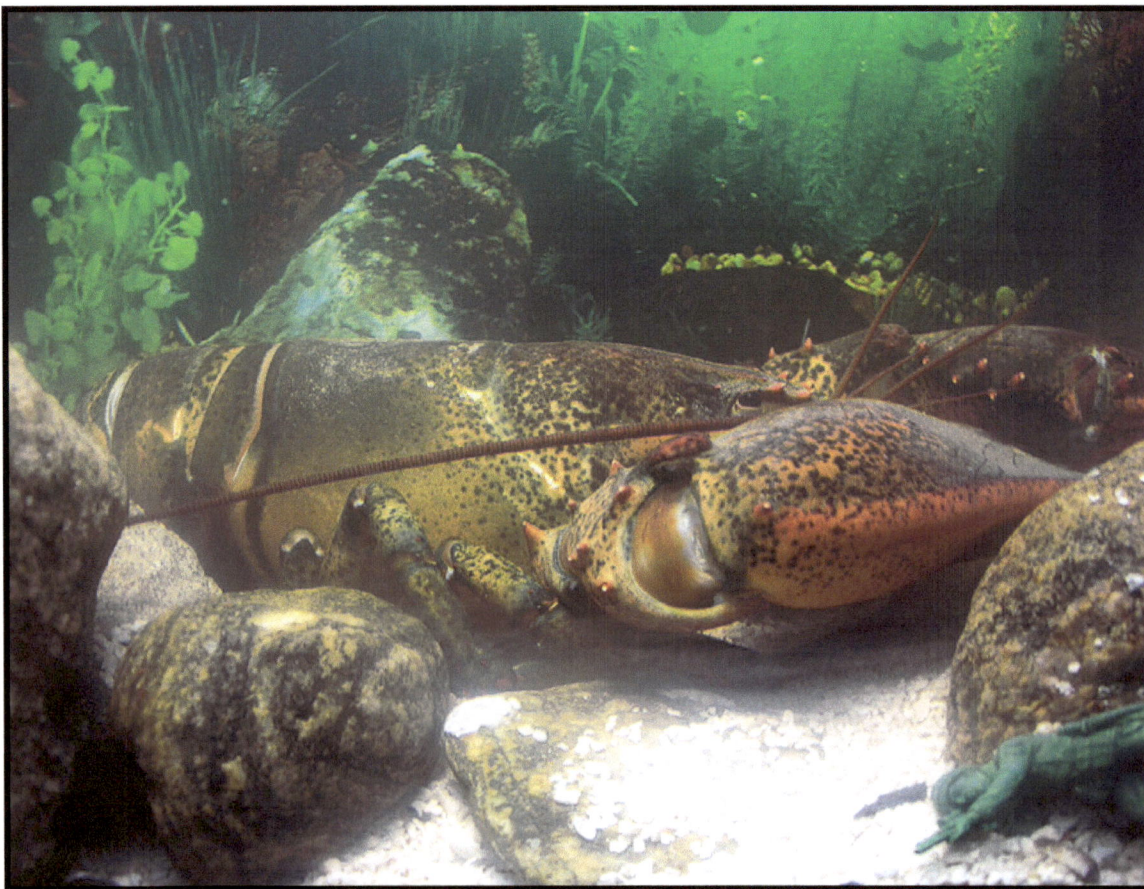

**Noofie, an 8-pound deepwater lobster from the
Canadian maritime in coldwater hibernation**

Now, armed with the information stated above, let's put our traps in the right places at the right times to maximize our chances of success.

- **WHEN?**
If you live near the shore, have access to a boat, and don't mind fighting bitter cold winter sea-spray, then you can leave your lobster traps in all year long. If you want to keep recreational lobstering just that, recreational, then you are best to put the traps in no earlier than the end of March. The very latest to leave them should be no later than November 1st. In my inshore lobstering experiences as a lobster diver and trapper, these seem to be the optimal date ranges of the calendar for recreational lobstering on Long Island Sound.

- **WHERE?**
Don't place all your traps in one spot. Hedge your bets and do as retirement investment bankers suggest, *diversifying!* Find rocky stretches of shoreline and inshore rock piles away from the beaten path and navigation channels. Drop some traps *near* them, not on top of them. Locate submerged reefs and nearby rock piles. Draw a map and a pencil-line that connects the dots (reefs and rock piles). Drop some traps along the sandy bottom along that pencil line, seemingly in the middle of nowhere. If you hit a mass exodus-march you'll find more lobsters in a single trap than you could ever imagine. Try dropping a few traps in "short-water", 2 or 3 feet. Places like near a stinking seagull refuge outcropping or near an old rotting pier in a lesser-known bay. All of these can produce some big old lobsters.

- **DEPTH?**
Basically, fish shallow in the cooler stretches of spring and fall, and deeper in the warmer periods of summer. Water temps will absolutely dictate where the majority of lobsters will, or will *NOT* be. Do yourself a huge favor early on in your quest for lobsters. Go on Ebay and find a Fish Hawk model #520 Temperature/Digital Depth Counter for about $20. Clip a 20 oz. bank sinker to the probe and send it down to the very bottom of the area you intend to set your traps. Bottom temps are ever changing in most New England inshore areas. Generally you're looking for bottom temps between 45 and 65 deg f. To be more specific, the best temperature range for active and foraging lobsters (as observed and recorded in my tank specimens) is between 48 and 54 deg f. As the shallow water bottom temps rise in the summer, seek rocky areas in the deeper waters.

One non-environmental consideration in placing your lobster traps is the proximity to other lobstermen's buoys. Although it is an "open ocean", some areas are considered personal property of certain lobstermen that have trapped there for long periods of time. When newly colored sets of buoys suddenly appear a turf war can erupt. In the old days this type of turf wars culminated in gunfire. Nowadays, it results in shouting matches and marine vandalism in the form of being "cut off", also known as having the buoy cut from the warp and loosing the trap.

You can avoid this by using some common sense approaches to placing your traps. First of all, do not drop traps near or on top of another lobstermen's trap(s) and carefully preplan the tidal swing of your buoy. Although your trap may physically hit the bottom far away from another trap, your buoy may float back in the tide and tangle in someone else's warp line. This is considered real bad form. Place your traps in such a way that there's enough room for a boat to safely navigate in between all the buoys. This shows a little courtesy for fellow lobster trappers and makes it easy for fishermen to navigate the minefield of lobster buoys. Many traps have been lost to honest fishermen having to cut propeller entangled warp lines to avoid being dashed on the rocks. Another technique used as a small courtesy to boaters is attaching a bank sinker to the warp line about 8-feet below the buoy with a plastic wire-tie. This assures that the line will sink straight downwards in all tidal conditions. This stops the line from floating a few inches under the surface during tidal swing, ensnaring boat props or sailboat keels.

Also, be advised that commercial lobstermen often set traps in multi-trap strings with a single buoy. Imagine laying 20 traps on the ground, in a row. Now connect them all to each other with 30-foot lengths of warp line. The total length of traps extending for nearly 2 football fields! The end trap is connected to the buoy line. One single buoy (sometimes two buoys, one from the other end trap) floats on the surface. When the single line is hauled, it brings up 20 or more, big commercial lobster traps spanning nearly 200 yards of line. If you see a commercial lobsterman's single buoy, realize that it is the tip of the iceberg. Look which way the bullet tip of his buoy is pointing into the water. It's pointing out the direction where 200 yards of lobster traps are laying on the bottom. Don't go bottom fishing in that area and definitely do NOT lay your traps there.

Put yourself in a commercial lobstermen's boots for a moment. Imagine trying to haul up your final string of traps after bouncing around all day, soaked in putrid rotting skate juice. The winch is groaning because of the excess strain put on it by what you assume to be a tangled line. One of the clutches burns out, another costly repair back at port, and you have to manually assist the pull. Your back and arms are screaming from a long 12-hour day at sea on a stinking lobster boat. You wonder why in hell you ever got into this miserable business in the first place. The $4.78 balance in the checking account is on your mind, as the cause of the smoking winch breaks the surface of the water. Some recreational lobstermen's trap is inextricably tangled, dead nuts in the center of your 40-trap string! Now, let's think about this for a moment. What are the chances that Mr. Recreational-Lobstermen will ever see that trap again? Actually, the chances of him ever seeing another of his traps are slim to none after his uniquely colored buoys are methodically hunted and cut-off by an enraged commercial lobstermen. Yes, it is an "open ocean" but there are certain common sense courtesies that all lobstermen must be aware of.

Another non-environmental consideration in trap placement is boat traffic and accessibility to the public at large. It is illegal to place traps in official navigation lanes, and a bad idea (at the least) to place them in well-used passage channels and throughways. As previously discussed, boat propellers and motor skegs also raise holly hell with lobster warp lines. Sailboat keels reach deep in the water, can snag warp lines and drag your traps far from the original set location before coming free. Unfortunately rocky structured seafloor, best for lobstering, is also best for fishing. An old fishing pal of mine once likened it to kids hanging around the 7-11 at night rather than some empty stretch of highway. "There's a lot goin' on at the 7-11," he'd say. The same is true for the fish, and fishermen know this well. They drift-fish through and around the rocky reefs and often drop anchor right among nests of lobster buoys. Sometimes an anchor will land on your trap or snag your warp lines. Before the advent of inexpensive fisherman's SONAR/GPS/Chartplotter underwater rigs, we knew that lobster buoy clusters meant "rocks" and "reefs". That is where we'd drop anchor and start fishing. More times than not fishermen snag expensive lures and rigs in your gear and have "rights of retrieval". They pull up your trap from the bottom and remove their entangled lures and rigs before sending the trap back down. During the time it takes to do this, the fishing boat (and your trap) will drift with the tide. Your traps always end up hundreds of yards from where you'd originally set them, covered in coils of fishing line, fluke rigs, and diamond jigs. If you set GPS waypoints for each trap location, be sure to run ever widening corkscrew search patterns for lost buoys.

One day I was checking and re-baiting traps on the boat gunwale as I drifted past two surly looking fishermen sitting in a small open boat. Their boat seemed to be anchored as I floated closely by them in the tide. It suddenly struck me that they did not have an anchor overboard. They'd tied a line to the top of one of my lobster buoys, using my trap as an anchor! At this point you have several options and courses of action available. You could pull the Glock .40 caliber S&W semi-auto pistol out of your sea bag and hit their boat just below the water line in a withering fusillade of gunfire. Or you could unleash a torrent of threats, insults, and vulgarity that would singe their hair. Or, on a more sophisticated scale, you could summon the nearby DEP officers in their big green gun-boat and have the two morons arrested. In that I'm a "recreational lobsterman" and do it strictly for recreation, and had eaten lobster daily all summer long. I took a different approach.

"How they bitin'?" I asked with a hi-sign wave of the hand. "Not so good today" was the answer, with upturned palms.

I held up the buoy of the trap I was about to throw over, pointing to the colors and said, "Hey, you guys are tied off on my lobster buoy. Can I check that one now, and you can tie up to this one if you want?" I heaved the trap overboard. The two men were dumbstruck. They said something like, "Ugh, nope, we gotta' go, thanks anyways". They untied my buoy line and slowly motored away. Now, in retrospect, I think you'll have to agree that this was the single best way to handle that situation. No one was shot or injured, nothing was damaged, and no one was arrested or parties to a long ugly civil suit. By chance, the lobster trap that they were tied off to had the single largest keeper lobster of the season in it. And in the end, I did not create a pair of vengeful enemies that would've returned in the night to cut off all my buoy tops. Instead, I made two friends that went away fully embarrassed by their stupidity, and will probably never do that ever again.

On the other hand and most maddening are the "Pot Raiders". These are common sneak thieves that commit the crime of larceny, plain and simple. They come in two distinct flavors. The first of which are the drunken fishermen and hoodlum teenagers. These petty thieves will pull up and rob your traps just for the fun of it. After a great day of boozing on the sound, or from late night zodiac boats, they find it hilarious to screw with lobster traps. These are easy to pull up on single trap strings and can be done with relative stealth. Sometimes they leave you a clever little keepsake as a sign of their trespass. A friend of mine put out two lobster traps to show his young kids how cool and interesting the ocean can be. He wanted to show them respect for the endangered environment. The kids loved pulling up the traps to see what type of strange stuff was inside. The fellow never actually caught a single lobster, but the kids loved playing "junior marine biologist" during every trip out. One day he could only find a single trap, the other was "cut off". The remaining trap was stuffed full of garbage, from Dunkin Donut refuse to used condom wrappers. This was a tad over the top for even the crudest "pot raider". My friend removed his trap and now uses it for a garden planter in his front yard. The kids have given up on the ocean, a sad chapter for sure.

The second type of "pot raider" is the hardened criminal. Thankfully they are rare and only work a specific area of the oceanfront. They are common street trash with absolutely nothing to loose. Time in prison to these folks is time well spent with regular meals, television, and air-conditioned workout facilities. They do not give a damn about the law, personal property, civil rights, or humanity in general. In one recent case, a fellow from Providence Rhode Island would make long trips, weekly, to the Southeastern Connecticut shoreline near the Rhode Island border.

He would launch a small boat in the dark of night and methodically raid each and every lobster trap in his path. Later returning to Providence with a trunk full of illegal lobsters, shorts included. He'd sell them on the street for $5 a piece. He raided the traps in both Rhode Island and Connecticut for quite some time. The multi-jurisdictional maritime and environmental protection agencies finally concerted their efforts to catch this brazen lobster thief. He was put away for a while, and then went back into business. He was finally taken into custody by environmental police at gunpoint one night when coming ashore with his ill-gotten gains. I'm told that several of the commercial lobstermen were laying in wait for him at night. You can rest assured that not one small piece of neither his boat nor his body would ever be seen again, had they caught him. I'm absolutely certain that many of these street urchins have mysteriously gone missing and slipped from focus in such a manner. He was fortunate to have been taken into custody by civil authority rather than popular authority.

A friend of mine was a law-biding sportsman. One of the fishing lines got snagged. They put the boat in reverse, and carefully motored over to the buoy that was bobbing from the entanglement. Knowing the unspoken rules, my friend attempted to raise the trap as quickly as possible in order to set it back near its original position. This was an area of extreme tidal rush and the trap was a heavy-laden four-bricker. My friend squeezed hard on the warp line, pulling against the tide with all his might to quickly retrieve the tube lure. His hands and fingers suddenly went numb and the warp line fell from his bloody hands. Five feet under the buoy, the warp line was meticulously laced with rows of double-edged razors, the thin Wilkinson type that you shave with. His hands, fingers, and tendons were sliced to the bone. This is a rare but extreme example of the extent that lobster trappers are willing to go in protection of their property.

Among the "eloquent" methods, there's a type of underwater marine technology that can drastically reduce trap raider theft, tampering, and vandalism. It's called a *Galvanic Timed Release* or *GTR*. These are small alloy clips that corrode (dissolve) at a given rate when submerged in seawater.

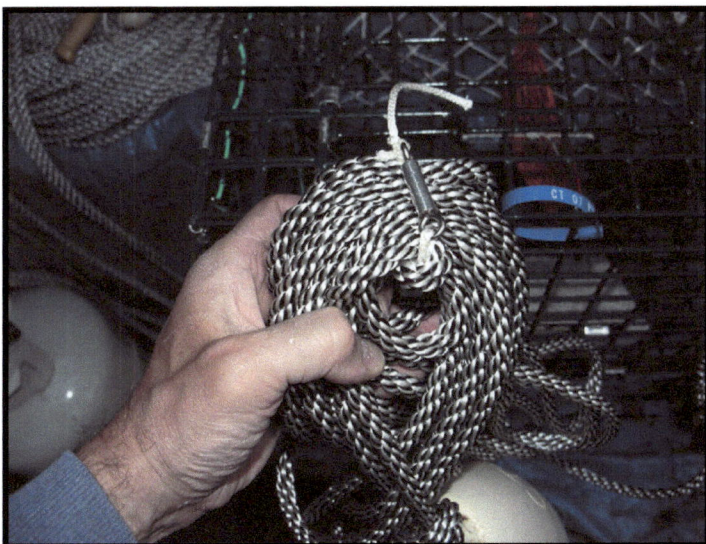

Galvanic time-release clip, strapped to lobster warp line

They come in sizes that will dissolve in specific time frames, from a few hours to a few weeks. GTR's are used in myriad marine applications. Used in a lobstering application, they allow the lobsterman to hide the whereabouts of his trap until the day and hour of pickup. For instance suppose that you wanted to place your traps in a remote location known to be lobster rich, but having high incidence of pot raiding. You elect to do a 3-night soak and pickup your traps around noontime on the 4th day. You coil up your warp line and buoy. Loop-tie the coil with a small length of twine clipped to the top of the trap with a galvanic timed release. Throw the trap overboard and the entire shebang, trap, warp line and buoy all sink to the bottom.

On the surface, there are no indications whatsoever of your trap's presence. In 96 hours, roughly 4 days from hitting the saltwater, the GTR corrodes through. The clip breaks free and the buoy pops up to the surface with your warp line attached to it.

GTR's work extremely well for certain applications, and not so well for others. There are a few downsides to using GTRs and I believe that I've experienced them all. First off, they cost about $1 a piece. This raises the ante and overall cost of lobster per pound. Using one of these in a commercial 50-trap string is far more cost effective than using one per each trap in recreational lobstering. Another minor drawback is the reliability of the corrosion rate. GTR's come with a complex chart of calculations, highly dependent upon water temperature at the depths you are fishing. You can take a wild guess at the bottom temps and hope that your buoys will pop up within a 6~8 hour range at best. Or, you can send a "FishHawk" submergible temperature probe to the bottom before setting each trap (a very time consuming process) to get a closer estimate on popup time.

The next major consideration when using a GTR is in attaching the warp coil to the GTR clip and trap top. If not done with extreme attention to detail, the GTR will corrode as planned but the coiled warp will get hung on the trap itself. Or if by chance the trap settles crooked on the bottom the warp coil can get snared on rocks. Either way, the buoy never surfaces and the trap is lost. The last inconvenience is the time that it takes to properly reset your traps with a GTR. I can reset a standard trap in about 2 or 3 minutes depending on weather conditions (commercial pros do it in mere seconds). Setting up a GTR on a trap takes me nearly 10 minutes of fiddling around at best. And every time I threw a GTR rigged trap overboard my heart sank with the trap, line and buoy, never knowing if I'd ever see it again. I no longer use GTR's and have only lost a total of 2 traps in the past 6 seasons of lobstering. One of these was lost due to tidal pull; the other was probably cut off.

The simplest tactic in safeguarding your traps is to find a place in waters near shorefront cottages, homes and office buildings. Here, your buoys are thought to belong to the cottage owners themselves. The presence of office personnel at lunch break or vacationing residents having a picnic is usually more than enough to dissuade pot raiders from tampering with buoys in the area.

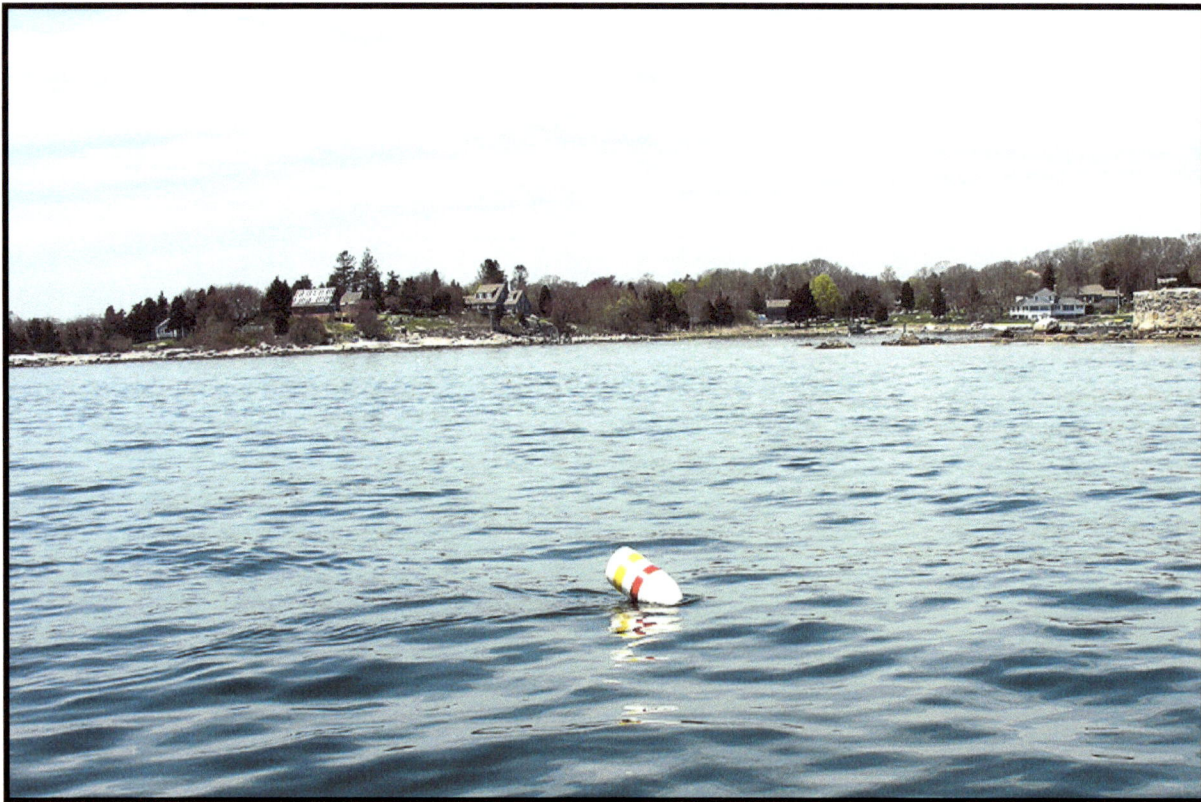

Place traps near waterfront cottages for security

In the cooler early spring months venture up into tidal bays and salt-river inlets to set your traps. We once visited some friends on vacation in the Niantic area. The grandmother of one of my friends reminisced about how she used to love eating lobsters in her younger days. Everyone knew that I was a night diver and we talked about deepwater lobster dives. I had my mask, snorkel, and dive light in the car trunk and offered to take a look around near the shallow inshore dock, expecting nothing more than a cooling dip in the water. The dock rested on 3 large boulders, the only structure in miles of shallow inshore sand bottom. Sure enough, I saw several small lobsters crawling around the rocks. A few minutes later I found a big 2-pounder lumbering along the sand near the rocks. That night the old lady ate fresh steamed lobster caught in only three feet of inshore brackish water. There were no lobster traps or buoys in or near that busy swimming area whatsoever and yet the lobsters thrived there.

One of the last considerations is in the process of setting the trap itself. A technique that I use all the time is to secure the trap hatch with plastic zip-strip wire-ties. I never leave port without a bag full of wire-ties. They are as important to me in resetting each trap as putting fresh bait in there. Zip tying the trap hatch serves two purposes, one for peace of mind and the other for security. Many times you pull up a trap with absolutely nothing in it. No spider crabs, no bait, no whelk, nothing! This is uncanny and you ask yourself how in hell something could've eaten all the bait and yet the trap is clean as when you bought it? This is maddening and in your mind there can be only one logical reason; trap raiders.

Actually, there are many other logical reasons, but it's easier to blame trap raiders than your own bad luck, poor location, or sea lice that can eat bait like battery acid. If you take 5 seconds to zip-tie the trap hatch to the cage, securely shut, then all doubt will be removed. Trap raiders will simply cut the plastic zip-tie without ruining your trap and steal your lobsters. When you pull up a trap with no zip-tie, you have been robbed, period. Reset it and go on to the next. When you pull up a spotlessly clean trap with the zip-tie in place? You are the victim of simple bad luck and sea lice. In either case your mind is put at ease and the doubt is gone. On a more physical security note, harbor seals have been seen and are known to raid lobster traps. They are extremely dexterous and can easily unlatch lobster traps to get at the tasty contents; both bait and lobster, within. A simple plastic zip-tie will keep seals out 99% of the time.

Inshore seal looking for a free meal in an unsecured lobster trap

HOW LONG IS TOO LONG?

*H*ow often should I check my traps? This is a very important question with many arguable answers. As previously mentioned, the true answers will come clear to you after 5 or 6 full seasons of lobstering. But if you can't wait that long I will give you some facts and revelations from my personal notes and experiences. The number of days that a trap is left underwater, or "set time", is called a "soak". If you put a trap down on Saturday morning and check it the following Monday, your soak time is 2 nights. Lobsters do not normally move around during the daytime and therefore the actual time that your traps are considered to be "fishing" is the overnight period. You can certainly catch lobsters in a single overnight soak, but maximizing the efforts required to check and re-bait a trap becomes really important after a while. There are two basic items that I use in combination when finding the right soak time for any given set.

The first of these is my current physical proximity to the shoreline and social circumstances. As a recreational lobsterman, many times you just won't be able to get out to sea due to other commitments. Thus a longer soak will have to happen whether you want it to or not.

Other times you may be near your boat with folks who would love to see how this lobstering stuff works. Children and adults alike are amazed at the bizarre sea creatures that crawl into lobster traps. Each new trap that breaks the surface is a unique exciting experience in itself like the one at right. During times like these, a short 1-day soak can be more fun without lobsters than the long soaks loaded with lobsters. One positive side to short 1 or 2 day soaks is that you don't normally have to open or re-bait traps without lobsters in them. The bait is usually fresh and you simply drop the trap back overboard with little adieu.

The second consideration is the time of year and water temperatures. Early season water temps are usually very cold at the bottom. Bait does not tend to decay and dissolve as quickly in cold water as it does in the warmer water.

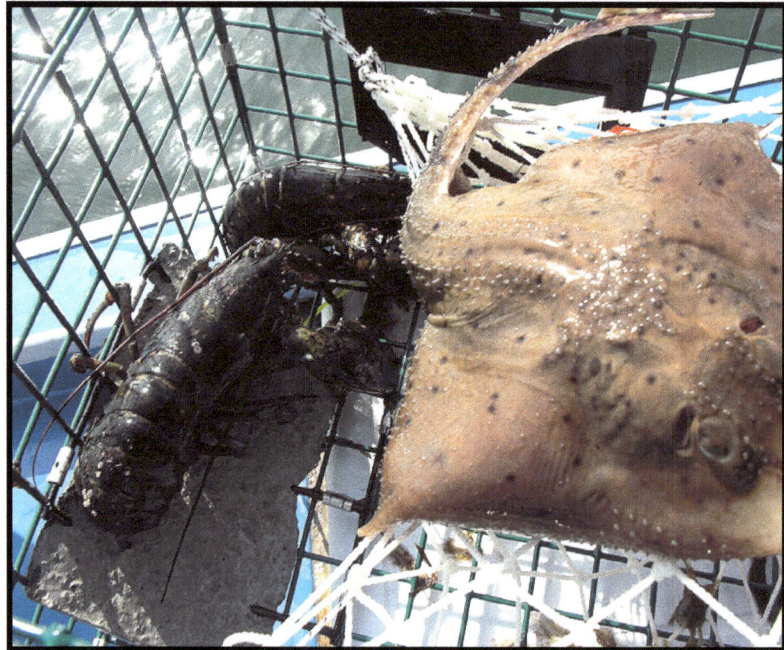

You never know what you'll find in a trap

After much heartache and back break, I managed to put a finite set of numbers on the issue of soak time. Obviously on the shortest end is a 1-day (one-night) soak. This minimizes the chances of catching lobsters. Making a long drive to the shore, launching your boat, expending energy and resources hauling traps on a 1-day soak is wasteful. If you happen to be there with eager faces, then the time and effort is well spent. On the long end of the spectrum, it seems that nine days is about the longest soak you want to have. Your chances of finding whole lobsters in the trap rapidly diminish after the 9th or 10th day underwater.

First off, they will get bored in the parlor compartment and given enough time, simply squeeze their way out. Lobsters, at first, appear to be stupid 2-dimensional stiff-legged slow moving slugs that waddle along the ground. In fact they are highly intelligent, flexible, 3-dimensional contortionists capable of logical reasoning and recall. If they want to walk out of your lobster trap's tangle of tight complex netting, they will absolutely do so! They will do it when it pleases them and not a moment before.

The worst outcome in leaving your lobster traps unchecked for long periods of time is cannibalism and mutilation. The bigger lobsters will tear each other apart and eat the smaller ones. You will eventually find hollowed out juvenile lobster carapaces, crushed claws and tail segments floating in traps left for long soaks as can be seen in figures below. These traps were found with hatch-doors tightly secured by wire-ties. No living lobsters were found inside the traps, only freshly slaughtered lobster parts. This evidence serves as undeniable proof that three things happened here.

Cannibalized lobster carapace

Cannibalized lobster claw

#1) Lobsters will cannibalize each other given the chance. #2) One or more larger lobsters were indeed present in the parlor compartments of these traps. #3) The larger lobster made good their escape after killing and eating the smaller lobsters in the confined parlor compartment with them. These findings were very saddening to me. A terrible way to end the life of a unique creature that had fought so hard to live the first 3 years of its life. It survived in a harsh environment that we couldn't begin to imagine. It had beaten nearly insurmountable odds, only to be torn limb from limb and eaten alive. Although this is one of the cold & hard facts of life under the sea, it is unacceptable to me personally.

There are no written laws determining a maximum soak time for lobster traps. One lobsterman I know left his traps, un-baited, in the ocean for 2 months while he was away on vacation. When he finally got around to re-setting them he was shocked to find several of them stuffed with big, healthy lobsters! I, personally, will not allow my traps to soak any longer than 10 days. If I know ahead of time that I will not be able to tend my traps for over 10 days, I will remove them from the water. Some of my fellow recreational trappers find this to be a huge waste of time and effort. I say, "Whatever floats your boat." And my boat floats on an ocean of respect for the American lobster.

Under almost all conditions, my catch logs consistently indicate that the optimal soak period is 3 nights. The exposure time underwater is optimal, the trapped lobsters are "fresh" and not likely to kill each other or have enough time to figure a way out. And, the bait seems to be re-useable regardless of time of year or water temp. The time and effort to reset traps on a 3-day soak is nominal. The reset efforts usually go much smoother than long soaks where traps are encased in kelp and other sea corruption too disgusting to describe. Again, this is arguable and there are many other points of view on this matter.

How long would it take you to clean and reset the lobster trap in the photo on the right?

Lobster trap strewn with sea sludge

LOBSTERMEN ARE GAMBLERS

*L*obstering is unique among all other fields, ocean & stream type fishing activities. But in the end it is simply that, fishing. It's like dog-track racing and has more incalculable variables and possible outcomes than logic can ever predict. Lobstermen are very much like pari-mutuel gamblers at greyhound races. They read the program with all the historical facts in it (their logs from previous years). They observe existing weather conditions. They talk to other gamblers (lobstermen) for general info on the race at hand. Any small tidbit of data to enhance the odds and possibilities of success is jealously guarded. They select a possible winning combination from the best guess scenario and make final wagers paid for with cash and hard work. There are no guarantees, promises, or "sure bets." The best wager can inexplicably fall flat on its face straight out of the box, while a 100-to-1 long shot can win by eight lengths. This is lobstering, plain and simple. Knowing how to put it all together can certainly increase the odds and probabilities that you will catch lobsters with the least cost and effort. The following is a list of major considerations that can increase the odds of successfully and economically catching lobsters. However, the only thing for absolute certain is that *nothing you do will guarantee it*. The sooner you understand and accept this fact, the sooner the sport of lobstering will become an enjoyable pastime rather than a maddening quest.

- ## Licensing & Registration

  Take a road trip to the nearest marine division office of your state's department of environmental protection. Do not simply printout an online form and mail it in with a check. A face-to-face chat with the DEP will give you priceless insight into the undertaking you're about to embark upon. Not only will you get all your paperwork personally handed to you, you'll also get an explanation as to what you're expected to do with it. Be sure to purchase at least two current lobster carapace measuring gauges from the DEP. Some pennywise lobstermen elect to make their own gauges from scraps of metal and bent rulers. It's a matter of time until they are in possession of $100 (a piece) illegal short lobsters by their own frugal stupidity. At $2 a pop, having an authorized DEP lobster gauge aboard is a very cheap piece of mind, when the big green gunboat pulls up alongside.

- ## Acquiring Lobster Gear

  You can buy all new stuff from shoreline warehouses and shellfish equipment vendors or you can look for bargains on Ebay and classified news ads. If you've been lobstering for a season or more, "used traps" are the way to go. They need close personal inspection and knowledge of the internal working structure, mechanisms and current escape-vent sizes. After a few seasons you'll have acquired hog ring and netting repair tools, and know how to use them. If this is your first season don't even entertain the notion of buying used lobster traps. Purchase brand new ones the first time and examine how it *SHOULD* look inside and out. You'll be sure of getting traps in perfect working order with all the current legal escape vents and other hardware. Consider starting out with one-half the total number of traps allowable by law. For instance, recreational lobstermen in Connecticut are limited to a maximum of ten traps. I fished with five traps for the first couple seasons. In this way you limit the initial outlay of time and money and still get to use an acceptable number of traps. You learn to deal with the logistics of tending a few traps and come up with your own clever methods to efficiently check, bait, and reset them. Add a few traps every season and eventually you'll find that tending the maximum amount allowable can be manageable.

- ## Miscellaneous Stuff

  The items mentioned above are all the basic hardware needed to go lobstering. However, as time goes by you'll wish that you had some other small accouterments to make life easier when tending traps from a 16' runabout in 3 ~ 5 foot rolling cross-chop waves. And, these little things need to be laid out and secured in strategic locations about the stern area. The first and most important item is a plastic 5-gallon pail. This multi-purpose container can be used to transport stuff to and from the boat, as a bait holder, a gunwale wash-down splasher, and even an impromptu porta-potty. I use a square shaped 5-gallon pail, which is easier to stow away in corners than the standard round ones.

The next most valuable tools needed are a pair of heavy-duty diagonal cutters and a fishing knife. Ideally, these should be placed in a gunwale mounted drop-in tool holder. They should be in a place where they can be quickly grabbed and replaced. You can get a medium sized pair of cheapo diagonal cutters from the "Dollar Store". These will be invaluable for cutting the wire-ties from each trap you pull up. A knife will work in a pinch but the "dikes" make it much easier. One huge pain in the neck to be contended with is a trap full of spider crabs, jokingly called "Long Island Opilios". These hairy, spider-like scavengers have long spikey legs that entwine into the trap's wire and netting. They are disgusting to touch and cannot be removed without a tussle. They have no commercial value and most predatory fish will not eat them. The novice lobsterman will spend 15 minutes or more, picking, cursing, and pulling at a trap full of spider crabs. Their legs & claws are seemingly welded to the trap wire. The fastest and cleanest way to remove them is with diagonal cutters. Simply snip the entwined legs off from the outside of the trap! The severed legs fall overboard, the body is easily removed and thrown away like a frisbee, and the trap is clear. As gruesome as this may sound at first, it becomes second nature after a while when dealing with those horrible "Long Island Opilios".

The best fishing knife for lobstering is the hard plastic handled cheapo "fisherman's knife" found at Dick's Sporting Goods for around $10. They come with a hard plastic scabbard that can be screwed onto some convenient location at the stern. Unlike the fancy, expensive "fillet" knives sold at specialty fishing stores, the Dick's cheapo knives have thick blades. It is almost impossible to keep a sharp edge on these blades, which is exactly what is needed for lobstering. You can rip-cut bait, pry apart frozen fish, pop open rusted containers and trap tops, stab spider crabs, cleave through stale grinder sandwiches or just about any function required of a good "stern-man". Always be sure to put it back in the scabbard after each use. If not, I guarantee that your knife will disappear in the hectic clutter of a lobster trap tending operation. Once when my dikes rusted solid I used the thick bladed cheapo knife to cut open trap wire-ties. Suddenly, the knife went missing about halfway through the trip. A week later when pulling the traps I found it, still wedged into the trap wire where I'd set it down several days ago. It had survived a violent ride to and from a week on the bottom of the ocean. A kiss of the grinding wheel and the knife was back in perfect working order. I used that knife until the blade was the thickness of an ice pick before giving it a burial at sea. It served me well for nearly 5 seasons before being replaced at a cost of about $12. In my humble opinion, there are no big-bucks fisherman's fillet knives on the market at any price that could've done the job of that discount knife from Dick's Sporting Goods.

Wire-ties are another onboard must. Purchase a 200 pack of the eight to nine inch types and store them in a place that is easily accessible from the stern without taking one single step. Make sure to secure the bag by weight or clip before leaving port. I cannot tell you how many times the boat was at WOT (wide-open-throttle) on full plane and I turned to see a glimmering array of 200 wire-ties flying out into the prop wash. These little one-way ties have as many uses at sea as duct-tape does around the house. Anything that needs to be battened down, clipped, attached, or joined can be done with wire-ties. The only thing that *CANNOT* be bound with wire-ties is the structural attach points of your lobster traps. I must admit that, on occasion, I've used small wire-ties to patch a broken internal trap net now and again. Although this would really have no impact on prolonging the life of a lost ghost trap, it is probably illegal in certain states. Thus, I would highly advise against using plastic wire-ties on any connective portions of your lobster traps.

- ## Storing your catch

Eventually the day will come when you do in fact find a keeper-sized lobster in your trap. After the photos are taken, the high-five handshakes are over, and the lobster has been passed around so many times that it becomes dizzy, you will have to store your catch. Up until now the logistics of storing a live lobster aboard boat was never an issue. Now, it is! The object of the game now becomes, getting the lobster ashore, intact and alive. These battle-hardened denizens of the deep become surprisingly fragile when out of the water. The effects of gravity, lack of oxygenation, and outright fear, stress them to the max. It's very important to minimize the "handling" time and get the lobster into a cool dark place (preferably in seawater) as quickly as possible. Burying your lobster in a box full of wet kelp and seaweed will suffice in a pinch, however a simple plastic cooler filled with seawater is better. *NEVER* store live lobsters in a cooler full of ice, directly atop the ice. The photo on the following page is exactly what NOT to do when transporting live lobsters. The lobsters in the photo below died before the boat reached shore, within 2 hours. It was my very first attempt at lobster husbandry. Standard freshwater ice-cubes will slowly but surely kill your lobsters. If a cooler full of ice is all you have, then place them in a plastic bag before storing atop ice.

**Never store live lobster directly atop freshwater ice.
The two above died before they reached the shore.**

Fill a cooler one-half way to the top with seawater, gently submerge the lobsters in the cooler and close the lid. The seawater stays cool, the lobsters relax in the dark, and the water won't splash out in rough seas. This is the most cost-effective, efficient way to store your lobsters in a small boat for the trip to shore.

If your boat has a "live-well" bait-storage tank with water intake and circulation port, then you've got your own onboard lobster pound! Check out the one at right.

Fill the live-well with seawater, activate the circulation system, and put the lobster in. Be sure to claw-band them if you have more than one keeper. It takes them about 30 minutes to shake off the shock of being captured. After this amount of time they will instantly set to their favorite pastime of killing each other. You'll find a live-well full of severed lobster parts when you reach shore.

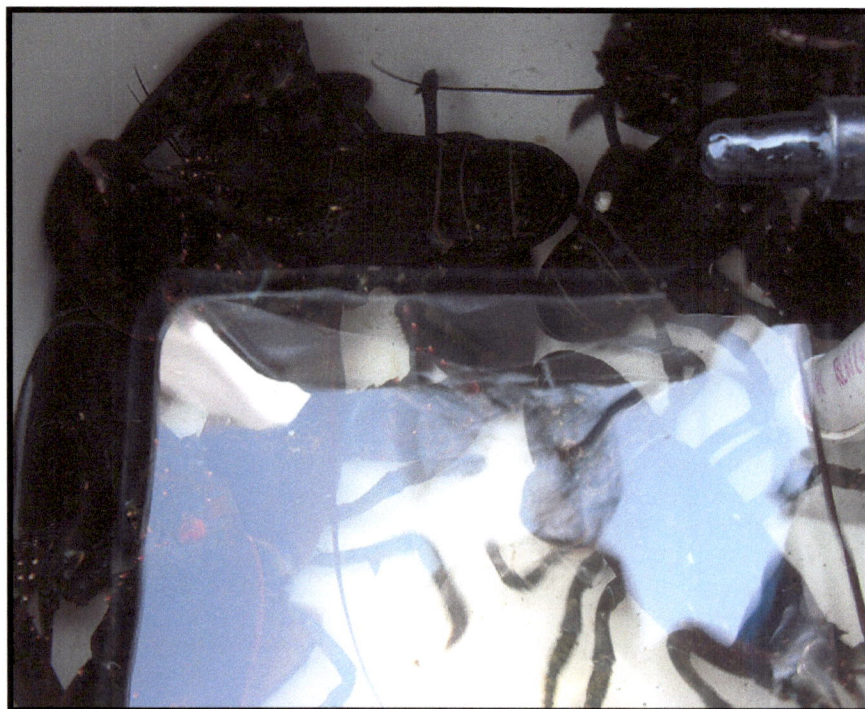

Standard fishing boat "live-well" used as lobster pound

Once ashore, simply lift the cooler out of the boat, put it in your vehicle trunk, and drive home. With this portable lobster repository, you can have some fun showing off your catch to neighbors, dockside tourists, and other fishermen. I suggest making a grandiose effort in carrying the cooler from your boat or at home up the driveway. Inevitably someone will ask; "What did you catch?" or "What's in there?" Take a deep, exhausted breath and set the cooler down. Stick your finger in the air and say, "Check *THIS* out." Then slowly open the cooler lid as if about to show something very secretive. Expecting to see some sort of standard finfish, people are always taken aback when they see one or more lobsters walking around the cooler bottom. The knee-jerk response of "WOW!" or "LOBSTERS! HOW COOL IS THAT!" is always rewarding, as you'll find out.

If you intend to cook and eat your lobster(s) the day of capture, then no more need be done as far as preservation goes. If however, you intend to keep the catch alive overnight, there are two simple ways to do so. The first and simplest method is to place the lobster(s) in the vegetable crisper bin of any standard kitchen refrigerator. I've done this many times when lobsters were overabundant. For some reason, they will live in a closed refrigerator crisper bin for up to a full week. Seawater moistened newspapers, lining the crisper bin seems to extend their life even longer.

The very best way to extend the life and freshness of lobsters at home is by keeping them in a cooler half-filled with seawater. The big trick here is aeration! If you leave a lobster in a 90-quart cooler full of seawater overnight, without aeration, it can be dead by the next morning. Purchase a small inexpensive goldfish or minnow aerator pump from any bait shop or pet store. Put the stone bubbler in the cooler with the lobster and let it run. The lobster(s) will survive comfortably for several weeks. If you drop pieces of clam or fish in there and change the water now and then they will survive for months! (More on this to follow in the section on setting up your own lobster aquarium) The only thing that can kill them at this point is if the water temperature exceeds 70-deg f. As a recreational lobsterman, you will often come home with only 1 lobster, not enough for a full family meal. Having a 90-quart aerated cooler full of seawater in the dark, cool garage or basement is like having your own mini lobster pound. Keep them alive and kicking until you have enough lobsters for everyone.

- ## Keep a Log Book!

Keeping notes on your lobstering activities is not only a good idea; it is a mandatory law in most New England states. The law in Connecticut requires that you submit a yearly "catch log" before you are eligible to have your lobster license renewed. The data required is somewhat cursory; dates fished, number of traps fished, number of overnight "soaks", amount of lobsters caught, and/or if taken by SCUBA diving, how many hours underwater.

As lobstermen are gamblers, we know it's best to keep records and charts of our activities on a much grander scale than that required by state law. Charting information "on the fly" during any given season will absolutely help you to make decisions during the following and subsequent seasons to come. Your logbook can be a simple hand-written diary in plain paper journal entries. Or, it can be a complex computerized database via mathematically pre-programmed calculating data fields. I use a Microsoft Excel spreadsheet type arrangement for entry and calculation of basic numbers and notes. I log the following data from each and every trip out to sea:

- Dates & Number of traps set
- Location of each string set
- Bait used in each trap
- Nights of soak time
- Keeper lobsters caught
- Short lobsters caught (and returned)
- Egg bearing lobsters caught (and returned)
- Comments, on each trap string & location
- Percentage of Keepers to throw-back ratio
- Running cost total (bait & trap repair)
- Running price total of keeper lobsters (based on average market per pound cost)

Obviously you don't have the time or 3rd hand to make these entries while at sea during trap setup operations. I keep a clipboard and pencil on the dash with a hand sketched map of my traps whereabouts and general location layout. On the map I've written all the buoy numbers (all have a unique number). As each buoy is pulled up, the helmsman jots down the stern-man's comments as he/she clears and resets each trap. Later at home I plug all the comments and numbers into the spreadsheet to update the running data and totals. It makes good reading during dark New England winters when you're counting the minutes until you can drop your 1st trap of the new season!

Pot #	Date Set	Location	Bait Used	Nights of Soak Time	Keepers	Lobsters Shorts	Eggers	Comments
3	May 30th	Tip of Golum Point	Frozen bunker, 1 can catfood	8	0	1	0	Cannabalized claws. Lobsters walked out of trap!! Too long soak
1	May 30th	South/West side of Mandrake Rock 12'	Frozen bunker, 1 can catfood	8	0	0	0	Cannabalized claws. Lobsters walked out of trap!! Too long soak
2	May 30th	Shallow East tip of Hosien Pnt!	Frozen bunker, 1 can catfood	8	0	2	0	hit rock! Dangerous area!!
1	May 30th	Shoreline due North of Mandrake-Rock	Frozen bunker, 1 can catfood	8	0	0	0	clean pot, nothing inside, bait gone.
1	June 7th	Shallow East tip of Bangalore!	Fresh bluefish & Fluke rack	9	1	0	0	1 pot robbed! Wire-tie gone. Male shorts
6	June 7th	East side of FL Can 18'	Fresh bluefish & Fluke rack	9	4	2	0	Loaded with LARGE, Hard-Shelled Male keepers!!
1	June 15th	Bingham Reef, center	Frozen bunker, 1 can catfood	2	0	1	0	2 night soak
6	June 15th	East side of FL Can 18'	Frozen bunker, 1 can catfood	2	1	1	0	2 night soak
1	June 17th	Allen Reef, center	Frozen bunker, 1 can catfood	6	0	1	0	1 big V-Notch Female with extreme shell-rot
6	June 17th	East side of Folley Pt 18'	Frozen bunker, 1 can catfood	6	2	0	0	Soft shells, pre-MOLT, shrunken meat inside!
1	June 27th	Allen Reef, center	Bluefish/Fluke DOUBLE-BAITED!!	7	1	1	0	Fluke rack in parlor! 2 big lobsters @ Allen!
6	June 27th	East side of Folley Pt 18'	Fresh bluefish & Fluke rack	7	0	3	0	Found small fishing boat anchored to my buoy..
7	July 4th	1 @ Allen Reef.. 6 @ Bingham	Fluke racks, frozen bunker	3	8			8 lobsters in 1 trap!! S/W side ripline of rockpile!
Total=> Lobsters	57	47%	<=Keeper Ratio	492	27	30	0	$491

Lobster catch-log entered in MS-Excel spreadsheet.

Banding lobster's claws is something that you should consider if you intend to store more than one lobster in a cooler or live well for over 2 days. Or, if you are going to cram a bunch of them, fresh from the traps, in close proximity to each other. When you first pull lobsters from a trap they become somewhat shell-shocked. They will not aggressively pursue each other in loose captivity for about 48 hours. However, in close proximity, for instance 10 lobsters in a 5-gallon live well, can't help but bump into each other's claws. They will snip and clip each other to pieces by mere reflexive accident. They should be banded.

Also, once dropped into a long-range storage tank or cooler, lobsters tend to initially "huddle" together in a corner. They become dormant for about 24 hours and then spread out to inspect their new environment. Eventually turf wars break out and they will mutilate each other and fight to the death just for the fun of it. A set of lobster banding pliers and rubber bands are fairly inexpensive and can be bought at the local shell fishing shop. It's a good idea to keep them in your "throw & go" bag just in case. Before using them for real, I strongly suggest that you practice banding things around the house. Try and put a band on your cats' forearm or your toddlers' thumb & forefinger. Soon you'll be on a bouncing wet deck trying to band an enraged crustacean hell bent on clipping your fingers off. This will be time well spent in practice.

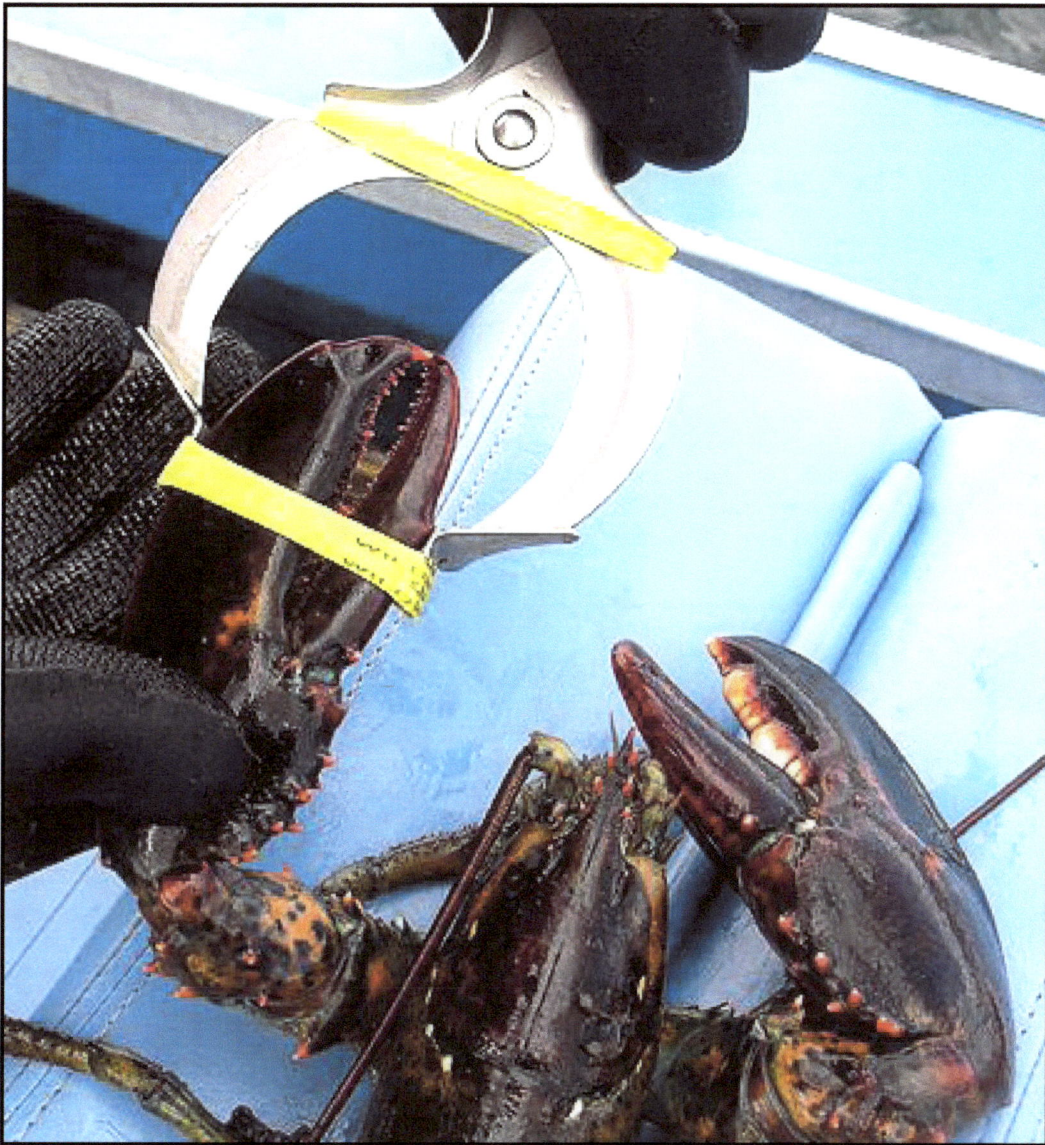

Banding a lobster claw

ARE YOU READY?

*W*e now have everything we need to try our hand at lobstering. We have the traps properly rigged, copies of licenses in waterproof baggies, and all the hardware needed to support a recreational lobstering operation. After scanning our Captain Seagull nautical charts we've got a good idea where to drop our traps and the water depths at high tide in those areas. Our boat is stacked with brand new lobster traps and we proudly display a lobster buoy.

This is the first set of the season, and in some cases, the first time you've ever dropped a lobster trap in the ocean. You're now nearing the first target area, near a rock pile or underwater reef. Bring the throttle back to neutral and turn the motor off. Sit quietly for a moment until the boat slowly stops its forward momentum and turns to drift with the wind and tide.

Look out over the back of your boat's stern and deck area. Take a deep breath of the cool, briny salt-air and enjoy a moment that most folks never will. At that moment you're no longer an electrician, or carpenter or admin assistant.

You are a lobsterman, congratulations!

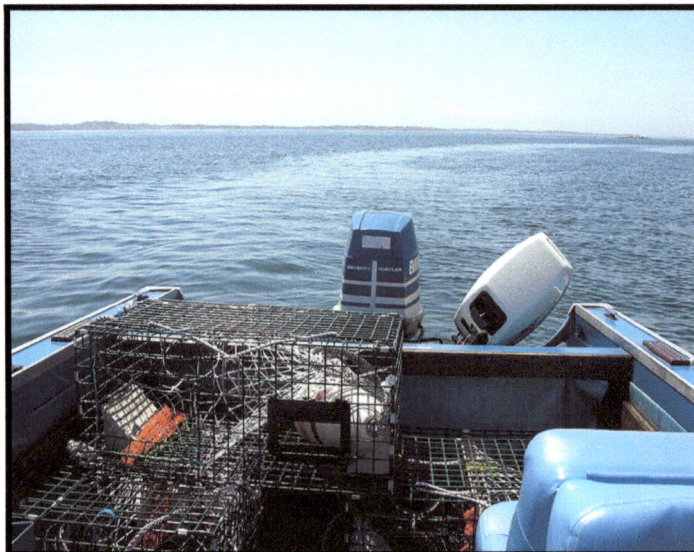

Lobster traps ready for 1st drop of the season

A well-worn 10-gallon cooler is loaded with bait-bags pre-stuffed with our opening bait array. Each bag contains ½ of a frozen bunker, 1 chicken drumstick, and a can of on-sale sardines with tin lid half-peeled open to allow the scented emulsion to leech out slowly. No bait bag would be complete without a round block of that compressed menhaden "sure-fire-lobster-bait" stuff that you bought online from a Maine bait dealer (see yellowish block in lower right corner of photo below). This magical stuff will not deteriorate in saltwater and is said to remain highly attractive for weeks.

Bait bag ready for action!
A can of catfood, sardines, last years frozen perch, and tablet of "last-forever" lobster attractant (note: does not work at all)

As weeks go by and you try different baits, you'll find that the simplest things seem to work best. If you have some freshwater bullhead carcasses, throw them in. If the local store has a sale on cat-food, put a can in there with lid slightly peeled back. Overall, I've had the best luck early in the season, when fresh saltwater game-fish racks are not available, using freshwater catfish carcasses and frozen bunker, mackerel, and herring. Stay away from the bizarre and/or expensive stuff.

When tending your traps, especially in the setting phase (dropping them in the water), it's really good to have a helper at the helm. It can certainly be done single handedly, but in this, your first few drops, be sure to have someone who is good at the wheel with you. Go over your basic plan like a military mission with your partner before you leave shore.

Be sure that your helper knows all the intricacies of your boat and especially the electronics on it. Every boat's motor starts and idles differently. There's nothing worse than having the motor stall out when you've got a heavy trap half way to the surface, in rough seas, with wind and tide pushing you onto shallow reef rocks, because your partner didn't know the low idle RPM sound of your motor.

It's a good idea to set a GPS waypoint at each and every trap dropped, regardless of close proximity to each other. If you intend to continue fishing this general area for several sets, it won't be necessary to erase and re-set GPS waypoints. These waypoints will be invaluable to you should the fog roll in, or you're looking for a lost buoy by setting up an ever-widening search circle using the last known GPS point for that buoy. I usually have fun with my helmsman (most times it's a helmswoman, my wife) and let them call out the final "drop" signal to me in the back. Once in the general area where you want to set, let them watch the SONAR screen for bottom topography. When they spot an up-spike on the seafloor (a rock, a mound, a small reef, etc) they yell out "NOW!" and kersplush! The trap goes overboard. It is HUGELY important to pay attention when dropping the trap. That's why I always personally do the drops. The first thing that you must be keenly aware of is the position of the trap as it hits the water. The bottom of the trap must be perpendicular with and hit flat on the water surface. Although traps are usually weighted in outside corners so as to make them land on the bottom, squarely with bottom down, this does not always happen. While SCUBA diving I've seen many, many lobster traps sitting on their sides, on their top or bottom ends, and even some sitting upside down! These traps were from both, single buoy recreational drops and multi-trap commercial strings. When this happens there is limited access and attractivity to the trap due to an opening being blocked or the bait bag being wedged in an odd position. A lobster will simply pass this trap by for another one with easier entry. When casting a trap overboard, do NOT give it the old porch-swing type "Heave-HO!" Grab it by both top outside corners and lift it completely overboard. When you look down through the cage and see the water surface level with the trap bottom, let 'er go! Watch the trap sink, squarely to the bottom. I've gone so far as to recover a freshly dropped trap and reset it when seeing it go out of sight on an odd angle.

The next and most important thing to watch is the warp line at your feet! This is first and foremost for safety's sake. I cannot overstate this enough. Especially so, when you have guests, children or pets aboard with you. Commercial lobstermen and Alaskan king crab fishermen call it "getting caught in the bight." Drop a heavy trap overboard, look away from the coil for an instant, and something is being violently wrenched over the side into and under the ocean's surface. It could be your arm in "the bight", or a child's ankle, or auntie Norma's big handbag full of sunscreen. Regardless of what it is, someone is injured or drowned in a most horrific manner if you do not *WATCH THE COIL!*

The closest I ever came to "the bight" happened one day setting out traps with a good friend. He was very boat savvy and a great boat handler. I'd stacked a ready-to-drop prep'd trap on top of the rear gunwale edge. We were slowly motoring around, watching the SONAR bottom scan for a rocky up-spike. We both stared at the screen, which showed dead flat seafloor. I said, "Goose it!" to do a quick zoom across the bay. He goosed the throttle and the boat came onto plane. I turned to see the heavy lobster trap fly overboard into the rooster-tail of prop-wash. The warp line peeled out in an instant, the buoy slammed into my groin and zipped overboard in a blur! I'd have been killed if I were standing in that coil which was placed, ritualistically, in the far rear transom well. Thank GOD!!

Always, always, *ALWAYS*, coil your warp lines when raising traps or before you drop them. Treat and consider a coiled warp as deadly as a coiled sleeping black mamba snake. Carry it gently, and place it as far away from people and as close to the gunwale as operational proceedings will allow in the space available, just like a sleeping snake. When retrieving lobster traps, I use a hand-over-hand method and methodically coil the warp with each inboard pull. When the trap breaks the surface, I lay the coil down inside the transom well, not on the floor inside the boat! I've accidentally dropped inbound traps in rough seas, and watched the warp coil disappear, loop after loop harmlessly flying out of the transom well. If the coil had been on the floor, "the bight" could've been quite painful.

You should make a ludicrous game out of this procedure as I did, and don't EVER drop a lobster trap without saying it. When kids are aboard, they get a big bang out of saying it repeatedly as we send trap after trap to the bottom. I refuse to even lift a re-baited trap from the deck until I hear this silly little rhyme, after which they all laugh like crazy and point to the coiled warp line where ever it is. After the first few unison chants of this, it gets old. But I can tell you that I do in fact think it and say it aloud when doing a trap set all by myself.

No lobsters to boil, 'til someone points out the COIL!

Your traps are now officially in the water. This is the last time that they will see the light of day (more than a few minutes) for the rest of the lobstering season. They'll remain underwater for the next months to come, until removed for the winter. As the very last trap sinks to the bottom and you toss its buoy clear of the motor skeg, take a look at the deck. It will seem eerily empty.

As you lay in bed the first few nights after dropping lobster traps for the first time, you can't stop thinking about them. You'll wonder if this is the night when a wild New England lobster will walk into your trap? In your mind's eye you can see a big 3-pound lobster in the kitchen compartment of your trap. His massive claws are ripping at the tough plastic bait bag. Another smaller lobster walks in; the big lobster spins around defensively and squeezes his big tail backwards. He falls into the parlor entrapment compartment.

Suddenly your spouse walks in, reminding you to bring out the trash and "Poof." The dream lobster evaporates for the time being but it's on your mind constantly until the time comes to check your very first string of lobster traps. And oh, what a day that will be. A big, lively, shiny hard-shelled lobster is waiting for you.

Big dream lobster, about to fall into the parlor compartment

The day finally comes when you pull out of port, set the GPS to the waypoint marked as "Trap#1" on your chartplotter. For some reason the boat, at wide-open throttle, cannot get there fast enough. You pull back the power to slow idle, the boat comes off plane and you spot the top of your first lobster buoy bobbing in the mild chop. The sheer joy of the moment is replaced with yet another of many logistical problems, namely, setting up an approach to a buoy pickup. It's something that you never think about at first. But, after you spend some time trying to retrieve buoys in rough water you'll find that the sea itself is a very strict teacher. One that is unbending in her rules and punishments.

Anyone can drive a small craft up to a buoy and grab it on a windless, calm, slack-tide sea. The challenge is to reach overboard with hand or hook in 3 ~ 4 ft chop, in a sustained 20 knot breeze, on an astronomical tide that's ripping along at peak flow. You must have a pre-planned method and stick to it. All small nuances of doing this in your particular craft with high or low gunwales and freeboard (the distance from gunwale top to water surface) heights will determine the exact way you should perform this operation. The following is a good way to start your operational planning and make small adjustments as time goes on.

Always intend on picking up your buoys from the *STARBOARD SIDE OF YOUR BOAT.* (The right side, as you're looking forward). Your helm and controls are on the starboard side. This will make it slightly easier for the helmsman to keep the buoy in sight as he/she approaches it. Someday you may be tending traps all alone, in which case it'll be nearly impossible to safely snag a buoy from the port side of the boat.

Keep the buoy in sight as you approach at a speed slow enough to barely maintain steerage. Imagine that you're trying to run directly over the buoy. The trick is to get the buoy to bump into the boat's prow just slightly to the starboard side at the waterline. When you (the helmsman) hear the buoy bump the hull and/or loses sight of it, *IMMEDIATELY PUT THE MOTOR INTO NEUTRAL!* If your approach speed was planned correctly the boat will have enough forward momentum to allow a safe pickup. If not, the buoy will eventually pop up in an unreachable position and you'll have to do a "go around" for another try. One other thing that you must never be tempted to do is this: *DON'T EVER PUT THE BOAT IN REVERSE TO TRY AND CATCH A BUOY BEHIND YOU!* If you forget or neglect to put the motor in neutral you may end up with a lead-core warp line welded to the propeller. At the very lowest RPM the line will instantly twist and choke the propeller to a dead stop. At worst it can render your motor totally useless. At the very best, it will require an hours worth of cutting and clearing to get back underway. I can personally attest to the latter.

If done perfectly correctly the buoy will momentarily disappear under water as the boat prow hits it. It will then pop up and roll along the starboard side of the boat at the waterline and someone grabs it by the loop handle. In less than ideal conditions, a small gaff-hook on 4-ft handle can be very helpful. When using a gaff-hook it's a better idea to snag the buoy by the neck (front end where the warp goes down into the water) rather than making a wild stab at the little loop-handle end swinging around in the air. When approaching buoys in rough conditions, take a look at the direction where the buoy is pointing. For instance, the buoy in the photo below is pointing to the right as the tide is flowing right to left. Drive the boat around the buoy to a position "up-tide / up-wind" from it. Then chop power to neutral and let the boat drift down ONTO the buoy. Ideally the boat will bump into the buoy dead amidship, on the starboard side, for easy pickup.

Buoy approach setup path

Now with the buoy safely in hand, most newcomers to recreational lobstering are wondering "Do I need some sort of ocean-going hydraulic winch to lift lobster traps into the boat?" Absolutely not! All the folks who've gone lobstering with me agree that pulling in the traps is the easiest and most fun part of lobstering. It is not like hauling up 500 heavy commercial traps from 200 feet of water. Recreational lobstermen pull up 10 traps or less, from depths of 10 ~ 40-feet on average. My 120-lb. wife pulls up all of our traps with little effort.

Back to the job at hand, or I should in hand. Being a frugal, pennywise New England Yankee I tended traps for several seasons without gloves and never needed so much as one surgical stitch. Working barehanded is doable and you'll find that saltwater is the most forgiving of any water, bacterially speaking. A couple of Christmas's ago someone gave me a new pair of 3mm SCUBA gloves that Velcro-seal high above the wrists. These gloves are so comfortable that they are a joy to wear, even on warm days. It makes the job of hauling in warp lines a piece of cake.

Lean your knees into the starboard combing pad and heave to. Hold the buoy with your right hand and lead the pull with your left hand reaching down towards the water. Drop the buoy into the transom-well or as far out of harm's way as possible. Make a circle with your left thumb and forefinger around the warp line. Pull with your right hand and slide the circle down the line toward the water, scraping off the water and weeds sticking to the line. Pinch the line and pull up with both hands. Feed the slack incoming line from your left hand back to your right hand. With your right hand, make a loose coil with each incoming yard of line like a cowboy coiling a lariat rope. Continue this process until the loop side of the trap breaks the surface. The warp line will now be somewhat clean of seagoing sludge and nicely coiled in your right hand. Carefully place it in the transom-well or as far back in the stern as possible out of harm's way. Remember, that coil is a sleeping black mamba!

Picking the trap up out of the water would be an unwieldy process were it not for the clever loop-handle bridle that you firmly strapped to the lower parlor side wires. Grab the loop-handle with both hands and take note of all your passengers and guests crowded around you at this magical moment. All are staring down into the water at the trap. When a lobster trap comes up from the deep, this moment in time, just before it is brought aboard, is magical.

Lift the trap out of the water and set it down on the rear gunwale top. Look to see if the wire-tie is still in place securing the trap door. If so, the trap was not tampered with. Snip the wire-tie with diagonal cutters and place it in a secure refuse receptacle. Putting plastics in our seawater is known to cause a catastrophic lobster scourge called shell-rot, more on this to follow.

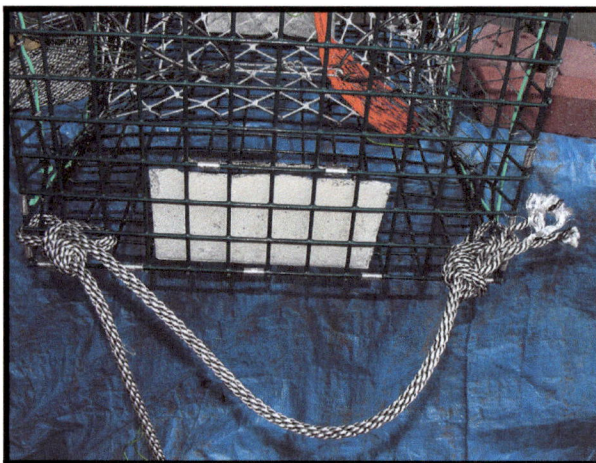

Lobster trap loop-handle bridle

As you unclip and open the top door absolutely anything can and will be in that trap. From flopping big game fish or cherrystone clams, to tail clapping lobsters. You remove and sort out all the keepable stuff from the ugly stuff such as weeds and spider crabs. Untie and take out the bait bag which may contain nothing more than a fused mass of fish bones and stinking goo. Remove any naturally non-biodegradable items, such as cat-food cans (place in refuse bucket) and toss the rest over the side. It will quickly return to the cycle of life in the ocean. Re-bait the trap and zip the door shut with a wire-tie.

Quickly recite aloud (in unison if guests aboard), *No lobsters to boil, 'til someone points out the COIL!* Look and point directly at the coiled warp line, pick up the trap and drop it overboard. I like to hold the warp line coil as it feeds out into the water, tossing the buoy clear of the boat as an ending note to another successful trap set. And that's all there is to lobstering, a piece of cake!

Now, with all this in mind, are you really sure that you want to be a lobsterman? Right about now, any normal person would be saying; "You gotta' be kidding me!" A normal person would have his or her calculator out, figuring the price of traps, buoys, line, fuel and bait. They'd add in the myriad ancillary items that are needed to accomplish the task, such as boat, motor, mooring & launch fees, licenses & registrations. Then the reasonable person would figure the amount of time, effort, and aggravation it takes to properly tend a measly few lobster traps once or twice weekly. When this reasonable person hits the total-sum key they'd give up on the crazy idea immediately. The price of each of the few lobsters that may (or may not) be caught would be somewhere between $50 ~ $100 per pound depending on circumstances described above.

But then again, some people realize that this is not a matter of price per pound, it is an experience of a lifetime. It is a challenge and an extreme privilege. It is something that most people have not and will never do. After you learn and understand the confusing volumes of environmental regulations and rules on lobstering, rig and set strings of your own complex gear, a day will come when you hold a lobster in your own hand. A New England lobster! Highly sought after and arguably prized as the single most delicious food on earth.

A lobster, caught by you and sitting in your hand like the one below. It may not be a perfect lobster, or even a keeper lobster but it is YOUR LOBSTER! Take a very close look at it and you'll find that it is unique among any lobster that you've ever eaten or seen at the store. It may have a dented claw after losing a game of claw-lock or it may have small shell "pits", the onset of epizootic shell disease (more on this to follow). It may even display one of nature's most amazing gifts, full regeneration of missing parts! All of these can be seen on the unique little fellow in the photo below.

You are now a personal part of a proud New England tradition, historically known the world over, spanning centuries. In a small way, you are now a New England lobsterman. Look at that lobster in your hand, a marvel of evolution and a million years of adaptation. Only the few people like you are able to understand and appreciate this moment in time. Precious moments that you will think back upon and fondly remember until the day you die. By all meaning and intents of the word, that one lobster in your hand is truly *priceless*.

Lobster with regenerating left claw & onset of stage-1 shell disease

THE LOGISTICAL REALITY OF LOBSTERING

*A*t this point you probably realize that, nowadays, the odds of coming out ahead monetarily through lobstering are slim to none. An underwater study performed by the University of New Hampshire also found some additionally disturbing facts about lobster trapping. Lobsters are solitary grouchy creatures by nature. They can easily escape from any man made lobster trap, given enough time and effort. The UNH marine scientist attached underwater cameras in and around their lobster traps. They recorded many interesting comings and goings of lobsters, which can be seen online on the lobsters/unh.edu website. The video, in time-lapse photography, shows large and small lobster crawling around a baited trap. Big ones and small ones enter the trap, nip at the bait bag, and easily leave the trap via main entryway rings. One of the larger lobsters falls into the parlor compartment and you would think he was inextricably trapped. But this was not the case. He roamed around every square inch of the parlor compartments walls, top, bottom and sides. Eventually he wedged his big claws into the watch-pocket tight back end of the parlor-drop netting. He slowly but surely squeezed his big body through the netting, and walked out of the trap, gone!

The study also claimed that a single lobster will jealously ward off all other comers and defend his prize (food source in the bait bag) until the bitter end, further reducing the odds of trapping a keepable sized lobster. The ending report stated that estimates of only 10% of the lobsters coming near the trap actually entered it. Of those 10% only 6% actually fell into the parlor compartment and were trapped. Putting this into a catch / ratio will make a very compelling case as to why you should *NOT* quit your day-job and go into lobstering on a fulltime basis; for every 170 keeper sized lobsters stumbling onto or near your trap, 17 of them will actually poke their heads into the entry ring. Of those 17, only 1 will fall into the parlor entrapment compartment.

All current logistics indicate that setting up a profitable lobster trapping operation are about the same as trying to set up a long running 5-star restaurant in New York City. The very best you can hope for is the indescribable taste of eating fresh caught New England lobsters, every now and then. But even this is not a guarantee. More often than not your lobster traps come up with nothing in them. The cold ocean water gushes out as they break the surface and come aboard totally empty, no bait, no crabs, nothing! In her book, "The Lobster Chronicles", lobster boat captain Linda Greenlaw sarcastically referred to this as "changing the water in the traps." As an old charter captain once said on the way out, "Ladies and gentlemen, we're going fishing. Catching, on the other hand, is quite another thing, not guaranteed." But sooner or later one of your traps will come up loaded with lobsters making it all worthwhile.

A trap with 8 or more keepers in it can restore your enthusiasm instantly!

THE ELKHORN RIVER INCIDENT

*T*ales of this ugly creature and its unique indescribably tasty meat started a craze that swept across the country. New England lobster was no longer used for fertilizer or fish bait and they could no longer be gathered by hand in any great numbers. The once shunned poverty food had become a highly sought after edible. By 1880, lobster had become a $430,000 industry and the prime natural resource of the state of Maine. It knocked cod, herring and mackerel to distant second place commodities. Visionaries and entrepreneurs of the time tried to take advantage of this new commodity. All sorts of unique experiments were contrived to make a fast buck or gain notoriety from New England lobsters. One of the most interesting yet little known stories began in the spring of 1873. Totally by chance, a calamity that occurred at the Elkhorn River in the state of Nebraska would be the start of lobster husbandry, as we know it today.

All modern sciences and technical advances stand squarely on the back of previous failures. So many times the best-planned experiments have gone completely awry. And yet, from the ashes, the solutions to vexing logistical and biological problems are gleaned by future generations. Often as not, the names of people involved in the initial failures simply slip from focus. Their names and deeds are forgotten and buried in the pages of time.

Many people have heard the names of renowned contemporary lobster biologists such as Jelle Atema and Diane Cowan. I wonder how many lobster lovers have ever heard the names of Livingston Stone or Marshall L. Perrin? These two men unwittingly became pioneers in lobster husbandry, over 130 years ago. With no modern scientific equipment they established, through abject failure, the ways and means by which we transport and sustain life in captured lobster today. This is their story.

Livingston Stone was born in Massachusetts in 1836. He was a highly intelligent man, graduated from Harvard, attended theological school and became an ordained minister. He eventually resigned his clerical ministry to pursue a career in his life's passion, "American Fisheries." Stone became a pioneer fish culturist and one of the founding fathers of "The American Fishing Society." He was named as the US Deputy Fish Commissioner and literally wrote the book of "Domesticated Trout" which became the standard operating manual for fish culture. Dr. Livingston Stone revered fish and aquaculture as John Muir did the Yosemite valleys.

Commissioner Stone and the state of California had conducted a very successful transplantation of eastern brook trout. The hearty brook trout survived the trip quite nicely, lived and multiplied "remarkably well" in cooler California lakes and streams. One report from the project stated; "Propagating the eastern brook trout was taken up in earnest and each year the Commission distributes thousands of these trout in nearly every county having suitable waters; they are now one of our most sought after fish." Brook trout are now among the easiest of the trout species to raise in captivity. They are strong swimmers and can survive in a wide range of water temperatures unlike other salmonide type fishes.

A hearty eastern brook trout.

Coming off this popular victory of man over nature, one of the first successful aquaculture transplantation projects ever, the California Fish & Game and Livingston Stone decided to press their luck. Commissioner Stone got the chance of a lifetime when the US Fisheries Department funded a project to design and build a special "aquarium car." In this first ever venture, "no expense or effort was spared." He had a blank check from the US Government to create his dream, a long-range mobile fisheries aquaculture & transplantation unit.

He started by acquiring a railroad fruit car from the Central Pacific Railroad Company. This railroad car was initially built for quick trips across the continent. It was 27 feet long and 8 feet wide. It was retrofitted to hold five tons of water and boxes of ice. The center of the car was jammed with large and small portable fish tanks, reserves of seawater as well as bulky barrels and crates containing lobsters, oysters, etc. The car also contained apparatus for aerating water, sleeping accommodations and supplies for attendants making the long cross-country journeys. The beds were located atop "large stationary water tanks" resembling oversized coffins.

According to official reports, the "car" carried nearly 300,000 valuable food and game fish, consisting of ten (10) species. In that plastic had not been invented yet, these tanks were made of "hard wood and smeared with a mixture of resin and tallow" in order to be watertight. It was later reported that these wooden tanks leaked constantly. I can only imagine what it must've been like, working as an attendant on that stinking fish car during an eight day coast to coast haul.

At precisely 2:15pm on Tuesday June 3rd, 1873, Livingston Stone's aquarium car departed from Charlestown, New Hampshire on its momentous trip to California. A small crowd of well-wishers cheered and waved white handkerchiefs as the heavy-laden railroad car slowly rolled out of the station. The Noah's Arc on rails contained: 60 adult black bass, 60 catfish, 60 yellow perch, 12 hornpouts (catfish), 1500 saltwater breeding eels, 1000 tautog, 20 striped bass, 50 yearling perch, 1 barrel of young selected oysters, 190,000 Hudson River Shad fry. The aquarium car also contained Livingston Stone, several other stalwart attendants, and *162 lobsters from Boston*, all making the long overland journey to California.

It is interesting to note several of Stone's comments pertaining to the lobsters on board that doomed excursion. On the second day of the journey, Wednesday June 4th Stone reported, *"All the fish are in good order, except the lobsters, which are dying in considerable numbers."* On the fourth day of the trip he reported, *"We entered Chicago on Friday morning, all the fish doing well except for the lobsters..."* By Saturday as the train pulled into Omaha Nebraska only 40 lobsters were reported to be "alive and in good condition." Dr. Stone did not mention, allude to, or venture a wild guess as to the cause of his lobster's high mortality in transit. As previously mentioned, the core biological requirements of Homarus americanus was not readily known in 1873. At that time the basic understanding of preserving a lobster was to keep it in a moist, cool, dark area. When Stone described the receptacles used for holding his lobsters, he said "six large *cases*, containing the lobsters.." There was never a reference or mention of the lobsters being kept within seawater in any part of his lengthy, meticulous reports. Also, his notes advised that lobsters should be kept at a temperature of 34 to 36 degrees Fahrenheit. From this we can assume with a fair degree of certainty that the "cases containing the lobsters" were indeed just that, dry wooden cases.

In 1873 the working nomenclature of the standard household food "icebox" consisted of placing a large block of ice in a compartment above the perishable foods. It was known that denser cold air from the melting ice would descend into the food chamber thereby keeping perishable foods cooled. The ice would slowly melt and drip into a pan on the floor under the icebox itself. This was new technology at the time, and we can assume with a high degree of certainty that Doc Stone used icebox technology in his lobster transport scheme. The large holding "cases" for Stone's lobsters most certainly were packed in heavy beddings of seaweed or straw and encased in ice placed atop the cargo. The ice was replaced as it melted. Possibly unknown to Stone (not mentioned in any of his notes) during this first venture was the fact that fresh water from melting ice was dripping onto the lobsters and slowly killing them. You, unlike Dr. Stone, are fully aware of this fact from a previous chapter and seeing the photo on page 60.

Also in one of his reports, Stone commented that *"most of the lobster are full-grown and heavy with spawn"* He had a cargo of heavy, egg bearing female lobsters, all of which were certainly stressed to the max and had little or no chance of surviving the trip. However, 40 surviving lobsters were on board the aquarium car when it pulled out of the Omaha Nebraska station on the evening of Saturday June 7th 1873. At that moment, it was a moot point whether 40 or 400,000 lobsters had survived. The train was heading for a cataclysmic ending. Miraculously, Dr. Stone survived the train wreck caused by the collapsing railroad bridge at the Elkhorn River in Antelope County Nebraska. A "great flood" during an April 1873 storm had weakened the bridge. Stone's first hand report of the event must be reprinted to give you the full impact of the event.

Imagine having "tea" (dinner) with him that evening as he sat in his beloved aquarium car. He was only hours from a success that would've propelled him into history, the zenith of his career. After reading this incredible tale of utter destruction and chaos, I feel it is best told in Dr. Stone's own words:

"After leaving Omaha, we stowed away as well as we could the immense amount of ice we had on the car; and, having regulated the temperature of all the tanks, and aerated the water all around, we made our tea and were sitting down to dinner, when suddenly there came a terrible crash, and tanks, ice, and everything in the car seemed to strike us in every direction. We were, every one of us, at once wedged in by the heavy weights upon us, so that we could not move or stir. A moment after, the car began to fill rapidly with water, the heavy weights upon us began to loosen, and, in some unaccountable way, we were washed out into the river. Swimming around our car, we climbed up on one end of it, which was still out of water, and looked around to see where we were. We found our car detached from the train and nearly all under water both couplings having parted. The tender (car for carrying fuel & water behind the engine) was out of sight, and the upper end of our car resting on it. The engine was three-fourths underwater, and one man in the engine-cab crushed to death. Two men were floating down the swift current in a drowning condition, and the balance of the train still stood on the track, with the forward car within a very few inches of the water's edge. The Westinghouse air-brake had saved the train. If we had been without it, the destruction would have been fearful. One look was sufficient to show that the contents of the aquarium-car were a total loss. Everything was lost. No care of labor had been spared in bringing the fish to this point, and now, almost on the verge of success, everything was lost."

A local newspaper, The Lincoln Journal, printed a much more lighthearted account of the event. The article, reprinted below, is actually hilarious if you can look at it from a Nebraskan point of view at the time. In 1873 the nation was going through a severe economic depression. All government spending and support for local communities had dried up. Imagine if you will, being impoverished by no fault of your own. There you are, standing destitute near the dusty railway station, and see a big expensive railroad car full of fish rolling past. Then watching this government pork barrel load of nonsense funded by the wealthy state of California crash into your favorite fishing hole. This sample statement from the article, in the writing style of the time absolutely slays me! I'm sure that Livingston Stone found little humor in it, but the dry wit is well taken nowadays, *".. a trestle gave way and the car containing the fish was precipitated into the Elkhorn, breaking the car to pieces and liberating the fish to our advantage and at California's expense."*

The Lincoln Journal lead story for June 8th, 1873 was entitled: *"The accident which let thirty thousand dollars worth of fish, great and small, into the waters of the winding Elkhorn."*

"Thus discourseth the Lincoln 'Journal' upon the accident which let thirty thousand dollars' worth of fish, great and small, into the waters of the winding Elkhorn. A car of little fishes collected in the east at a cost of $30,000 was precipitated into the Elkhorn River by the Sunday accident. The oysters were fished out and roasted by the wrecked passengers. The tautogs will not survive, but there is a large assortment of escaped swimmers that will live and flourish. We suggest to those fish a trip down the Platte and up Salt Creek. We can give them a little brine, and cool shady retreats, and if a few county bonds would be an inducement we'll vote some. We should like to see the mighty shad, and the salty cod, the silver eel, and the Massachusetts cat, sporting in the depths of our tawny river."

"Some time in the early seventies, probably in 1872, the legislature of California made an appropriation to be expended by the state agricultural society to stock the waters of that state with choice varieties of fish of such kinds as were not then found in California. Accordingly, a carload, consisting of three hundred thousand in number, was purchased from Seth Green, the famous fish breeder of New York. These consisted of such varieties as the tautog, the black bass, the striped bass, the perch, the walleyed pike, the silver eel, oysters, lobsters, and trout. The car was in charge of Livingston Stone, Assistant United States Fish Commissioner. The bridge over the Elkhorn was weakened from the great flood that followed the April storm of 1873, and when the train drawing this car was crossing the bridge a trestle gave way and the car containing the fish was precipitated into the Elkhorn, breaking the car to pieces and liberating the fish to our advantage and at California's expense."

"The first settlers found the Elkhorn stocked with such varieties of fish as pickerel, catfish, two or three kinds of suckers, buffalo fish, bull-head, sun-fish, and possibly some other varieties. This accident added to the waters of the Elkhorn the black bass, silver eel, perch, and wall-eyed pike, and possibly one or two other kinds. The trout did not survive, and recent efforts to plant trout in the Elkhorn have not been successful."

IF AT FIRST YOU DON'T SUCCEED

*S*uffice it to say that no New England lobster survived the initial 1873 overland transplantation attempt. Americans however, cannot stand loosing or being told that something couldn't be done. Somehow, the good Dr. Stone came up with funding to build a second aquarium car. To commemorate those that had died at the Elkhorn River, it was decided to try the entire drill all over again, on the same dates of the following year in June of 1874. In this venture, Dr. Stone employed a skilled assistant and purveyor of lobsters, Mr. Marshall Livingston Perrin. Perrin was in his final year at Harvard and had to petition the board of directors for a leave of absence to attend this grand "expedition." His request was granted and he embarked on a cross-country adventure that would change his life forever. After the trip, I sincerely doubt that he ever had anything to do with lobsters for the rest of his life.

During initial meetings Stone and Perrin meticulously went over every detail of lobster handling and storage during the ill-fated 1873 attempt. Perrin labored with each facet, in minutia, to come up with the very best logistical plans and methods to keep lobsters alive during a cross-country train ride. He kept a very descriptive journal of his plans, how things were constructed, the trip itself, and final conclusions. In a report to the California Fish Commission, Mr. Perrin explained the entire coast-to-coast trip starting in Charleston, New Hampshire on June 3rd, 1874 with 150 New England lobsters. His observations lead to the fundamental understanding and practical procedures that we use today in the transportation of live New England lobsters.

150 lobsters were purchased from the Johnson & Young Lobster House in Boston, MA. The owners, Samuel & Francis Johnson and James Young were given Mr. Perrin's highest praise for the special attention they took in crating the precious cargo for the trip from Boston, MA to the aquarium car's departure point in Charlestown, NH. The lobsters were packed in seven pine boxes, measuring 3 ½ feet long, 15 inches wide, and 15 inches deep. The boxes were divided in two tiers, upper and lower, by a thin wooden divider. 11 lobsters were placed in each of the tiers, except one that was only partially filled. On the trip to New Hampshire the lobsters were not bundled in straw or any other type of packing. They were simply laid on the wood with sponges over them and all around them. This was initially called a "regrettable mistake." Mr. Perrin subsequently tested the longevity of lobsters packed in straw against that of lobsters lying flat on wood and packed in wet sponges. There was no difference regardless of method used in this circumstance. 35 pounds of sponges were procured for packing purposes. In Mr. Perrin's own words, "The sponges were soaked with seawater and each lobster was completely hidden by the wet sponges. Salt water was poured upon all the lobsters, and all the sponges newly wetted once during the trip to Charlestown. The lobsters were all alive when reaching Charlestown" The last item loaded for the trip to New Hampshire was 6 casks of seawater, exactly 149 gallons as stated in the Perrin report. This reserve of seawater was freshly acquired in the Boston Harbor, just beyond a place referred to as "The Graves" for reasons of purity. It would serve as the only seawater refreshment source for all lobsters throughout the entire cross-country trek.

On the morning of June 4th, 1874 the lobsters had reached Charlestown, NH, all alive. They were carefully removed from the boxes used on the inbound leg from Boston and were placed in twelve waiting boxes on the aquarium car. These waiting boxes were each partitioned into 12 "apartments." The apartments were 6 inches deep and large enough to "admit" one lobster. The bottoms were bored with an augured-hole to allow drainage. A handful of wet straw was placed in each apartment and a single lobster nestled upon the straw. Sponges dripping with seawater were then placed above and around each lobster ".. until it was quite concealed from sight and from dry air by this stratum of wet sponges."

The apartment filled crates were stacked one upon another and lined up against the aquarium car walls. Each day of the overland journey, the heavy crates were taken down and each lobster carefully inspected. The sponges were completely removed from each apartment and seawater squeezed out of them onto the lobster of that apartment to check for signs of life, such as "..by blinking its eyes and stretching its claws, perhaps moving its body a little." The sponges were then dipped in seawater and rearranged around each lobster as before. The boxes were replaced against the car walls and seawater poured over each stack. This laborious process was done every day, twice a day.

Two remarks made by Mr. Perrin in his description of the daily lobster attendance procedure spelled doom for his fragile charges. One of his comments was a prophetic deduction of things to come. He stated, "It (the daily changing of sponges) was slow work, and the lobsters were too much exposed during the operations." He was absolutely correct. He'd have been better off keeping the apartment lids shut, lobsters insulated, and routinely dousing them with seawater. Continually exposing the lobsters to the ambient warm air within the train car would have a disastrous effect on survival rates. The knock out punch, unbeknownst to Perrin was a procedure also being performed during the twice-daily lobster repack operations. In his own words, "Pieces of ice which another person had been breaking up meanwhile (during the straw repack) were strewn over each box, among the apartments and sponges, to keep cool the water in the sponges and the moisture in the straw and around the lobsters." The melting freshwater ice acted like poison on the already overstressed lobsters. They were doused twice daily with a substance that is tantamount to battery acid. After reading Perrin's comments on page two of his report, it became clear that the mortality rate, in the end, would be nearly 100%. I knew this before reading his ending summation. Sadly, I was correct.

As predicted, the mortality among the lobsters started on the 2nd day of the journey, numbering only three. The lobsters' mortality rate accelerated rapidly through days three, four and five. Simple math showed that all lobsters in the apartment crates would be dead exactly one day before arrival in California. Perrin realized that some drastic change must be made. As the apartments were about to be repacked one warm afternoon in the middle of the country, Perrin made a bold command decision. He ordered the heavy lid of a large saltwater tank containing striped bass to be pried open. The seawater in this large, permanently mounted wooden tank was being aerated by a clever mechanical scheme. A pulley belt passed down through a hole in the car's wooden floor and looped around the train's wheel axle. As the train moved along, the spinning wheel axle turned the belt. The upper end of the belt was looped around a set of "air-forcing pumps" which aerated the saltwater in the tank. Ergo, the very first aquarium aeration device was born!

Sixty of the remaining live lobsters, about one half, were placed in the aerated saltwater tank. Unbeknownst to Perrin or Stone at that time, this was the solution to all their logistical headaches in long-range transportation of lobsters. The only problem that they would've initially encountered is in the fact that they did not band the lobster's claws. They were of the mindset that lobsters experience less stress if their claws are not constrained and all lobsters aboard were un-banded. Their assumption is true to a small degree, but the un-banded free ranging lobsters would have torn up the stripers and each other within 48 hours. Unfortunately this would be a lesson learned another day, as the fickle finger of fate once again intervened. A day after the sixty lobsters had been moved from dry apartment crates to the aerated saltwater tank, the heavy lid was again removed and cargo checked. Perrin was obviously delighted to report that, "The lobsters in this saltwater appear to be doing *VERY* well," as we in the 21st century know that they would've been. The next afternoon Perrin was filled with great expectations and high hopes as he went to check the lobster tank. He found that the heavy tank lid had not been secured properly and had collapsed into the tank itself. It took several men and much effort to raise the heavy lid out of the water. Many of the lobsters and stripers were crushed and killed outright by the falling lid. All the rest died by "some external calamity common to them both." Regardless, it was a complete loss.

Perrin went into great deductive conjecture as to the reasons why the lobsters and stripers that were not killed by the lid may have died. His first thought was that the wooden tank's sealing mixture of tallow and resin might have been mildly toxic, thereby poisoning the occupants. He questioned whether the ratio of lobsters to striped bass living in close proximity might have had some effect on overall mortality. He mentioned the fact that ice was placed atop the tank to cool the water without "diluting" it. Reading between the lines, Perrin seemed to realize that a large amount of ice-water runoff going into the saltwater tank would be a bad thing. The small amounts that certainly did leak in would however, have no great effects on the volume of seawater in the tank. The final note made by Perrin was indeed the true cause of death in the lobsters not crushed by the falling lid. As it fell into the tank, the lid destroyed the seawater aeration pumps and hoses. He noted, *"The impure air was confined inside (the water) for some time without being replaced by purer air."*

Let's fast-forward 135 years in time to 2009. A pair of fresh caught New England lobsters come to the surface in one of my traps. I decided to preserve them overnight for the next day's dinner. Two 60-quart coolers full of fresh seawater are brought ashore to preserve the two lobsters. A few common starfish are also brought ashore to show the kids at dinner the next day. One lobster is placed in each of the individual coolers along with the starfish. I decided not to put small aquarium aeration pump bubblers in the coolers for this short overnight stay. The next morning, 18 hours later, I found both lobsters and all the starfish completely belly-up dead! A single, fresh from the ocean lobster placed in 60 quarts of cold, non-aerated, seawater had suffocated in less than 18 hours. So completely had the lobsters depleted oxygen from the water in both coolers that it even killed die-hard starfish? There is no question in my mind that Perrin's lobsters and striped bass had died from suffocation due to aeration pump failure caused by the falling tank lid.

Perrin concluded that *"This incident should not be considered a fair experiment and as deciding whether lobsters cannot be transported healthily, in an open tank of salt water, into which air is continually forced, without changing the salt water itself, and kept constantly at a low temperature."* His conclusion was right on the money. He'd inadvertently invented the first viable lobster transportation system without knowing it. The changing of the seawater itself was not an issue. The only things that really mattered were simple; keep lobsters in seawater, aerate the seawater, and keep it cooler than 70 degrees Fahrenheit. He had it right! The lobsters in his wooden tank would have lived healthily for up to a month or more had the lid not crushed the aeration unit.

Perrin carried on as best he could and the expedition continued. The death of those 60 tank-lobsters *"reduced the number of lobsters materially"* so he noted. This, yet another terrible act of God, had a very negative impact on morale, as well it should have. Perrin knew that once again, the jig might be up. The joy and positive comments in his journal ceased. His notes became cold, strictly clerical scientific notations for the record. He abandoned the idea of placing lobsters in any of the remaining seawater tanks due to the unknown factors as to why the un-crushed specimens had died in the lid collapse. The dry box apartment arrangement continued for the surviving group of lobsters. He doubled the effort to keep these lobsters as cool as possible by piling 500 pounds of ice on "slats" placed atop the apartment crates. Unfortunately, he also doubled the amount of freshwater ice used to re-pack each lobster tightly in its apartment box. He carefully monitored each re-packing, removed the dead lobsters, the numbers of which increased with each passing re-pack. He reported that now, upon each re-packing, between one-third to one-half of the residents were found dead. This is not surprising owing to the freshwater and warm air exposures during each re-pack. When running out of seawater in spare barrels, he used tank seawater to wet the packing sponges instead of simply chucking the lobsters in the tanks. Had Perrin ripped the lid off any of the several remaining aerated seawater tanks and deposited the lobster therein, his woes would have ended. But, with the limited biological data on Homarus americanus at that time, the poor man had no idea of this.

As a side note, I was interested to know if Perrin, Stone, and the other attendants cooked and ate the dead lobsters? They had a few kitchen accouterments in the aquarium car for human comfort such as small cooking devices. It would've been a waste to simply heave those large, freshly dead lobsters out the car door as it sped cross-country. But, apparently, that's exactly what they did. Perrin commented, *"At every time of re-packing, one third to one half of the lobsters were dead and had to be thrown away."* They were simply tossed out the train car door. At that time it was thought that a lobster instantly turns toxic at the moment of mortality. In reality I've eaten lobsters that have died in captivity, up to 3 days after their expiration (being well chilled) with no unpleasant taste or tummy ache.

On Monday June 8th only 20 lobsters were left alive. Perrin was beside himself. He grasped at straws trying in vain to figure out why the damn lobsters were dying on him. He was a man of great logic and tried to make sense of why this was happening, hoping to halt the extinction that was numerically only a few hours away. Marshall Perrin was vexed and frustrated to distraction. He'd had enough of New England lobsters, which had become the bane of his existence. He'd had to jump through hoops and call in favors back at Harvard to get a leave of absence for this miserable train ride. And now, in his eyes the sonuva' bitches were dying to personally spite him! Although his journal contains no exclamation points or vulgarity in its final printed form, I can only imagine the language he used to fellow train riders as lobster after lobster died inexplicably. The following is an excerpt taken directly from his report. See if you can read between the lines of what he REALLY wanted to say.

He wrote, *"There were only 20 left alive and there is no regularity in their dying; those treated most carefully and faithfully die as readily as the neglected; and those handled much, live as well as the undisturbed. After the fifth day crowds of lobsters take offense at something, and revenge themselves by dying. The reason of their death was wrapt in mystery. Numerous experiments always failed to bring any regular results, and nothing certain could be gleaned from them. Theorizing about lobsters' chances of life is vain when applied in practice. There seems to be a wide diversity in their constitutions, though unseen and imperceptible. Certain lobsters live well and persistently, while others destined to die beforehand do so irregularly and for an unassignable cause."*

This was one of the first powerful realities that I found, over 100 years later, in conducting my own experiments with lobsters living in captivity. They are, in many ways, very much like us humans. Some are smart and some are dumb. Some are hearty and some are weak. Often times the healthiest ones will die from within perfectly controlled aquatic conditions without reason. From my observations, it seems that some captive lobsters simply die from what I call "a broken heart." Like some humans, POWs for example, in captivity, far from friends, family and home, they just die. There is no readily apparent scientific explanation and I can understand how this fact drove Perrin crazy during the last hours of his trip.

Perrin now spent most of his time theorizing about means by which future ventures like this may succeed. He envisioned some type of "refrigerating apparatus" to replace the "primitive" methods he now used to cool the lobsters. He noted, *"Great harm was done every time the car doors were opened and destructive warm & dry air inevitably and injuriously rushed upon them."* In retrospect he reported that the apartment box arrangement was a failure. He eventually removed all straw and doubled the size of apartments. He had the few remaining lobsters completely packed in seawater soaked sponges, top, bottom, and sides. The mortality rate decreased with this new spacious arrangement as the lobsters were able to stretch and became less stressed in packing. He noted that unrestrained lobsters have the best chances of survival, and he did not band the claws.

On Wednesday June 10th, 1874, the aquarium car stopped at Ogden Utah. A surviving, healthy pair of New England lobsters was given to Mr. A. P. Rockwood, the Salt Lake City Superintendent of Fisheries. This very precious pair of lobsters was placed into the Great Salt Lake. They may as well have been dropped in a pot of boiling water, outright. Fisheries Superintendent Rockwood knew as much about the salinity tolerance range of New England lobsters as he did of the soil composition on Uranus. The lobsters died within the first hour of their release in the Great Salt Lake.

Pulling out of Utah, the Perrin / Stone lobster express now contained only 8 living lobsters and 1 pail of salt water. Not wanting to drain tank water supporting the striped bass, Perrin arranged for a shipment of Pacific coast saltwater to be delivered at a meeting point in Beowawe, Nevada, on Thursday June, 11th. He noted in his journal, *"The ideal condition of (keeping) a lobster is, unrestrained, very cold and disturb them as little as possible. Lobsters can easily be killed with care."* As my old pal would often say when a perfect solution was found or stated: ***"BINGO!"*** Perrin had the correct combinations for long-range transportation of New England lobsters. Of course, this would not help him in the waning hours of this 2nd failed attempt to transplant New England lobsters in California.

8-lb. American lobster in perfect transport conditions: cold, highly aerated, seawater

150 years later, after much experimentation, I found that Perrin's theory on the transport of live American lobsters was absolutely correct. Put them in cold ocean water between 40~45 deg f, aerate the hell out of the water continuously, and keep them in darkness with cooler lid closed. ***THEY CAN EASILY LIVE FOR MONTHS IN THIS CONDITION, WITHOUT CHANGING THE WATER!***

Nine days after 150 lobsters were taken from the Atlantic Ocean near Boston, Massachusetts, only 4 were alive upon arrival in San Francisco Bay on Friday, June 12th. That afternoon the 4 surviving lobsters were ceremoniously released from a wharf in Oakland, California. They crawled into the bay and were never seen again. Perrin noted that it would've been better if the California Fisheries Commission had ordered them released farther out to sea as opposed to simply throwing them off the wharf for publicity's sake. He surmised that the deeper water would be cooler and more "salty." He also noted that two of the four lobsters were heavy with spawn (eggs under the tail). Although these females probably died, he wrongly theorized that the eggs would continue to mature and later hatch regardless of the dead parent they were attached to. This assumption was based on the knowledge that lobster eggs are fertilized at the time of excretion not thereafter, like fish. He had no idea of the extreme care that a berried (egg-bearing) female lobster goes through trying to keep her clutch clean, aerated, and protected. Once a berried female dies the first thing to deteriorate or scavenged for food is the tender eggs attached to her abdomen.

Marshal Perrin concluded that the long-range overland transportation of New England lobsters would be impossible without considering the following. First, that a dedicated "express car" be set up for the sole purpose of transporting lobsters. The many stops and cargo loads / unloads from the aquarium car exposed the interior temperatures to dry heat. Next, that the jarring disturbance of lobsters during transit is detrimental. They should be packed only once and continuously dosed with cool seawater throughout the trip. Finally, he stated that in order to fully determine and remove the many "needless evils" in transportation of live lobsters, more trips (experiments) of this nature would be required.

Perrin returned to Harvard after this failed project and graduated later that year. He moved to a small town in Massachusetts where he wrote a book on the history of Germany and tutored school children. I would wager that this man had nothing to do with lobsters for the remainder of his life. In reality, Marshall Livingston Perrin was a true pioneer in the live transportation and maintenance of New England lobsters.

Soon after the 1874 failure, several other lobster transplantation projects were attempted, unsuccessfully so. Each attempt was a death race against time. As transportation methods became speedier, solid shipments of New England lobsters numbering in the hundreds reached the West Coast. They were released in California and Washington State. They were also released in the brackish waters of Chesapeake Bay, Maryland. None, not a single one of these lobsters, were ever seen again, back then or today. The farthest southern point known to have had New England lobsters is North Carolina. The northern most range was discovered when a British lobsterman was fishing the far western ocean area of Great Britain. He found a New England lobster (Homarus americanus) in his trap, which also contained a British lobster (Homarus gammarus).

LOBSTER AQUARIUMS AT HOME

*O*ne spring day, after a highly successful lobstering trip, I came home with more lobsters than we could eat in 2 sittings. My wife had just gone shopping and the refrigerator was chock full of groceries, both crisper bins were jam-packed to overflow. There was no room to store my lobsters in refrigeration so I left them in a 60-quart cooler full of seawater on the back deck. I dropped a small ball-shaped stone aeration bubbler used to keep trout minnows alive in the cooler for the hell of it. After taking out what we thought to be the last pair of lobsters for a second dinner, I closed the cooler lid and forgot to turn off the aeration bubbler. It was early springtime and the outside temps were very cool.

Things got hectic around the house and I forgot to clean and put away my tote cooler. Two weeks later my wife yelled at me to "get that cooler off the deck." I opened the lid and looked into the brownish seawater to find a pair of lobster antennae sticking out of the water. They were whipping around trying to reach up for me. When I touched the tips of the antennae, a pair of lobster claws came flying up out of the water trying to kill me! Apparently there was an odd numbered lobster left in the cooler; we'd never seen it when removing the other lobsters in pairs previously. It had lived in a few inches of aerated seawater on our deck for over two weeks.

By chance, I had been cleaning a pair of brook trout at the time. I brought a trout head out and dropped it in the cooler. The lobster instantly grabbed the trout head, brought it to his mouth, and started eating it greedily. We watched the lobster pick, tear, and consume all but the jawbone, and then I put the lid back on the cooler. Everyday my wife would go out to look at the lobster, and everyday he'd jump up out of the water trying to grab her with his claws. He'd just look up and stare at me but seemed to hate my wife. I got a few miles of verbal torment out of this. Even she thought it was cute how he'd jump and snap at the sight of her. We kept him out there for another week or two and the darn thing just kept on ticking. The seawater in the cooler was horribly dirty from rotting leftover foodstuff and excrement, but as long as the aeration bubbler kept pumping oxygen into it, the lobster thrived nicely. This is when the bright idea struck me to set up a short experiment just for the hell of it. The "short experiment" lasted for several years and had a major everlasting impact on my life.

I found a used 55-gallon aquarium tank on Ebay for $20, set it up on a basement workbench and filled it with fresh seawater. We put a small aeration stone bubbler in the water and we were ready to go to the basement. The rancid seawater in that cooler reeked as I reluctantly reached in and snatched the feisty lobster out. He was highly charged, twisting and turning to get a claw on me as I dropped the little bugger into the big 55-gallon tank. He instantly tail-snapped his way to the farthest bottom-corner available. Sitting on a curled tail, his antennae whipped around wildly and he brandished both gaping wide claws menacingly.

Edward Scissorhand hated the author's wife.

We watched him for an hour or more in sheer amazement. *A wild caught lobster in an aquarium at our own home!* From the first moment he was with us, we started learning things about lobsters that most folks will never know in a lifetime of merely eating these strange, secretive creatures.

Throughout the next day, we could not help but going to the basement to "see what the lobster's up to." One thing you immediately notice is how keenly aware that lobsters are to human presence. It's definitely not just a "movement awareness" thing, as our cat and dog were constantly sniffing around the tank edges which went unnoticed by the lobster.

As soon as my wife entered the room however, the lobster went on full alert. He tracked her movement with his lightning quick scissor-like claws, hoping to get a bite of her through the glass. We named the lobster Edward Scissorhand after the character in Tim Burtons' 1990 classic.

When making sporadic walks from one side of the tank to the other, the lobster didn't seem to like the shiny glass tank bottom. His walker legs skittered and slid on the bottom glass as he moved about. I went to Petco and bought a 20-pound bag of "Substrate" mix. This is made of crushed seashells, beach pebbles, and sand. The packaged mix is extremely dusty and had to be thoroughly rinsed in a big cooler with fresh water several times before putting it in the lobster aquarium. Even after numerous rinsing, the substrate created a cloud of dusty water in the tank that completely shrouded the lobster from view. I went to Wal-Mart and got an Aqua-Tech 30-60 Power Filter for about $30. This unit worked perfectly for the mission at hand. It filtered and cleaned 50+ gallons of caustic seawater inside a harsh environment filled with creatures having highly destructive hydraulic scissor hands. The Aqua-Tech 30-60 is easy to set up, easy to clean, and has worked for 3 years without stopping. The milky water from the initial drop of substrate was cleaned to crystal blue clarity within 24 hours of filtering. Now we could sit and clearly watch the lobster go about his daily and nightly business.

Watching an American lobster in captivity in your own home presents an endless source of amusement and amazement. Even now, after years of having had a lobster aquariums, I could not walk past the tanks without stopping to see what they're up to at that moment. After seeing just about every notable move or action that lobsters are known to exhibit, they will do something totally odd. They are all as unique as human fingerprints and have personality traits that become individually distinguishable after you watch them closely for a while. They are capable of working out the logistics of problems that perplex them and coming to solutions that never cease to astound me.

One such problem that Edward Scissorhand managed to solve was the matter of human hands being able to snatch him up from the ocean floor as he was walking across the mid-tank area. My wife, an expert lobster handler, would routinely reach in the tank and gently lift him off the seafloor just to aggravate him. The cranky little lobster hated her, and it was funny to see how angry and wild he'd get when she touched him. After a few days of this, he'd had enough human harassment and figured out a way to defend against her hand coming up behind him in the standard rear-carapace grab.

Upon seeing my wife enter the room, Edward immediately ran to his burrowed tank corner. He curled his tail under as tightly as possible and squashed back into the corner. When Ms. Human Hand came towards him, he rolled backwards on the curled tail shell. His carapace was pressed back upright along the tank corner and both deadly claws thrust upward. There was absolutely no safe way to get hold of this lobster at this point with a bare hand so my wife stopped hassling him. That lobster figured out how to use his environmental assets to create an absolutely perfect defensive position and posture. Of the many lobsters I've observed in captivity, Edward Scissorhand is the only one that has done this.

Edward figured out this position by which no human hand could touch him.

A couple weeks later I put 3 more fresh caught lobsters into the tank with Edward, all unbanded. At that time I had no idea how vicious and territorially protective these creatures actually are by nature. They all backed into the same corner and huddled in a heap. I later observed that this was a classic action taken by recently handled lobsters being dropped into an enclosed area. Look at the lobsters in your local grocery store cooler tank. Most will be piled atop each other in the corners. After a few hours, they broke the huddle and started to feel their way around the tank bottom. Upon bumping into each other at this point they courteously stepped aside and let the other pass with no trouble. A few hours later they separated as far apart as possible, and started doing something that we found to be incredible. We've now seen it countless times, as it is a favorite pastime of all American lobsters, and even after 3 years I cannot pull myself away from watching lobsters do this thing; *BURROWING!* They are tireless little bulldozers that can move any amount of gravel in little or no time.

Lobster bulldozing gravel out of the burrow.

They use their small walking legs to scoop up gravel under them. Then they use their jaw mandibles like the front blade of a bulldozer to push the substrate up into mounds all around them. They are like little soldiers methodically building ramparts for a strong defensive foxhole position.

You can depend on the entire seafloor of your aquarium being rearranged every 3rd day as if by the tooth fairy. Rocks, substrate mounds, underwater toys, and aeration bubblers will all be moved about completely. They are tireless workers. And regardless of how clever you are to hide the aeration hoses, they will be found and snipped when you least expect it. So be prepared to replace them.

When you watch this tireless worker, you can't help but wonder where do they get all the energy?

Maintaining a lobster aquarium at home requires very few things. Among them are the big 3: salt water from the ocean, the right temperature, and oxygenation. The most important facet is water temperature. An American lobster survives in temps as low as 34° f and will not survive one single degree over 70° f. They prefer water temps anywhere below 65° f, the cooler the better. Water cooling systems are available but they're complex & costly. In the hot New England summer months, you can use plastic pales full of tank water, frozen. Just rotate the blocks of ice in and out to keep the temps around 62° f to 68° f. The lobsters gather under frozen the blocks like a beach umbrella. They'll snap at it like some sort of alien ship floating overhead, which gives them something to do.

Oxygenation is one thing that is a must. Given enough water, you can go 2 days without it, and then all sea life will cease to exist. A small battery operated minnow bubbler will do in a pinch, but you'll need an aquarium sized plug-in electrical one for the long haul. Be sure to get a 6 or 12-inch long stone bubbler and hide it under the rocks. Regardless, they'll dig it up and march it around for fun. Often a lobster will perch themselves atop a source of bubbles. This is the way they recharge themselves, letting the bubbles go through their whiskers and lungs.

Salinity in water is not a problem when living near the coast. The best water supply I've found is going to the shore and scooping up several gallons of dirty seawater. The natural nutrients in filthy sea slosh are the best! Once back home the clarity filters out with the Aqua-Tech, and you have the best salinity ever. Do not attempt to "make" seawater with chemicals guaranteed by Petco, or any other company. It tried it only once. The salinity meter was within range, the temps were perfect, and the chemicals were metered spot on. It had catastrophic results that I won't forget. Other than an aquarium big enough to match the lobster(s), some substrate, and an air bubbler, you should be all set. One thing that you should know about lobsters. If you intend to keep 2 or more lobsters in 1 tank, without a divider, you should keep them banded. I can tell you for fact that they will tangle, and both will end up mutilated, if not dead. Captive lobsters in this book were only allowed to get together in controlled face-offs. To do other than this is tantamount to animal cruelty. Once in your care, a lobster is a wild animal. Treat them with due respect.

WHAT DO THEY LIKE TO EAT?

*W*hat do lobsters like to eat the most? Well, they will eat just about any type of protein-based substance. This fact always causes me to digress and recall a story that my father told me as a boy when he worked at the US Naval salvage dockyard back in the 60's.

As he told it, one morning the old man arrived at work and found quite a commotion going on near one of the submarine docking berths. Two state policemen, several shore patrolmen, and local wrecker services were all gathered at the dock looking down into the deep water just off the pier edge. He joined the crowd and saw a pair of US Navy divers in the water. They'd hooked up the end of the wrecker cable to something sitting on the bottom of the mucky submarine berth. Apparently some foolish man had gotten drunk, gone out joy riding and was reported missing several days previously. The wrecker winch pulled tight and eventually the trunk of a large sedan emerged from the cold saltwater. The entire car was slowly hoisted from the bay and dragged onto the submarine berthing edge. As water gushed out of the open windows, both state policemen approached the car, then turned away and wretched. The victim was still sitting upright in the driver's seat. His head had been eaten to the skull as was his neck and shoulders. The two burly Navy divers climbed up the gangplank in full gear. They walked over to the car and shook their heads at the dead man's stupidity. One of the divers reached in the backseat of the sedan and pulled out a pair of large five-pound lobsters. One of the lobsters had tatters of the victim's shirt draped over its claws. They offered the lobsters to the state policemen as either evidence or dinner. According to the old man, "Them state cops turned green, and ran off, puking their brains out." The hardened Navy divers simply walked off in clanking gear with the lobsters in hand, for lunch back at the Marine barracks. Point being, lobsters will indeed eat anything of protein base, ANYTHING!

I found that frozen bunker also called menhaden, a large New England baitfish, is most commonly used for recreational lobster trapping. They are also used as bait when game fishing for striped bass or bluefish. You can purchase 6 pre-frozen bunker in bags for about $5. The oilier fish types like mackerel, herring, and bluefish are also considered excellent lobster bait, however, they cost slightly more than bunker. Commercial lobstermen use all combinations of these fish types depending on availability and current cost. Commercial lobstermen of Narragansett, Rhode Island use skate. Skate are a small stingray type junk fish found in great numbers along the sandy coastlines of New England. If you take a day trip to the Galilee, Rhode Island, and the lobstermen's tourist dock in mid summer, you'll be knocked off your feet by the aroma of decaying skate. They are packed into blue plastic 50-gallon barrels, salted, and left out in the sun. Lobstermen then string up 4 or 5 skate using a big spike-like sewing needle for hanging bait within individual lobster traps. Imagine having to go elbow deep into these rotting barrels of goo on the pitching slippery deck of a lobster boat. They must re-bait 500 or more traps during each trip out to sea. Better yet, on a roasting hot August day in waves the size of your house. And we complain when lobsters are $6 a pound?

Once the "recreational" lobster trapper decides on a bait type, then the problem of acquiring and storing it must be dealt with. Unless you can acquire a cost effective, constant source of bait, you should give up on the prospect of lobster trapping. Hey, who said lobstering was going to be easy? If it were easy, then everybody would be doing it, right?

There are a few professional lobster bait companies offering inexpensive alternatives to traditional bait methods. One of these is a compressed ground fish tablet, about the size and shape of a fat hockey puck. It is impregnated with bunker and mackerel oil and guaranteed to last for several weeks under saltwater in a lobster bait bag. I ordered a few of these in my initial experimentation with lobster baits. I was not overly impressed with the initial results in lobster attractivity. However, the longevity in caustic saltwater was amazing. These tablets held together in one spongy chunk for weeks and weeks until I finally threw the things overboard.

I'd heard that cat food would attract lobsters and gave it a try. Initial experiments of placing a single frozen bunker (cut into three pieces) and a can of opened cat food proved to work well in the early, cold-water months of March, April and May. As the water temps got warmer, the cat food seemed to loose its attractivity. Bait will also last longer in colder water than in warmer water when it seems to melt or rot away more quickly.

Every trip out requires fresh bait for each trap. In order to keep costs down, you must come up with economical alternatives to buying it at the local bait & tackle shops. In that I was fishing for blues, stripers & fluke regularly, I recycled the carcasses into lobster bait rather than maggot fodder in the trash can. I found that freshwater fish carcasses such as trout and catfish also work for lobster bait although they seem to dissolve quickly in saltwater. After filleting a fish, you simply fold the rack and put it in a ziplock plastic bag. Ideally, you'll need access to a freezer compartment, additional to the family refrigerator. The family refrigerator freezer will work nicely, but the gruesome appearance of big bluefish eyeballs looking out can be upsetting to spouses. It is illegal to bring in game-fish filets therefore, you cannot rebait traps with that day's catch. You must bring your catch to shore in one piece, clean it on shore, and set aside the carcasses and racks for the following lobster trapping excursion. If you're good with a fillet knife, you can get unlimited access to fresh fish carcasses by cleaning fish at the docks and marinas. Of course, the time and effort doing this would be better spent working a few hours of overtime to simply purchase lobster bait.

Fresh smelt, a favorite lobster food

I conducted extensive tests on what types of bait (food) that American lobsters are most attracted to and which food they prefer to eat. Yes, there is a difference here as strange as it sounds. Some foods wildly attract them to the "hunt". Once obtained, if they were in a moderate state of hunger, they would discard the food or bury it in the sand. Other foods have reduced attraction but when they discovered it during random prowling, they would greedily consume it even when they weren't hungry. I found this to be very odd at first and thought it to be an anomaly due to captivity feeding. As time went on, the strongest surviving captive lobsters in my environmental aquariums became completely adjusted to life therein. They were for all obvious intents and purposes "right at home". I monitored their "hunger state" closely as they were fed at regulated time frames.

My group of specimen lobsters was taken from a wide geographical home range. They consisted of two large 7lb. males from the deep Canadian Maritime near Nova Scotia, a pair of chix from Maine, and a 2lb. male from the inshore region of Long Island Sound. After several months of monitored feeding, eating patterns, and food preferences, some very interesting realities became clear.

Initially, it's important to know the answer to a question that people often ask "How long can a lobster go without eating?" Canadian lobstermen and marine biologists have done exhaustive tests and seasonal experiments to determine that *a lobster can survive up to a full year without food*, given the right conditions. The "right conditions" primarily consist of 2 things.

1) That a lobster's shell is hard and it is meat-full.
2) That the water temps are very cold (35~40° deg f)

It was found that lobsters caught under these 2 conditions could survive quite nicely for up to a year without any noticeable degradation in meat quality, firmness, or taste. Lobsters are naturally programmed to survive without food for extended periods of time. It has been reported that as the water becomes extremely cold in the winter, lobsters go into a form of hibernation and stop eating. Also, that under these extreme conditions, they will curtail all unnecessary movement and secrete themselves in rocky burrows or under the sand. Not surprisingly, I observed these exact same traits in specimen lobsters when the tank water temps plummeted during a deep winter cold snap.

As the water temp in the tank dropped to around 40° deg f, the larger deepwater lobsters (from Canada) were first to slow down and nestle into the substrate between the rocks. They rarely got up to walk or move about the tank. The smaller Maine lobsters were next to hunker down in what appeared to be a form of suspended animation. They did not actively seek food. However, if food chunks were literally dropped onto them, they would grab it with walker leg claws, draw it to their mouths and eat the food hungrily. They would not move from the burrow and once eating was done, they resumed suspended animation.

As water temps got down to a hand stinging 38° f, the inshore Long Island Sound lobster slowed down a bit. Curiously, he only exhibited hibernatic torpidity during the daytime and was fully active at night unlike all the others. In the water, nearly as cold as ice, he marched around briskly, antennae inquisitively swaying about. This may simply have been an anomaly or it could be a trait unique to lobsters dwelling in shallow inshore cline. In that I had no other inshore specimens, it was (as of this writing) impossible to determine which of these are true.

How can a lobster survive without food for a year or more? They are able to survive on energy reserves stored within their own bodies. Their *hepatopancreas* (good word to use in a marine biology-101 essay) otherwise known as liver, tomalley, or the green-stuff, contains huge amounts of life sustaining nutrients. It is the stuff that helps the lobster purify and digest the food he eats. This is the key to their long-term survival in a food-depleted environment. The lack of tomalley in a store-bought lobster indicates that it has probably been in captivity for a very long time without food. Their body assimilates the nutrients stored up in the tomalley.

It's now suggested that pregnant women, nursing mothers and women who may become pregnant do NOT eat tomalley (liver of the lobster). It is the lobsters' natural way of filtering out contaminants from its body. All others should limit their tomalley consumption to 1 meal a month. With the official warning being noted, you should also know that tomalley is considered to be one of the most delicious parts of a New England lobster. It is used as a flavor-base for stuffings, casseroles, and myriad other seafood applications. I can only describe its unique flavor in these five words, "the true essence of lobster". In my family this green ambrosia always causes a scramble trying to grab the lobster with the most tomalley in it. The photo below shows tomalley in its cooked state, a bright greenish color. In its natural, uncooked state it is a grayish dark green. As an aside, note the blob of white yogurt looking stuff on the right side of the photo below. You often see this cottage-cheese stuff inside of cooked lobsters and floating in the water that you cook a lobster in. It is totally edible, but somewhat tasteless; it's the lobster's blood.

Hepatopancreas, aka: tomalley or "the green stuff"

As with all facets of the amazing New England lobster, their eating rituals are quite complex. Many small factors come into play, all of which are inter-related. Aside from pre and post-molt stress, a lobster's hunting and feeding patterns seem to be affected by two major conditions, namely water temperature and hunger state.

I must admit that I could not in clear conscience starve a lobster under my care, to death, in the name of research or for any reason whatsoever. Thus, for the parameters of this experiment, the longest that a specimen went without being fed was 14 days. The test was performed in the months previous to deep chilled water, causing what appeared to be a form of hibernatic slowdown.

Hungry lobster, relentlessly on the prowl

During the test, lobsters going 14 days without food showed absolutely no signs of lethargy, stress or degradation in vigor whatsoever. They did however show an increase in activity, interest in prowling, and rooting through substrate. This is no surprise as the longer they went without food the more they sought it.

They became ingenious in finding food sources that I'd never thought of within their environment. One lobster dug up an old quahog clam that had been living beneath the substrate. I'd dropped it in the aquarium months before and forgot about it. It survived nicely until a big lobster on a 14-day fast cracked it open and ate it, including most of the shell!

Every square inch of the underwater environment was scoured for the most minute naturally edible material. To this end, the lobsters were not the least bit shy nor did my presence deter them whatsoever. They performed one amazing feat after the next right before my very eyes. The 2 lb. male lobster from inshore Long Island Sound, for instance, set his sights on a large starfish that had made its way to the top of the tank glass to escape the carnage (seen above). He jumped and grabbed for the starfish's lowest limb for a few minutes. Realizing that this strategy was not working, he set to full speed head-on charges of the tank divider, a plastic pane with large holes cut in it. His big claws were too heavy for an upward burst and his body toppled over backwards like a kid falling off a rock-climbing wall. He gave up on this tactic and marched away to pout in the corner. An hour later I came back and was dumbstruck by the scene. The diehard lobster was relentless as are most American lobsters in pursuit of whatever endeavor they undertake. He'd managed to push a boulder, easily 3 times his size, across the substrate into a position below the starfish (above). In order to physically perform this task, he'd bulldozed the sand from in front of the boulder, and then pushed it into the dip created. Now he used the boulder like a stepping stool to easily grab the starfish. An absolutely amazing display of what lobsters are capable of. Whether the lobster actually used (and is capable of) logical reasoning, or this was simply a matter of luck through an act of abject frustration (lobsters often push rocks around), I do not know. I do know for a fact that when lobsters become bored or hungry they are capable of things that truly defy logic and our human imagination.

In the end, the lobster pulled that starfish down and walked it to the corner of the tank. I thought that it was most certainly curtains for the starfish, but once again, the lobster did something quite unusual. It gingerly handled the starfish and made one quick surgically accurate snip! It removed one of the starfish's five arms and ate the single spoke. The lobster then brought the starfish to the area of the tank where it was taken from earlier. He released it with 4 remaining arms. A day later the starfish was back at his lofty perch clinging to the tank glass top with 4 healthy arms. Interesting point being that, unlike most of us humans, lobsters will not eat more than they need for one feeding. Also, unlike some of us humans, they seem to appreciate the need to preserve natural resources that can sustain them at another time, another day, even when that resource seems readily abundant.

The other hungry lobsters started to scissor the barnacles off the sea boulders (below). After they snipped them off with pincer claws and cracked them open, the barnacles were then eaten whole. I watched one of the hungry lobsters eat a saltwater snail. As mundane as this may sound, it too was an amazing process to watch.

It was one of the larger lobsters. It held a snail about the size of a dime in the tip portion of its massive crusher claw. Instead of smashing the little snail to bits outright, the lobster applied well metered, slightly increasing crusher claw forces. It applied just enough force to delicately crack into one outer chamber at a time.

As one chamber would crack, the lobster reached up with a walker leg claw-tip. Like a person who'd just cracked open a walnut, gently picking up the meat with thumb and forefinger, the lobster brought the bits of newly exposed meat to its mouth with walker leg tips! This went on until the last snail chamber had been broken open and eaten. It was an awesome display of the discreet control that a lobster actually has over its powerful claws. They can cradle a soft starfish or amputate a human finger at their behest.

Making a meal of rock barnacles

The aquarium tank bottom became completely littered with broken shells, remnants of crushed appendages, and other carnage left from hungry scavenging lobsters. I sighed to myself thinking what a mess this will be to clean up after the experiment had ended. A day later I went to the tank and found it totally clean! The lobsters allowed the mess to exist for 2 or 3 days. They then buried all the broken shells and discarded materials in the substrate in one evening's work. Boulders, aeration bubblers and other tank ornaments were completely rearranged. It looked to be a totally different underwater environment than it was the day before with no mess. These creatures will never cease to amaze you.

Eventually food was dropped into the lobster tanks after several fasting periods consisting of 14-days, 7-days, 3-days, and 1-day. I found it more interesting to observe "how & when" they ate, rather than "what" they ate. The food types used in these tests were among the following:

- **Fresh salmon**
- **Fresh bluefish**
- **Frozen bunker**
- **Frozen mackerel**
- **Fresh herring**
- **Fresh codfish**
- **Fresh flounder**
- **Fresh tilapia**
- **Fresh smelt**
- **Fresh sea scallops**

- **Mussel clams**
- **Cherrystone clams**
- **Fresh large shrimp**
- **Canned cat food (Friskies beef & chicken)**
- **Fresh/frozen tautog**
- **Freshwater trout**
- **Fresh striped bass**
- **Fresh scup (porgy)**
- **Fresh chicken (leg meat & skin)**
- **Live green crabs**

After the 14-day fasts, they all responded wildly as soon as a food chunk hit the water. They tracked it down instantly, and greedily ate it. The type of food was irrelevant at this juncture. All food was quickly found and eaten regardless of type. As always, the lobsters did not engorge themselves. They ate only enough to satiate themselves and discarded the rest, always bringing the discards to the farthest end of the tank away from their home burrow. Some of them bulldozed a hole in the substrate and literally buried the leftover food like the classic dog burying his bone.

During several 7-day fasting period tests, lobsters were moderately active and seemed more interested in pushing each other around, their favorite pastime, than prowling about and digging into the substrate for food. They did not go about obsessively crushing barnacles or digging for clams as they had in the 14-day fasting tests. When food was dropped into the water, they would approach the food and quizzically examine it. They'd make a curiosity-grab at it and eat the food, with enthusiasm dependant on what the food actually was. I'll have more on this to follow.

Lobster's favorite pastime, boxing with each other!

Overall, in a controlled environment, it seems that lobsters were at their optimal health and vigor state at a point of between 3 and 7 days without eating. This of course may vary due to the effects of molting, water temps, and mating found in the wild.

After a 3-day fasting, the lobsters seemed to be at their peek activity level. They poked around, had brief skirmishes with each other, more on the "bump n' run" basis rather than the "locked up life or death" type engagements. They busied themselves with trying to figure out an escape route from their confines. To this end they left no small avenue of escape untested. This is another interesting obsession of the New England lobster.

As food was introduced into their midst, they reacted the same as in the 7-day fasting tests. They tracked down the food, brought it to their mouths, took a few nibbles, and quickly discarded it. Generally speaking, the action of a lobster that has not eaten for a period of 3 to 7 days is about the same, excluding certain types of food that will also be discussed later on in this chapter.

After a 1-day fasting, the lobsters generally were not as active as in longer fasting periods. They tended to hunker down in burrows and rocky crevices for longer periods of time between movements from place to place. Only one of the test specimens briefly ate at a food source dropped in front of him. All the others reacted the same by initially repulsing the foods placed near them. They would not seek or intentionally go near fresh foods laying on the substrate.

I had some fun with one of the lobsters during his 1-day fast feeding. He was sitting pat in his rocky burrow, obviously not the least bit interested in eating. I dropped a juicy chunk of fresh codfish atop his head. His antennae flailed and he jumped up at full attention, antennules wildly sniffing the water. He quickly found the offending codfish chunk and picked it up with his mandible arms. He did not so much as take a taste of the fresh cod. He angrily marched the piece of cod out to the farthest reachable corner of the aquarium and flung it away! He did not simply drop the cod; he literally arched his back inward, convulsed upward, releasing the cod at the apex of the upward jerk. It looked like a kid throwing a ball underhandedly. The cod chunk flew upward in the water and landed as far away from the lobster as possible. He spun around, stormed back to his burrow, and nestled back in. I reached into the tank, picked up the cod and dropped it back in front of the surly lobster. Once again he immediately repeated the same exact process of carrying the chunk to the same distant corner. This time, however, he simply dropped it and returned.

I did this several more times and the lobster did the same thing over and over (below). As I dropped the cod in front of him a 5th time (just to see how long he'd keep up the act), he sat staring at the big white piece of codfish, inches from his face. His eyestalks slowly retracted inwards and his flickering antennae folded backwards over his shoulders. He was like a human who had had enough nonsense and was shaking his head and sighing in disgust. It was hilarious. Slowly, half-heartedly, he got up yet again. He picked the cod up with the pincer tip of a walker-leg, and hobbled the thing, once again, to the far corner of the tank. He dropped it back in the far corner and stared straight ahead at the cod for a long minute. As if to be saying, "Go ahead, make one move; I dare you!" Eventually he returned to his home burrow and hunkered in. I removed the cod from the tank and saluted the lobster.

American lobsters are very particular about how they eat. They have definite set patterns of behavior that at first are not apparent to the general observer. Of the many nuances, two are most pronounced and obvious. The first being that they will not eat gluttonously, consuming more than they need for a single meal. The second is that uneaten food is ALWAYS carried far away from a lobster's home burrow and dropped or buried. This reflexive habit is a survival technique used to keep scavenging predators and other hungry lobsters far from their resting places.

Overfed lobster moving fresh codfish away from his home burrow

Favorite food choices were assigned numeric values according to the lobster's observed preferences and eating interests. The data was noted as objectively as possible. It was then sorted and charted to show the foods that lobsters most like to eat and which foods lobsters are most attracted to. There was an almost imperceptible difference in the two, however, quite noticeable at some times during fasting feeding tests.

Lobster food preference test results

	Foods that lobsters eat, in order of preference.		Foods that lobsters are most attracted too.
1	Mussel clams, cracked	#1 **	Mussel clams, cracked
2	Smelt, whole/fresh	#1 **	Bluefish, fresh
3	Bluefish, fresh	#2	Mackerel
4	Tilapia	#2	Cat food, canned
5	Flounder	#2	Green crab, crushed
6	Scup	#2	Herring
7	Striped bass	#2	Chicken legs & skin
8	Codfish	#2	Cherrystones, cracked
9	Mackerel	#2	Bunker, frozen
10	Herring	#2	=========================
11	Tautog	#2	** ALL OTHERS **
12	Cherrystones, cracked	#3	SIMILAR ATTRACTION
13	Shrimp, fresh shell on	#3	
14	Sea scallops	#3	
15	Green crabs, crushed	#3	
16	Bunker, frozen	#3	
17	Trout, freshwater	#3	
18	Salmon	#3	
19	Chicken legs & skin	#4	
20	Canned cat food	#4	

It should be noted, once again, that these results were obtained from lobsters in captivity and under completely controlled environmental circumstances. The effects of tidal ebb and flow, ever-changing water temperature ranges, seasonal food type availability, and molt cycle could certainly cause deviations in the data observations above. That being said, I cannot, however, imagine those deviations in any great amount having a major impact on the items listed and the preferential order of their listing.

Although the numerical list orders a lobster's favorite eating-foods from 1 to 20 it should be noted that four definite sub-group patterns were noted within the 20 food items. For instance, the items listed as #3 through #11 (bluefish, tilapia, flounder, scup, striped bass, codfish, mackerel, herring, & tautog) were eaten with about the same enthusiasm. Differences were, in most case, imperceptible. The next sub-group appeared to be from item #12 through #18 (cherrystones, shrimp, scallops, green crabs, bunker, trout, & salmon). The final and bottom ranked sub-group is items #19 and #20 (chicken/skin and canned cat food).

The top 2 items that lobsters prefer to eat are cracked blue mussel clams and fresh smelt. I can say with a high degree of certainty that this finding will stand true under almost any condition or environment where an American lobster will seek his food. When the juices of a freshly cracked mussel clam enters the water, all lobsters immediately perk up and go on the hunt. They quickly devour the internal meat and then go about grinding up and eating most of the thin mussel shell itself. A lobster's body requires calcium found in clamshells. It is easier for them to chew and digest the thin mussel clamshell than it is to do so with the thicker cherrystone clams (finishing in the 3rd group of preference order). It is possible that controlled aquatic environments may not contain naturally occurring calcium, therefore elevating their apparent lust for mussel clams.

Fresh whole smelt is a delicacy that lobsters seem to cherish. They do not instantly go wild upon the initial presence and scent of smelt like they do with cracked mussel clams. They do, however, quickly locate it and bring it to their mouths. After the first taste (or close smell) of fresh smelt the specimen lobsters all seemed to be floored (stunned) at their good fortune. The same as a person who bends down to find a winning lottery ticket on the ground at their feet. The lobster will greedily start eating the smelt in the place where it was found. He/she then makes a beeline back to the burrow or closest shrouded hiding place with the prize. In this way they are assured not to be disturbed by other lobsters in possession of that winning lottery ticket. The lobster jealously guards the smelt. Some specimen lobsters seemed to eat the smelt more slowly than other foods, as if actually enjoying the taste. Smelt seemed to be the only food that a lobster would tend to eat more of than they actually needed for a meal. Any other food would have been discarded after lesser amounts had been consumed. Not so with fresh smelt for some reason.

The items listed above, the food that lobsters seemed most attracted to, come in 3 main sub-groups. Group #2 (the 2nd most attractive to lobsters) appeared to be items #3 ~ #5 (mackerel, cat-food, and crushed green crabs). These 3 items present a tantalizing oily slick that quickly infuses into the water. Mackerel makes a nice edible find, however, cat-food crumbles into dust. That only seemed to frustrate the lobsters when they encountered a small bit of it on the substrate. Crushed green crabs, once found were quickly eaten, including most of the calcium-laden shell. Group #3, containing items #6 ~ #9 (herring, chicken, cherrystones & bunker) seemed to run a close 2nd behind group #2. Fresh, bloody bluefish appeared to be the #2 best overall option for baiting your lobster traps. They sought it quickly and loved eating it.

Of the top two favorite food preferences, (fresh smelt and mussel clams) only one could not be resisted or passed up, even when a lobster was "full" from a short 1-day fast. By no accident, the top #1 most "attractive" food to the American lobster specimens in this experiment happened to be the same item. This item is also a favorite among human seafood lovers and served at some of the finest restaurants. Using it for lobster bait would seem foolish to some of us. However, if you are strolling along a rocky beach, snorkeling or boating near a craggy reef, be sure to gather some clusters of this incredible lobster food. Crush some up for your lobster trap bait-bags, and sauté the rest in fresh garlic and red Cabernet Sauvignon wine with crusty French bread. A favorite of the human and American lobster alike, the edible, the incredible, **BLUE MUSSEL!** Scientific name: *Mytilus edulis*

Blue mussels, a favorite of lobsters & humans alike

KNOWING HIM IS TO LIKE HIM

*A*fter watching lobsters in their natural environment and in captivity for 50 years or more, you start to get a slight inkling of how they operate and why. Knowing the lobster is to understand what he likes and what he dislikes. Once you understand this, you can make a logical wild guess at where they go and what they do when they get there. For instance, did you know that lobsters spend most of their time grooming?

They are very clean animals and do not like having dirty shells and undercarriages. While "off-duty" and not on the prowl, lobsters cup their tail flippers downward onto the bottom as seen on right. In this resting position their entire body lifts up off the seafloor. It promotes water flow up through their gills and makes breathing easier for them.

When in confined areas they will wave their walker legs, fanning the water for enhanced aeration and breathing. This is similar to a human sitting on a hot porch waving a hand-fan at their face.

Cup tail ventilation & grooming stance

In this tail perched resting position, a lobster will always inevitably start grooming itself. They extend both claws and press them downward to elevate their bodies even further. Then the walker legs vigorously go to work. All eight of the walker legs start working in pairs or singularly. The front pair of walker legs, having pincer tips, will twist upwards and scrub the claw and wrist shells. The first time that I observed this, I thought the specimen had gone berserk and was dying from strange convulsions. Finally, the lobster did something that I'd seen my cat do a thousand times when cleaning itself. He folded both antennae (whiskers in my cat's case) down and grabbed them between his walker leg pincers. He slowly pulled the antennae up and through the leg pincer tip. All the seafloor substrate dust flew off the antennae and it popped away clean as a whistle. He then ran both of his feathery nose antennules through clenched mouth mandibles cleaning them, too. The lobster methodically did this to his mouth feathers and all his appendages. He then started on his undercarriage with the mid-body walker legs. He picked, scratched, rubbed and generally dug at himself until all kelp strands and foreign material was gone. He then used the rearmost walker legs to cleanse the abdomen (tail) section. It was interesting to note that the rearmost walker legs of a lobster are fully rotational and double-jointed. Initially I thought the specimen's rear walker legs had been broken in battle as they twisted fully upward and started cleaning the top of the abdomen (tail) shell.

This grooming ritual in American lobsters is actually reflexive. It is somewhat of a nervous habit much like a person who twists their hair when in reflective thought or conversation. I noted this when observing several specimens engaged in half-hearted shoving matches in my lobster tanks. As they poked claw tips at each other, their rearmost walker legs would twist upwards and scrape at their own shell tops and undercarriages. Clearly this was an act of nervous habit, as it had absolutely no advantage in the playful combat at hand.

Probably the most important thing to understand is how a lobster locates his food. A lobster's sense of "smell" is extraordinary. Their sense of smell and taste are basically one and the same. Obviously they cannot "smell" food like we do in the breeze. They "taste" it in the water around them using tiny but powerful chemosensory hairs in their antennules, the feathery whiskers on their nose (Fig #5). If you watch a lobster very closely you'll see his/her antennules flickering almost constantly. Look even closer and you'll see that they seem to flicker in only two directions, up & down. If you really press your face to the lobster tank glass, you'll see that the downward thrusts of a lobster's antennules are very forceful and repetitive. The reason being that lobsters have a row of very fine sensory hairs along the bottom edge of its antennules. As these hairs are rapidly rammed forward & down they collect concentrations of particles from the water from which the lobster is alerted to the things around him. The three most important things that lobster antennules pick up are, #1 trace particles of food, #2 another lobster that is a threat, and #3 another lobster who is a suitable mate.

If you have a lot of time on your hands, and the local seafood clerk doesn't mind you pulling up a chair in front of his tank with your magnifying glass, you may actually get a quick glimpse of what lobster antennule chemosensory hair looks like. Look at the rare photo in figure #5 below. It was taken at the instant before this lobster was about to snap his antennules down for a water particle collection sample. If you look really closely you can see the particulate matter in the water as well as very small particles already trapped in his chemosensory hair on the bottom edge of his antennules.

Fig 5: Lobster trapping scent/taste particles on tiny chemosensory hairs along bottom edge of antennules.

They're also able to sense taste through the front pincer-enabled walking legs, often using these to sniff around the bottom for edibles. The following is an excerpt from my notes on maintaining lobsters in captivity. Quite by chance, while observing two of my favorite specimens, Edward and Titan, two large male lobsters, a peculiar thing happened:

"One day the local seafood market had a sale on fresh dressed smelt. This was the first time in a long time that I'd seen these tasty little seagoing minnows for sale. I purchased about ½ pound and brought them home. I cut a smelt into two pieces about two inches long. Up until now, I'd been feeding the lobsters by softly skewering the fish pieces on a plastic tie-wrap end, attached to the end of a length of monofilament fishing line. I'd jig the fish piece up and down in front of the lobster until he would feel it with antennae and snap it down with a claw. As I was about to do this with the smelt, my wife came in and said, "Just drop it in the far end of the tank; they'll march out and find it."

I told her that they'd wait until after dark to seek it out and that I wanted to see them eat, as we stood there at that time. She matter of factly said, "They'll find it right now; I've been feeding them when you're not around for weeks now. Watch this."

So, she took the smelt and dropped them in the far ends of both of the lobster's sections. Edward and Titan were as always when they see me near, hunkered down in burrows wearing stone faces. The smelt bodies did a slow fall to the bottom and sat there, completely out of the lobster's field of view. There was no visual way that they could have seen the smelt being placed in the tank. My wife said, "Now just stand still and watch this" About 15 seconds later both of the lobster's antennae started swaying around. Their feathery antennules whiskers wildly fluttered and they walked from their burrows in full daylight with us watching. They did not walk all around the tank bottom in a hunt and peck fashion as I thought they would because they did not see the smelt fall into the tank. The smelt fell in behind them, completely out of their sight.

They emerged from burrows and urgently walked DIRECTLY to where the smelt was laying. They snatched up the food, spun around and quickly returned to their burrows to consume their prizes. There was no hesitation in their step. There was no question as to the fact that food was actually on the bottom at exactly that moment. They knew without feeling with antennae precisely WHERE the smelt was lying. The most puzzling part of this amazing display is how they knew all this without looking or touching?

The answer can only be in their ability to detect minute "scent" particles within the water itself. Watching them eat the smelt (which they love more than bluefish) I tried to make sense of how ultimately discrete a lobster's sense of "smell" must truly be. I tried to analyze and understand what I'd just seen.

Each lobster's side of the tank consists of approximately 30 gallons of saltwater, a 60-gallon total. There's a pair of large 60~80 gallon Aqua-Tech dual water filtration units sitting above both sides of the tank. These units suck up tank water through 1" intake pipes located near the aquarium bottom (inches from where the smelt landed). They constantly suck up seawater from the bottom of the tank, and force it through a series of carbon filtration screens. At the top of these units the cleansed water is pushed out a pair of dual output ramps, and the clean water splashes down in a pair of gushing waterfalls atop both lobsters.

On the bottom, inches from the back of the filtration intake pipes, there is a pair of 12" aeration bubbler stones emitting a constantly gurgling curtain of fresh air bubbles. The top of the water over both lobster burrows is constantly boiling and swirling with miniature water vortices. And yet the lobsters knew exactly when those smelt hit the bottom and precisely where they landed by scent particles in the water currents, alone!

I can only put this in human terms as follows. It would be like a farmer standing in a field of 10-foot high corn stalks on a pitch-dark night and being able to smell exactly when dinner is served back at his ranch house, over 100 yards away. And, being able to walk directly to the kitchen door blindfolded. And, doing all of this with ease, in the winds of a catagory-3 hurricane."

As you can see, lobsters have no problem locating food by the slightest whiff from distant locations and know the shortest route to get to it. Although they'll scavenge for food and eat dead carrion to survive, lobsters highly prefer fresh killed sea fare. People often ask how come these garbage-eating scavengers can taste so darn good? The fact of the matter is that they do not eat garbage. They have more fresh edible foods at their disposal than we will ever know. They eat certain types of fresh seaweed (garden salads!) and just about all types of living things that dwell in their seafloor realm (sushi!).

They are compulsive housekeepers, constantly fanning the bottom debris from their burrows with coursing swimmeret water blasts. The few impure foods that lobsters do consume are immediately filtered and cleansed as they pass through their liver, also known as the tomalley or "green stuff". Making a short story long, this is why they taste so darn good.

Mating, prowling, eating, and fighting are what lobsters "do" for a living and not in this particular order of preference. The actual order would be something like this, prowling, fighting, mating, and eating. American lobsters absolutely love to fight with each other. This is the one thing that they do with unbridled passion whenever and wherever the opportunity exists. Few humans ever witness these nightly battles occurring in darkened, deep undersea arenas. When two or more lobsters encounter each other they immediately begin a wild swordfight with their large antennae. The object of this pre-fight ritual is to get a general estimate as to how big the other guy (or gal) actually is. This wild slap-fest goes on for a few minutes as seen in photo below.

Lobsters sizing each other up before having a good fight!

It seems that a secondary objective of this violent antennae palpation event is to slap the other guy in the eye! When one of their eye-stalks gets whacked with an antenna, it protectively retracts down into the carapace eye socket and the lobster does a slight involuntary convulsive shiver. The other lobster (the one who scored a direct hit on the eye-stalk) often appears to sense his/her good fortune, and will then advance to the next stage of the fight, which is claw thrusting.

Claw thrusting looks similar to a pair of Japanese sumo wrestlers when they initially clash in the middle of the fighting ring.

Both claws are usually pinched shut, fully extended out front in tandem and pressed together for mutual support. One or both of the combatants will run full speed at the opponent trying to jam his claw tips into the other lobster's face. Interestingly enough, more times than not, at this point of the game, both lobsters keep their claws closed. The battle at this point is usually kept to pushing, shoving, and boxing with each other in a contest of overall size and strength.

It seems that there are 2 objectives during this second stage of engagement. The first objective is to jam a claw tip into the eye of an opponent. The second and most important objective is to maneuver both claws underneath the opponent's body and physically push or lift him up off the seafloor, similar to the rules of Greco-Roman wrestling. Once lifted from the seafloor, the winner is usually determined and understood by both combatant lobsters.

Once a lobster is lifted off his legs and loses contact with the seafloor, he usually affects a frantic escape attempt. He goes into a wild, tail snapping reversal and flies away backwards, moving as far as he can go from his opponent. He sits for a moment, collecting his thoughts, and tries to bolster his wounded pride. Usually, this defeated contestant will soon race back into the fray for a second shot at the title. Sometimes he wins, but if he loses a second bout, he will usually call it quits and retire to fight another day.

A perfect example of two lobsters engaged in their version of Greco-Roman wrestling can be seen below. In this photo the lobster on the right got the bright idea to attack from the high ground. His opponent countered with a powerful left uppercut, which eventually pushed the attacker off his lofty perch. Note the topmost lobster's walker legs. He is franticly trying to grasp the surface of the rock. He was ultimately dislodged and flew away in defeat. Interestingly, this lobster made several more advances for engagement. Each time, he walked around the boulder, never again over or upon it. He knew the old human adage, "Fool me once, and shame on you. Fool me twice, shame on me!" Lobsters have long-term recall, which is a huge asset to their overall survival in the wild.

Lobsters vie for dominance in a classic wrestling match

If no certain victor emerges, this 2nd stage-wrestling match will go on for hours and even days. Sometimes both lobsters will mutually agree to take a time-out to rest up a bit before slamming back into each other. I once had a trio of small chick sized lobsters. When I placed them in the tank, they literally hit the ground running and instantly took to fighting each other. They pushed and banged into each other from all angles and directions. They were relentless. When they got tired, they all rested quietly next to each other, side by side. As soon as they were re-charged the fighting continued. It was fascinating to watch, and we referred to them as "The 3-Stooges".

The 3-Stooges..

On occasions when the size and fighting skills of combatant lobster pairs are equally matched, the fighting will sometimes progress into a 3rd stage of engagement.

Biggest loser at the "Claw-Lock" game

The gloves come off, figuratively speaking, in this stage. They become far more aggressive as both claws separate and open wide. This becomes dangerous to both combatants as winners and losers are often seriously injured. They often engage in a dangerous game of what is called "claw lock". In claw lock, they grab onto each other's claws and squeeze down hard. Like 2 humans shaking hands and seeing who can squeeze hard enough to squash off the other guy's thumb! The lobster having thinner claw shell-thickness ends up with cracked or debilitated claws.

Sometimes the lobster with stronger claw muscles can lose the initial claw lock game due to shell thickness. He will usually retreat to heal his wound and fight another day. Look at the old claw-lock veteran in figure on the left. This guy just didn't know when to quit!

Sometimes, however seldom, the weary pair will call it quits at this point. More often than not in long running equal size battles, the struggle escalates into the final phase, deadly combat. In this end-all phase the lobsters are not interested in wrestling or poking each other in the eyes. They are interested in only one thing, namely getting an open claw around the other lobster's weakest parts. They do this in order to crush, avulse and sever the other lobster's body as completely as possible in the quickest, most vicious method available to them.

Lobsters fighting in earnest, deadly physical combat

A classic end-game opener can be seen in the photo on the previous page. They go for the opponent's face, trying to crush the entire frontal carapace off. This killing blow seldom occurs due to the sensitive parts in that area. A lobster will feel the enemy's claw on his face and quickly respond with powerful tail thrust movements. Many times, however, as the offensive claw snaps shut, it will crush and remove a nose-spike, large antennae, or antennules.

American lobsters are always keenly aware of scent in the water around them. As was previously mentioned, the feathery nose antennules are always snapping downward trying to "smell" the things around them. They are constantly taking note of conditions that may be noteworthy for their immediate physical well being. This is especially so when engaged in combat with another lobster.

At first glance, this would seem tactically unsound. When engaged in phase #2 hand-to-hand combat they wisely tuck their large antennae backwards, tightly over their shoulders. This keeps them away from the enemy's frantically clipping, hydraulic-strength scissors. Why then won't they also safely tuck away their delicate antennules? The reason is valid; however, it is totally imperceptible to the human eye.

Lobsters use their powerfully scented urine for many purposes, not unlike a dog marking his territory by urinating on a passing fire hydrant. Many animals do this, including large cats. Lobsters however use this method of communication far more extensively than most other animals on earth. An American lobster's urine carries more messages about him/herself than the spoken word could ever tell. It tells of who he or she is, in as specific detail as a human fingerprint. It tells of a lobster's physical state, his or her current intentions, and much more. Probably one of the most powerful uses of a lobster's urine emission by females is to completely seduce and mesmerize larger aggressive males. One squirt of her powerful pheromone laced urine, *INSTANTLY* turns any violent male lobster into a whimpery puppy dog at her beck and call. More on mating rituals will follow.

When engaged in mortal combat, lobsters continually urinate in each other's faces! They urinate out of two small nozzles located on the lower section of their faces just ahead of the large mandible arms.

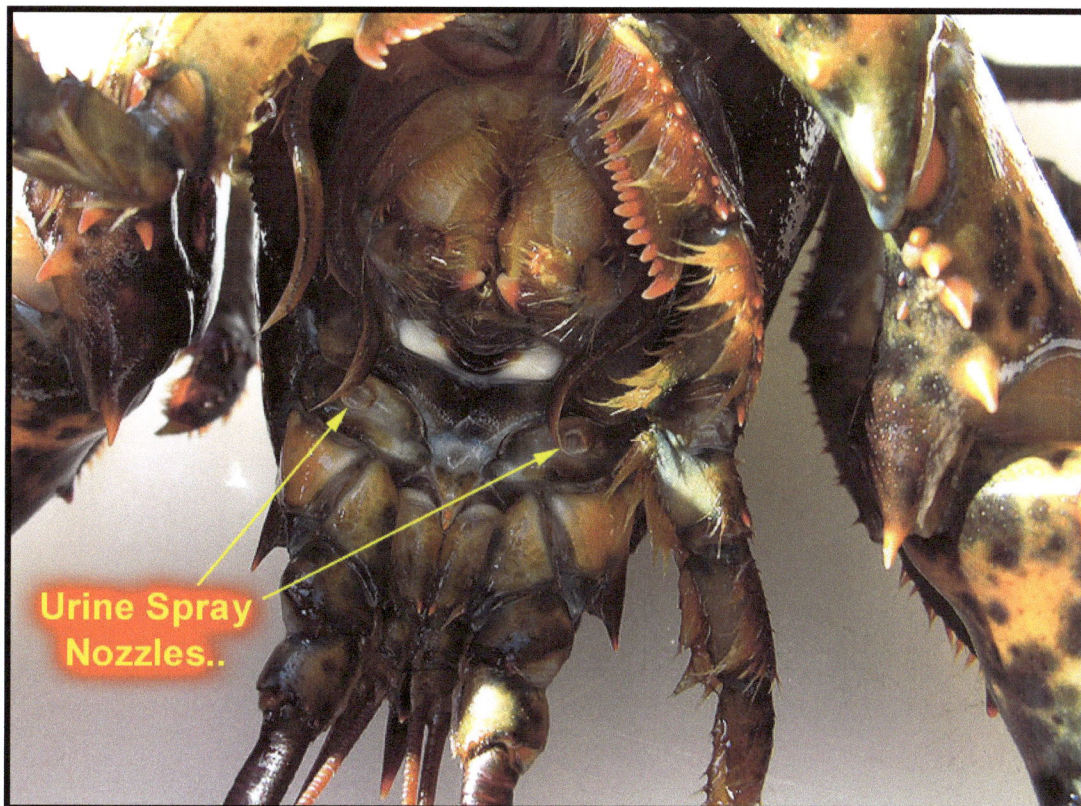

Lobster urine emission nozzles underneath the nose-spike

As the fight progresses, their antennules monitor the scent of the adversary's urine to see if he is hurt, experiencing fear, or becoming, more physically aggressive. Flight or fight calculations are made during running battle from samplings of an opponents urine scent. After a winner and a loser have been determined, in the case where death did not occur, both combatants make mental notes. They maintain a short-term recall of the fight, how it was fought, who won, and who lost. This recollection will remain with both lobster combatants for a period of about 2 weeks. This amazing recall is based solely on one unique set of chemicals. These chemicals are specific and unique. They are found in a lobster's urine. The lobster that lost the fight will turn tail and refuse to voluntarily engage with another lobster that has beaten him in the previous 2 weeks at the approaching whiff of the winner's urine. Conversely, the winner will recognize the urine scent of a defeated foe and aggressively pursue him with reckless abandon.

In phase #4 of battle, the tangle of snapping claws continues. Eventually, by chance or by planned attack, a walker leg or wrist joint will fall into an opponent's gaping crusher claw. The appendage will instantly be amputated and slowly flutter to the seafloor. This usually concludes hostilities as the amputee makes a frantic retreat. In some cases the stress of phase #4 battle, combined with severe injuries and open amputations, can lead to the death of one or both combatants. In captive controlled environments such as lobster aquariums, the victor will often relentlessly pursue the vanquished lobster and cut him/her to pieces, one bite at a time, until they are dead.

This lust for hand-to-hand combat is why you often see market lobsters with missing antennae or being among the one-clawed "cull" types. You may be shocked to know that *THIS* is the reason why lobstermen put rubber bands on their lobster claws. It's to keep their cash crop from killing each other. It is *NOT* done to protect you (the innocent seafood customer) from getting your fingers snipped off when you reach into a carry-bag full of un-banded lobsters.

Another curious condition was noted when lobsters are engaged in phase #2 (or higher) of their combat struggles. They get into a state of total fixation. Nothing is more important to them than the other lobster in front of them, not food, not other lobsters, nor human intervention. Lobsters in captivity are very sensitive and in tune to the presence of humans. A light bump on the tank glass with the bottom of your hand will usually send a lobster scrambling to the far corner on full defensive alert. During one wrestling match between a pair of small male lobsters, the fighting was getting somewhat out of hand. I tried to break up the pair with a long wooden-handled tank cleaner rod. I tapped them; I banged them with rod, and finally tried to physically pry them apart using the rod as a lever. They would NOT disengage, nor could I physically pull them apart with the large wooden rod. I reached in up to my shoulder with one arm and physically slapped their carapace tops with my hand. They acted like I wasn't even there, both going for a killing face-hold on the other. I finally had to reach in the tank with both arms to try and separate this pair of small 1lb. lobsters! They would not release their respective grips on the other and I lifted both out of the water and set them down on the bench. They continued to fight for several minutes in dry air on the bench top until they ran out of breath and released their mutual grips. Still, they did not clamber away in fear of death by suffocation. They both stared each other down with menacingly raised claws. This is the length that lobsters will go to kill each other, given the chance.

Several curious observations were noted after watching many hours of lobsters tangling with each other. One remarkable pattern indicated that male lobsters normally adhere to the nuance of specific escalation throughout the combative phases. Among male lobsters it is similar to human kids saying, "I dare you.. I double-dog dare you!" They always started off with antennae whipping, then progress to pushing, and so on. When a female lobster fought with a male lobster, things often went differently. Female lobsters took a no-nonsense approach to the fight. They went from the opening phase of antennae whipping directly to deadly claw open combat. Also, they did not tend to hang around and fight as long as male lobsters would. Rather than pressing her luck, when a female lobster appeared to be on the loosing end, SWOOSH, she was gone. If a female lobster won the fight, she did not pursue the loser, as was the case in most male vs. male fights. She'd simply turn and strut away as if the fight never happened. Male lobsters are constantly looking for a good fight. Females will only engage if they are totally bored or are cornered by another lobster.

As with all things in the natural world, every creature's inherent traits are biologically ingrained. We all have a purpose for being in our genetic makeup. These reasons are most often for the survival of that particular creature within the environment in which they live. After reading this far, you can certainly see that the lobster has many, many unique genetic characteristics. All, except one of these, will help their species thrive and enjoy a long survival into the future.

It seems odd, however, why these creatures absolutely *LUST* to engage each other in mortal combat! Certainly, the old postulates of "survival of the fittest" and "selective breeding" do come into play here to a certain degree. But one would think that most of the dwindling or fragile species like the lobster would have learned to curb their self killing instincts to a point where deadly combat seldom if ever occurs. This is not so with the indefatigable American Lobster. They would rather fight than eat or mate. The last existing pair of Homarus americanus on earth would instantly fight each other to death given the chance. This is what they do for fun. The American lobster's credo and approach to life is simple: "Fight to live, live to fight!" In retrospect, I suppose that American lobsters are not unlike human beings.

The American lobster's mantra:

Fight to live, live to fight!

It should be noted that throughout these tests, no lobster was purposely subject to any harm. Each had their own aquarium or sectioned-off portion of the aquarium. They were allowed to fight under controlled supervision. Only once was a lobster so hell bent on getting to the other that he literally pushed a rock (the size of the one above) into a glass wall one night. He broke through the glass (I've since used plexiglass) and they tore each other to pieces. They were among my favorite pair, both full of life, and capable of showing me things that defied imagination. Now they are dead, which hurt me deeply. They truly lust to fight; it's their way.

EATING LOBSTERS THROUGHOUT THE MILLENIA

*W*e now know a little something about a lobster's comings, goings, and how to catch them in the wild. To further enrich our appreciation for this unique creature, it is important to understand its history from a distant past perspective. We've already discovered that there is absolutely nothing better than the deep oceanic taste of a freshly caught, locally grown, New England lobster. With this in mind, we'll start our historical journey at a place in time, long before written records, when a starving humanoid first encountered Homarus americanus.

In the 1770's Europeans and American colonists referred to tomatoes as "Poison Apples". It was grouped in the botanical family of Nightshade, a deadly poisonous plant. Poison apples were avoided well into the 1800's until a distraught suicidal man once tried to kill himself by eating a tomato. Obviously, the attempt failed, but he lived to describe what a sweet, vine-ripened tomato actually tasted like. In the early 1820's this intriguing tale was finally put to the test in front of the Salem, New Jersey courthouse. Colonel Robert Gibbon Johnson stood in front of the courthouse at high noon and publicly consumed an entire basket full of ripened tomatoes. Mouth covered with tomato juice, he swiped a puffy white shirtsleeve across his dripping maw and flipped his palms up. The stunned crowd of 2,000 spectators waited for nearly an hour to see him drop dead in his tracks. He didn't die and the US Supreme Court would later officially classify the tomato as a vegetable fit for human consumption and exportable as a prized United States commodity.

Unfortunately there are no records as to who consumed the first lobster. One can only use logical deduction and a lively imagination to envision a scene that may have taken place, long ago. So, we must digress several hundred years to the time when a bedraggled upright walking humanoid first spotted the shoreline of the area now known as New England. The hairy fellow was clad in stinking animal skins. He'd been struggling through the dense inland thicket for several days without food. In his primitive mind, he cursed the day that he got the bright idea to leave the safety and comfort of the cave he called home for a long walk in the woods. He was lost in an inhospitable land with only a sharp stick for defense. Suddenly, he breaks through to a clearing on the shoreline of an endless expanse of water. He peers out at an unimaginable scene that takes his breathe away. Water extending from his hairy feet out into infinity is hard for his logic to contend with. Bone dry and thirsty from a long day's march he scoops up and greedily swallows a handful of the water at his feet. It instantly gags him, he wretches convulsively for several minutes, and falls onto hands and knees in the seawater. What manner of liquid poison had he consumed?

He sits on the shoreline staring at the ocean for several hours and experiences primal human emotions that rock him to the core. Ultimate despair, grief and loneliness set in. An hour later, the second most powerful human survival emotion grips him; abject hunger, starvation, and a desire to eat at any cost. Thoughts of his home cave, friends, and times past are replaced with pangs of hunger and the urge to eat. Cautiously wading into the brackish water, past the swaying kelp gardens, he spots an outcropping of wet mossy stones. A large shiny black-shelled bug-like creature is crawling along the top of the rock pile. The creature is about three feet long, head to tail, and weighs about 20 pounds. It has a pair of massive hands with which it is crushing a big quahog clam. The starving human stealthily closes on the creature with curiosity. He doesn't know if this strange animal will take flight like the inland prey that he's hunted so many times. The big bug casually picks clam meat from the shell with its huge mouth mandibles. With a fearsome grunt, our starving friend leaps from the water and covers the big bug with his chest and arms. The creature is knocked off the rock and pinned to the sandy ocean bottom for a moment.

The man is surprised with the ease in which he'd made the capture. He comes to a kneeling position in the water and blindly reaches for the hard-shelled creature in order to take a closer look. The feeling of euphoric success disappears in a flash of blinding, gut-wrenching pain in his left hand. Two of his left fingers are crushed and severed off at the bloody knuckles by the pincer claw of a 20-pound lobster. He rises up on two feet, bellowing in agony. The lobster holds onto the stump of his severed fingers and tries to reach across with its crusher claw to clip off the entire hand. Adrenaline floods the human's system and his fight or flight instincts kick in. With super-human strength, he uses his one good hand to grab the lobster by its massive carapace. Tearing its grip from his body, he rears it up over his head, and smashes it down on the rock pile. The lobster hits the rock pile with a sickening splatter and is killed instantly. The man cradles his bloody left hand and the pain soon subsides, as the nerves from the two-digit amputation are gone.

Luckily for him, he is standing in New England seawater that has natural anti-bacterial, clotting and healing capabilities. If he were in stagnant pond water, the staff infection in his hand would have killed him within a few weeks.

Pangs of hunger replace the dissipating pain and adrenaline. Cautiously he examines the bug-like creature laying smashed open and upside down on a mossy rock. A mound of clean fleshy meat is protruding from the underside of the cracked tail section. It reminds the man of an inland turtle that he once smashed open and ate. He pins the creature's body down by stepping on it with his hairy foot and tears a chunk of fleshy meat from the tail shell. He smells the flesh and it has no hint of rancidity. He licks the flesh and it has a clean and slightly salty taste. Not knowing what to expect, he gnaws off a full mouthful of raw New England lobster tail meat. After several cautious chews, he swallows. Unlike the sinewy inland turtle, this meat is tender, somewhat sweet tasting, with a slight flavorful hint of saltiness that he'd never experienced before. He chews off another mouthful and much to his surprise it tastes better than the first! Some green, pasty, goo from the bug's insides seemed to have added a flavor unlike any he'd ever tasted. He scoops a handful of the green goo out of the lobster's crushed thorax and brings it to his mouth. The stuff has a smooth mellow flavor with a slight brininess, not like the gagging taste of seawater. He carts the giant smashed lobster to the shore and sets it on a boulder. The large claws intrigue him. They are dangerous and must be destroyed. He pummels the crusher claw with a rock. It eventually cracks open, exposing a ball of white flaky meat. He finds this claw flesh to be the most tender and tasty meat that he'd ever eaten in his long 17 years on earth. This creature's meat is easy to chew, even with his few remaining rotted teeth.

Not only did our bold Neolithic friend survive his first encounter with an American lobster, he also became one of the oldest survivors of his time, living with eight fingers to the unheard of age of 32. The moderate climates and abundant shoreline food sources where he took up residence sustained him in a healthy form not seen by any of his inland predecessors during that period. His favorite food became, ironically, the most plentiful and the one that nearly killed him upon first encounter. Unknown to him, the flesh of lobster is high in natural proteins. It is abundant in essential vitamins and minerals now known to promote healthy bones and enhance neural synaptic and brain activity in humans. It is low in cholesterol and high in Omega-3 fatty acids known to reduce heart disease.

Eventually, other inland humans came to the area, haggard, hungry and broken. He was the master of this mysterious shoreline wilderness and revered as a godlike life-giving being by those who arrived there, on deaths door. Before his passing, he showed others how to handle lobsters. Placing a stag's leg bone in the crusher claw of a beached giant lobster was enough to show the power and potential danger that these creatures possess. The thick deer bone would snap like a twig and smash into powder.

Held by the very end of the tail and lifted off the ground, a lobster was helpless. Its heavy claws hung as useless appendages once held aloft by the tail. From this position, he showed them how to kill a lobster by thrashing it against a rock. After four large 12-pound lobsters were killed, they were dragged back to the beach where a fire was burning in a dugout sandpit. The old survivor had found these bug-like creatures to be even more palatable when cooked than when eaten raw. Hickory sticks were soaked in seawater and laid across the pit in a criss-cross pattern. Without presoaking, the sticks would quickly burn and collapse into the fire. Our prehistoric lobster lover also found that the smoking hickory branches added a delightful flavor to the cooked bugs. All four smashed lobsters were then carefully placed atop the grid of hickory sticks. He learned that simply throwing them into the fire would contaminate the meat with sand, charcoal, and other tasteless materials. The dripping lobster bodies would sizzle and spatter for 30 minutes or so. As the shells turned crimson red, they were pulled off the smoking hickory stick grid and placed on a large, flat, table height beach boulder. After cooling down a bit, the lobster's claws were all methodically cracked open with a stone. Green tomalley was hand-scooped out and smeared over the mounds of puffy opaque tail and claw meat. And so the wisdom of our first lobster eater was passed on to the ages.

This may not be the exact turn of events, but it surely embodies some of the elements that happened during this first encounter between man and lobster. One thing that we can definitely be assured of is that lobster claws in some form, mauled one of our ancestors. This is not a matter of "if"; it is a matter of "how severely" he or she was crunched. I can only wonder what sounds, before formal language, were shouted when a 20-pounder snagged their thumb. Perhaps something like *"YOU NO GOOD ROTTEN %@#$"* in caveman vernacular?

At any rate, time marches on for the union of man and lobster. From this inauspicious beginning comes a time of ambivalence. On the one hand, the lobster is truly an ugly sucker. But on the other, its meat is edible, palatable, and contains all the nutrients and life giving qualities to sustain a human being. Thus, we've made a tenuous agreement with the lobster: *We'll eat you only when we absolutely must.*

In 1615, explorer Captain John Smith wrote in his description of New England, "You shall scarce find any bay, shallow shore, or cove of sand where you may not take many clams or lobsters or both, at your pleasure and at many places load your boat if you please." We now fast-forward to one of the first documented lobster dinner festivals. It took place in 1621 when the Wampanoag Native Americans treated the Pilgrims to a fall harvest feast. The Pilgrims weren't doing so well at the time, and the boss man, Governor Bradford, sent his best marksmen out "fowling". He'd hoped to save face by adding a few ducks and geese to the mountain of foods brought by the Wampanoags. Whether in fact they bagged a turkey or two is not really known. What is known however is that the term "turkey" itself was used at the time to describe any sort of wild fowl. Paintings and accounts of that first American fall festival all pretty much indicate one thing for sure, that New England lobsters and clams were most abundant on the menu that day. It was reported by a Plymouth resident, complaining about the colony's lack of food diversity, "there was a time when the only thing you could have was a lobster and a cup of water. And then for a change, a cup of water and a lobster."

From these factual accounts we can assume that lobster had been a common staple among New England shoreline tribes for many years before the first Thanksgiving. In fact they were so readily available that Native Americans used lobsters to fertilize gardens and as fish bait. I recall reading a well-preserved old farmer's diary that described a long wagon trip from the cornfield to the shoreline. Lobsters were shoveled with wooden pitchforks from the beach onto the wagon. Once the wagon was filled to the sideboards, the lobsters were carted back to the field, chopped or ground up, and flung along cornrows for spring fertilization.

During colonial times lobster was called "poverty food". They were easily harvested by hand in tidal pools and along rocky beaches. No one of the colonial time would ever admit to eating lobsters. It was considered to be a shameful disgrace, the lowest form of destitution and impoverishment. Lobsters were fed to penniless widows, orphans, indentured servants, prisoners and residents of insane asylums. It was said that during the Revolutionary War, British POWs rebelled over being fed a constant diet of lobster. Eating a spider-like lobster was akin to eating rats. Most migrant workers' and indentured servants' contracts contained a clause detailing the exact amount of meals per week that said worker could be fed lobster, usually 3 times weekly. After a backbreaking 18-hr. day of veritable slave labor, workers preferred a bowl of gruel or leathery tough beef to a pair of steamed lobsters. As hard as this may be to imagine, it was reflected in the written terms of their working agreements.

One of the strangest ironies in the rags to riches story of the New England lobster exists in factual penal history and current statistics. In the early days of the New England penal system, it was officially deemed to be cruel and unusual punishment, to serve lobsters to prisoners more than once a week. Nowadays, lobster is probably the most frequently requested "last meal" for prisoners about to be executed. But times being what they are, some states now limit death-row prisoners with a last meal consisting of $15 or less. I'm sure that at least one death-row prisoner of the 1700's had tried to come to grips with his upcoming demise and considered this one thought, **"At least I won't have to eat another lobster & clam dinner!"**

In the 1700's this lobster & mussel clam dinner, was hated by all

By mid-1800, our country's infrastructure was making huge advancements. Rough, but accessible networks of roadways and railroads connected most major cities across the country. Due in full part to the burgeoning transportation systems in America, dwellers of the interior states were able to visit the never before seen New England shores. They could experience breathtaking rocky coastlines leading to an endless expanse of seawater. Local cuisine was always an intriguing challenge to visitors from the hinterlands.

Clever New England innkeepers used good old Yankee ingenuity to marginalize costs in a new market, later to be called "Tourism". Making the most out of the least, they fed these wide-eyed tourists lobsters! Lobster meat was served in many forms outside of the shell. Casseroles, pies, skewer-grilled, and smoked were among the many lobster meat styles of serving. Unlike today, Inns and eateries for tourists had no telltale signs of a lobster in shell form. This disgusting thorny exterior generally remained hidden from view whenever the meat was served, for obvious reasons. Eventually, the flavor and tenderness of lobster surpassed the visual revulsion caused by its nauseating bug-like appearance.

Returning to their inland homes across the country, tourists described to friends and family something that they had eaten on their first ever vacation. It was a delicate meaty food that was easy to chew, even with decayed teeth. It was sweet and had a slight salt brininess that tasted like the smell of deep New England ocean water. They tried to describe what this fantastic tasting creature looked like and eventually produced a souvenir brought home on the long 8-day trek. This souvenir would be passed around, examined and appear in single-room classrooms around the country. It became a family conversation piece for years to come. It was placed over the hearth until it became paper-thin brittle from the heat. Eventually the huge crusher claw of a large New England lobster finally cracked and broke into pieces from age. Another enjoyable trip to New England would be needed.

A pair of large New England lobster crusher claws for home display

NEW ENGLAND LOBSTERS vs SPINY LOBSTERS

*T*he majority of New Englanders have never eaten a spiny lobster. In our book a "lobster" has two big claws and mostly come from the state of Maine. Few of us have ever seen a living spiny lobster and fewer yet have ever held one. The truth of the matter is that spiny lobsters, cousins of our clawed lobster, lead equally complex lives and are in their own right as edible and delicious as any lobster in the world.

In 1976 my wife and I ordered a pair of spiny lobster tail entrees at a 4-Star South-Florida restaurant. We'd been eating New England lobster 3 times a week back then and this was the first time we'd ever eaten a spiny. Our recollection for many years after that was that the spiny lobster tail was rather bland and tasted more like fish than lobster. This was a very long time ago and the memory of that first taste of spiny lobster stayed with me until recently. For purposes of this book, I could not give an unbiased representation of "what a spiny lobster tastes like" without a fair and thorough assessment. To this end I was able to have a fresh pair of Florida spiny lobsters (panulirus argus) shipped to my house.

I called Todd at Florida's Finest Seafood in Lauderhill, Florida at 1:00pm on a Tuesday. At 11:00am the very next day, less than 24hrs. later I had a pair of fresh, whole, 2lb. Florida spiny lobsters on my doorstep. For about $50, they were a bargain in my book (literally). The two lobsters were tightly packed in frozen gel-packs and styrofoam. They were not alive on arrival, but were obviously fresh from the water. I then purchased a pair of similar sized live New England lobsters and spent the day comparing these interesting species, Homarus americanus and Panulirus argus.

North vs. South, New England lobster (top) & Florida spiny lobster (bottom)

The first thing I did was to place my nose on these fresh lobsters and take a deep smell of both. The scent of New England lobster I knew so very well. It has that brackish inshore saltwater smell, like standing at the tip of Stonington Point (Stonington CT) and taking a deep breath in the breeze. The smell of the spiny lobsters sent to me from South Florida had a distinct scent that surprised me. I expected a sort of highly salt concentrated warm Mediterranean water type smell, like the surface water of my last snorkeling trip to Aruba, but I was wrong. Curiously enough, the Florida spiny lobster smelled like deep, cold, ocean water. It reminded me of a recent trip to Gloucester, Massachusetts. We were standing on the Maritime trail, overlooking the dark green open ocean. The brisk sea breeze coming in from the Georges Banks was blowing in our faces. The smell was unique. It had a distinct plankton enriched deep oceanic cold-water smell. Strangely enough, this is the smell of a Florida spiny lobster.

When first laying hands on a spiny lobster, you quickly learn how it got its nickname. There is no way to grab a spiny lobster barehanded without getting stabbed. At the end of my daylong comparison testing, after handling the panulirus, both of my hands were shredded from cuts and stabs. The carapace top is lined with rows of forward pointing razor sharp hypodermic needle tipped spines! The eyes stick out from under a pair of thick horns that are absolutely deadly. Given the choice of having my thumb squashed by a New England lobster claw or fully impaled on a spiny lobster eye-horn? I'll choose the New England crush every time!

The painful business end of Panulirus Argus
The Florida spiny lobster

The carapace and leg shells of Panulirus Argus also seem to be much harder than that of Homarus americanus. It is like super hardened thick plastic, almost as hard as glass. When fully hardened, like the pair sent to me, the carapace could not be bent, dented, or broken with your hand or nutcrackers. I finally had to use a ball-peen hammer to break the carapace shell. It shattered like a glass Christmas ornament.

The first huge noticeable difference between the spiny lobster and the clawed lobster is the spiny lobster's large solid antennae. They are the size of cigars at the base and are lined with forward pointing sharp spines. When next you see a picture of someone holding up a spiny lobster by the antennae barehanded, imagine the pain that they're hiding with a big smile. It's like grabbing a rose bush with one hand and running your other hand backwards down the stalk. Notice the thick fur-like sensory cilia hair lining the inside edges of the spiny lobster antennae below and the smaller separate pair of "feeler" antennae used to more discretely locate food and surroundings in the spiny lobster's world.

Florida spiny lobster antenna stalk

This creature has become highly adapted at survival in its specific warm water environment. It obviously does not need arms with powerful claws for defense. The spiny lobster, unlike the New England lobster, seems to be completely covered in sensory reception devices. It is most certainly fully aware of its total underwater presence and surroundings.

The pointy tips of the spiny lobster's legs are covered in a thick cilia hair. This gives the animal an extremely sensitive touch in understanding exactly what it is walking over, finding minute edible portions of food, or deciphering messages in water particles around him on a very discreet scale.

The shell thickness of a spiny lobster's small legs is that of the clawed lobster, but they are much harder and more brittle. They feel like the plastic barrel of a ballpoint pen tip.

Spiny lobster leg tip covered in cilia hairs

Unlike the New England lobster, the bottom coloration of the Florida spiny is bright white with a smattering of brown and red camouflage spots. They also have a row of needle-sharp spines on the tip of the lower point on each tail (abdomen) segment.

The underside of a Florida spiny lobster

As you inspect the underside of Panulirus argus a little more closely, you'll find a dazzling array of pleopod swimmerets. They are big, colorful and puffy!

Colorful spiny lobster pleopod swimmerets

The next thing that caught my eye in comparing New England and Florida spiny lobsters is their tails. I'm talking about their true tail fins, the five flat flippers at the end of their abdomens. They both have 5 tail fins; a single fixed fin in the center and a pair of pivoting fins on either side of center. The trailing edges of all five fins on both species are tipped with soft hair-like cilia fur.

Florida spiny lobster tail on left, New England lobster tail on right

There are two major differences between the tails of a spiny lobster and a New England lobster. The first of these is the coloration. Each is colored from a top-down view to assume the background-camouflaged color of its specific environment. For instance, look at the New England lobster tail on the right side above. It is a dark mottled soft mish-mash of brownish green. If you were snorkeling along the top of a shallow New England inshore reef, the ocean bottom below you would look exactly like this lobster's tail segment! On the other hand, if you were snorkeling in the bright crystal clear waters of Aruba or southern Florida, the sparkling sand and coral bottom would look exactly like the lobster tail on the left above.

One big difference between their tail fins is not immediately visible but can be felt in the pliancy. The New England lobster tail fins are shell-like and as hard as an extension of the upper tail (abdomen) shell itself. The spiny lobster tail fins are soft and pliable as any normal fish's tail, as can be seen below.

Panulirus argus spiny lobsters have soft pliant tail fins

After all the outward appearance differences were noted, it was time to get down to the meat and potatoes of the matter; namely how edible are these two lobsters and what do they taste like in comparison? Being a lifelong New England lobster fan, I wanted to set up an unbiased side-by-side test in order to give the spiny lobster a fair shake in the matter.

Both test specimens were about the same size, weighing in at approximately two pounds each. The spiny lobster's tail was slightly larger than the clawed lobster tail, but the clawed lobster made up for the weight differential in claw meat weight. Two separate kettles were used to avoid cross-contamination in the cooking process. One inch of tap water was put in both kettles and the lobsters were steam cooked for about 15 ~ 20 minutes. They both took on the reddish shell color of normal cooked lobsters, except that the spiny lobster was a more light orange shade of red.

Cooked New England (left) & Spiny (right)

Throughout the cooking process I took several whiffs of the steam rising from both kettles. They both had unique and distinct scents similar to that of the fresh individual pre-cooked lobsters. The New England lobster steam smelled like the brackish salty seashore of Stonington, CT. The spiny lobster steam smelled like the deep oceanic waters of Cape Ann, Massachusetts.

They were fully cooked (not overcooked) in the same amount of time and removed from the kettles. The New England lobster was, as always, simple to remove from the kettle. Its outer carapace was smooth and easy to handle. The spiny lobster was painful to handle as every square inch of spine covered shell surface gouged deeply into my hands. The antennae are like a pair of thorny rose bush vines waiting to rip your flesh with the slightest misguided sweep.

Handling a cooked spiny lobster can be treacherous!

As far as edible portions of meat in similar sized spiny and New England lobsters, I found that the spiny lobster tail contained, on average, slightly more meat than the New England lobster tale. This is due in part to the large connective strands of muscle (meat) that run the full length of the spiny lobster's inner carapace and attach to the large antennae stalk bases as seen in the photo below.

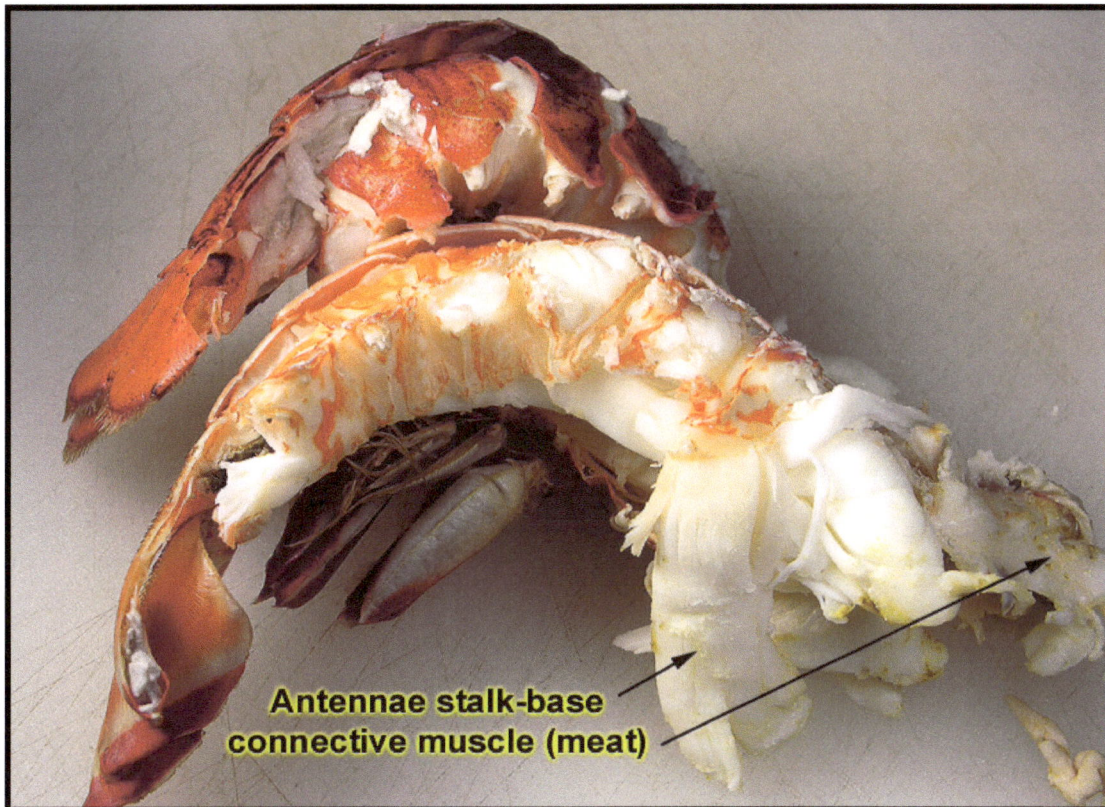

Cooked lobster tails; Spiny lobster in front, New England lobster tail in back

I found that there were two large dollops of tender meat inside the antennae-base shell joints. Cracking the spiny lobster's faceplate open to get at this meat however, was not a task for the thin skinned. I cut my fingertips to shreds trying to get at this sweet meat as seen in figure below. Also, the spiny lobster's small walking legs all seemed to contain thick, tender strands of tasty meat, similar to the New England lobster legs.

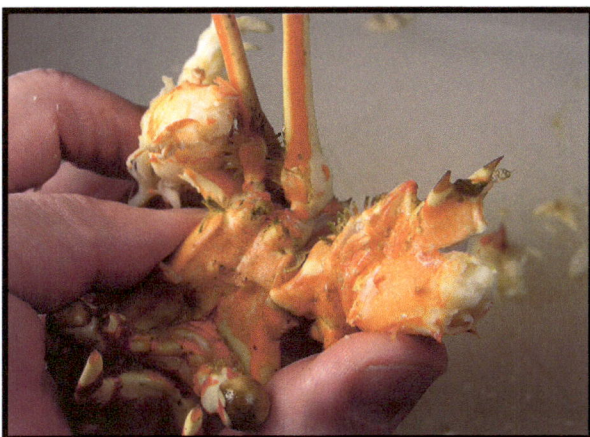

**Tender spiny lobster meat
in antennae stalk bases**

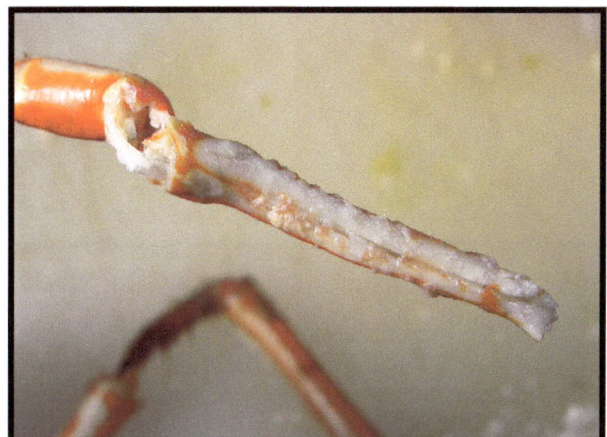

Strands of meat in spiny lobster legs

When the meat from both lobsters, with nearly similar overall body weights, was completely shelled out, it was placed on side-by-side plates. It became clear that the New England lobster contained slightly more edible material than the Florida spiny lobster as can be seen in the photo below. This is due in large part to the claw meat found in New England lobsters.

Lastly, the most important part of comparison between these two kings of the crustacean world is the taste test. The first comparison was of the tail meat only. I trimmed off small cross-sectional medallions from the tail portion of both these lobsters and placed them in small ramekin dishes. This first taste test was set up by me, for me, and I took a personal oath to be fair in my assessment. I had some melted Land O' Lakes butter fresh lemon wedges, and sea-salt nearby, but did not use it initially. For a palate cleanser I chewed a small saltine cracker and washed it down with Poland Springs seltzer water, and then gargle-rinsed with tap water.

After slowly chewing, tasting and swallowing small test samples of both types of lobster tail meat, twice, my personal findings astounded me. By a slim but clear margin I found Florida spiny lobster tail meat to be better than New England lobster tail meat. Allow me to clarify the word "better". The spiny lobster tail meat was clearly smoother in texture, far easier to chew and more tender. In fairness to the New England lobster, however, this could be due to a simple luck of the draw with regards to the individual lobsters that I'd purchased at that time. I've eaten New England lobster tail meat in the past that was fork tender and some that was as tough and chewy as shoe leather. This was in fact the first spiny lobster (both spinys were the same in taste and texture) I'd ever eaten. But they may have seasonally differing textures also. The one thing I found that would seem to be a constant in both lobsters is the taste and overall flavor. The New England lobster tasted great to me. It was a regular, good old New England steamed lobster. A flavor that I've known and loved for over 50 years, like putting on a comfortable old pair of shoes. When I tasted the Florida spiny lobster tail, I was devastated. Its lobstery taste, as I would call "lobster flavor", was slightly better than the New England lobster's tail meat! This was undeniable even after several palate cleansings and more taste tests. This was upsetting to me, so I decided to set up a true "blind" taste test among random participants at my workplace.

Edible portions of similar sized New England lobster (left) & Florida spiny lobster (right)

I carefully trimmed the sinewy red outer skin covering from all of the lobster tail meats and cut them into small cross-sectional medallions the size of quarters. I also trimmed the New England lobster claw meat and cut them into similar sized portions. All were placed into separate ceramic ramekin bowls. The bottoms of which were marked with "F" for Florida, "C" for Claw meat and "N" for New England. They were all slightly warmed before the testing began.

When I asked for volunteers to taste fresh lobster, my coworkers who normally make themselves scarce when there's work to be done, came out of the woodwork with raised hands. I selected ten of them at random. Of the bunch, all had eaten New England lobsters previously. Only one had ever eaten a Florida spiny lobster several years previous. Five of the tasters claimed to be crazy about the taste of lobster. The other five said that they were "so-so" on seafood and could take it or leave it.

Young and old, the taste testers acted like kids getting to determine which type of candy was the sweetest. I speared out test samples on double-ended toothpicks. They obligingly closed their eyes and allowed me to place a tidbit of lobster meat in their open mouths. The initial reactions of these blind taste testers were quite interesting.

The ranking in blind preference for the most "lobstery" tasting samples took a clear and almost unanimous vote. Of the samples marked "F" and "N" (tail meats from spiny and clawed lobster), the testers scored 9 to 1 in favor of sample "F", the Florida spiny lobster! Five of those nine took some time to discern which sample they preferred most, ultimately choosing "F". The other four testers chose the Florida spiny tail meat instantly, claiming it to be "definitely more tender and lobstery tasting". Some of the comments made about the actual taste of Florida spiny lobster tail meat were: "Definitely more tender", "It has a slight nutty taste", "Yep, this here's the New England lobster meat, I could tell that instantly, you can't fool me", "It tastes a little bit like tender sea scallops."

Interestingly enough, the sample marked "C" (New England lobster claw meat) was rated as "the most tender of all and slightly more tasty than samples "F" & "N". Ergo, New England lobster claw meat ranks highest of all in both the flavor & tenderness category. Four of the ten testers tried a small amount of tomalley from the cooked New England lobsters. All four of them agreed that the flavor of tomalley is heads and tails more lobstery tasting than any and all of the samples provided.

At the end of the day it appears that the Florida spiny lobster tail tastes better on the "lobstery" scale than the New England lobster. I guess it's a matter preference and taste. My wife has bluntly told me for years now that she'll take an Alaskan king crab leg over any type of lobster, any day. Each to their own, I suppose.

RED'S EATS

Lobsters and humans have come a long way. Now let's go to a small town called Wiscasset, Maine. Here you will find a small shack, about the size of your garage. It's a food shack, with a small window that you pass money through and get food pushed back. Although there is no signage that says what it specializes in, it has a simple sign that says: "Red's Eats."

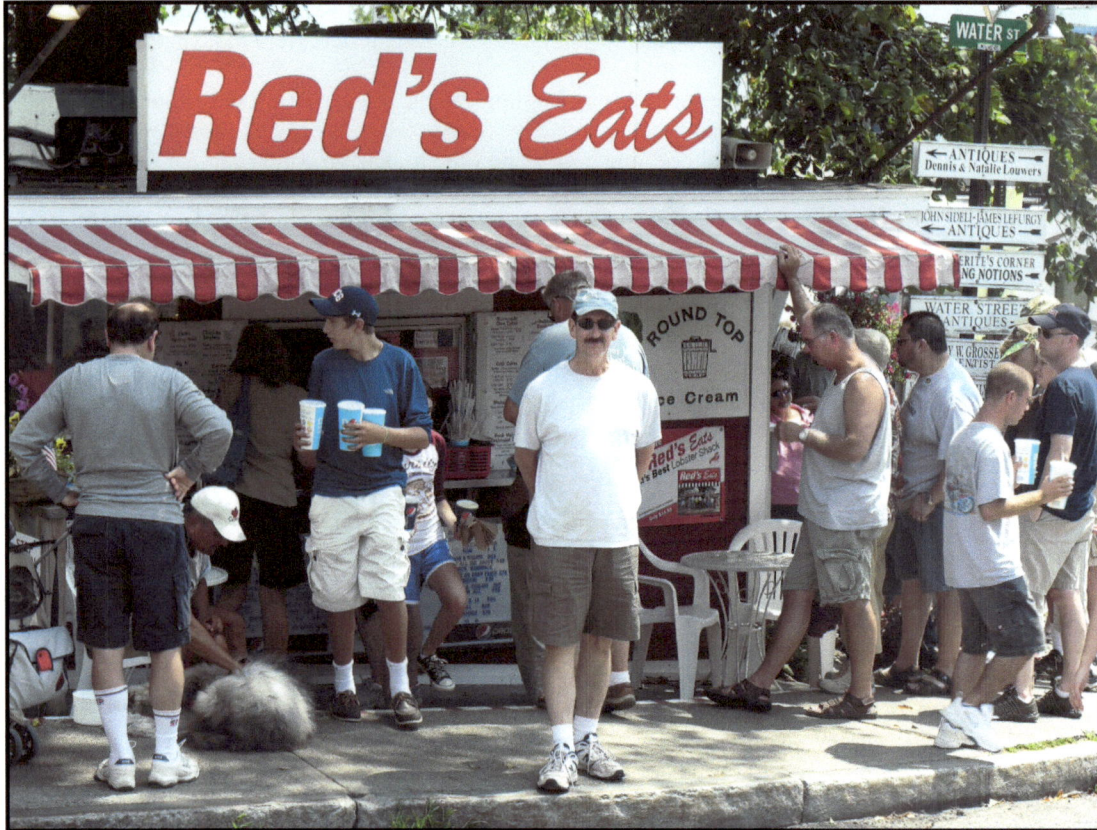

Red's Eats is a roadside diner that has operated since 1938, originally in Boothbay, Maine. In 1954 it moved and is presently located at the corners of Water Street at Main Street in Wiscasset, Maine. There is no inside seating but there are several outside tables and chairs in the back. You can see the size of the place above, and the lines stretch to my left and behind the building. There is always a waiting line, it's just a matter of "how long" the line will be. Always expect to wait at least an hour; that way you won't be disappointed. When I first went there on my way to Rockland, Maine I didn't know what to expect. So we fell into the long line that went down Main Street, about an hour and a half from what I figured would be just another tourist rip off. After all, every roadside diner in Maine boasts of the best lobster roll in the "world".

But, this place had something that was strange. It was the one that was mystical from all others. Just across the street was a sprawling lobster place. It had lobster rolls, lobster dinners, lobster *EVERYTHING*. And, it didn't have anyone in line waiting. A couple of the folks in line gave in and walked across to an unknown fate. They walked right up to the counter while I hung in at Red's. My wife even tried to dissuade me with a promise of no lines at "the place across the street". I almost gave in but, no. I was in it for the long haul and I don't care if my legs buckle, I'm going to have a Red's Eats lobster roll!

The place across the street

It was August in Maine and the heat was roasting. The line moved slowly and we all shuffled forward toward the prize. The Red's Eats folks came outside with trays full of water for the people in line. I thought that was a nice gesture that they didn't have to do. Now rehydrated & reinvigorated we pressed onward toward the finish line.

Debbie is in!

Finally, I made the corner of Water Street. This is the only place I saw a sign saying anything to do with, or any mention of, a lobster roll. Good gosh, I hoped that this was worth the wait. And besides, "Debbie was in!"

I explained to my wife (also named Debbie) that her namesake was in. At this point you've said everything that you could possibly think about saying to one another standing there. So my comment was met with a deadpan look.

By the time I made it to the counter, we knew the people in front of us and the people in back, intimately. It was an hour in the sun, but it seemed like an eternity.

The line starts at the right, but worth the wait.

The moment of truth finally came when standing before the smiling woman inside the little window. She was just as cheerful as if I was the first one there. I had plenty of time to practice saying the magic words but it came out wrong. The moment had come and I totally forgot what I wanted. She explained it all to me, calmly, and I tried again (I guess the sun was too hot). "I'll have 2 lobster rolls, one with butter & one without."

The real lobster roll is simply lobster meat, cooked and ever so delicately tossed in mayonnaise. It's served cold. It is always served cold. At Red's you may have melted butter with it, but not on it. The bun is toasted on a grill and the meat is added. A few minutes later my number came up and I got what I'd waited for.

It was everything that I'd hoped for and more. The meat was piled high on a large golden toasted bun. You could hardly see the bun for the lobster meat. Both lobster rolls were exactly the same except that one had 2 cups of drawn butter next to it. I figure that the meat of one lobster roll was at least equal to a 2lb. lobster picked clean, each! They included the claws and the tail cut in half. This came with a plastic knife & fork if you so desired.

Red's Lobster Roll

The meat, unlike any you've ever eaten, was somehow, tenderized? 2lbs. of lobster meat (tail & claws) was absolutely delicious, fresh, fork tender, and without a doubt the best I've ever eaten. At first I thought that maybe they'd gotten a bunch of good ones. I've gone back there, several times over the years and each time it's the same. I've tried lobster rolls up and down the coast and none of them remotely comes close to Red's Eats.

Debbie (the Red's Eats Debbie) was kind enough to autograph a copy of the little booklet and a Red's Eats baseball hat that I wear today. It said: "I hope you like lobster.. Best wishes, Reds" I read what she'd written while waiting for my order and had to snicker. I winked at her and said, "Oh yeah, I like lobsters; they're our friends", and we laughed like hell.

We had a mission that trip and stopped at Red's on the way up. On the way back I couldn't help myself and stopped by again. This time it was 9am. I figured to beat the crowd about 2 hours before opening. There were already 4 people waiting. So we all hunkered down and got to know each other. They were Asians from New York City. They'd driven all night long in search of some good seafood. I assured them they were in for a treat and they wouldn't be disappointed. Neither will you if you're traveling on Route #1 through Maine in the small village of Wiscasset. Stop at Red's Eats and don't worry about the waiting line. I can honestly say that a Red's Eats lobster roll is bar none, the single best lobster roll made today. Watch this video if you get a chance:

http://www.youtube.com/watch?v=E5tDe-XPWvo

THE MAINE LOBSTER FESTIVAL

Now, let's talk a little bit more about eating lobsters. Let's go to August 13th, 2005. It was a very special "Lobster Eating Festival" held in Kennebunkport, Maine. The day was filled with unique lobster type events, presentations and live entertainment. The highlight of the festival was the 2nd annual World Lobster-Eating Championship. This contest was no silly backyard farce. It was a no-nonsense, official World Championship event sanctioned by the International Federation of Competitive Eating (IOFCE), headquartered in New York City. Professional competitive eaters, who were hell-bent on winning, stood behind a long table filled with steaming red lobsters. Competitors were partnered off with some of the fastest lobster shuckers alive. They had exactly twelve minutes to shuck and consume as many New England lobsters as they could. The World Championship was in the balance. A hush fell over the crowd as the master of ceremonies dressed in dapper straw hat, suit & tie, looking like the classic carnival barker, called the starting countdown. "FIVE! FOUR! THREE! TWO! ONE! *HONK!*"

Shuckers ripped lobster meat from shells in a blur of motion trying to keep up with the professional eaters. Lobster juice and tomalley flew through the air and splattered spectators out into the first several rows. The crowd roared, cheering on their local eating heroes who were doing their very best to keep up with the world-renowned professional eaters. As the official clock's sweep-second hand struck 12 minutes, the ending horn sounded and all eating ceased. Engorged mouths full of lobster meat had to be chewed and swallowed to signal the official ending consumptive action by all contestants. Careful tallies were tabulated, rechecked, and certified for each competitor before the final results were announced.

3rd place went to Eric "Badlands" Booker. Mr. Booker, a resident of New York City is a huge man, weighing well over 300-lbs. He is currently ranked as the 10th best competitive eater in the world by the IOFCE. His hands are the size of catcher's mitts. Badlands Booker had eaten a total of 25 lobsters in 12 minutes.

A man named Jason "Crazy Legs" Conti placed 2nd in this historic event. Conti is a unique individual to say the least. He's a multi-talented, world ranked professional eater. He's featured in a short film entitled, "Zen and the Art of Competitive Eating" by Crazy Legs Conti. He wolfed down a total of 32 lobsters in the time allotted to capture 2nd place.

98 lb. Sonya Thomas ate 44 lobsters like these in under 12 minutes!

The contest winner is currently ranked 5th in the all-time competitive eating world directory. Weighing in at a scant 98 pounds, her name is Sonya Thomas. This diminutive phenom is known among the hulking competitive eating professionals, as nearly unbeatable. Her short, lithe frame was dwarfed in between all the gargantuan lobster eaters. In the end her bowl was not half-full, it was empty. Sonya Thomas had broken her own existing World Record by eating 44 (*forty-four*) New England lobsters in 12 minutes! She bested Badlands Booker, a towering giant who is over 3 times her size, by a full 19 lobsters.

For her effort Thomas received $500 cash and more importantly, she was awarded "The Claw". Many notables including former world champion Kevin Cross, a Maine resident, have held this highly coveted championship belt. As of this writing, Sonya Thomas remains the undisputed official IOFCE World Champion eater of New England lobsters. She is known as the Black Widow, and the leader of "The Four Horsemen of the Esophagus."

Now we fast-forward to August 4th, 2011, the scene of the world renowned "Maine Lobster Festival" in Rockland, Maine. The people of the city of Rockland have done a great job to showcase the state of Maine and the abundant seafood of this community. This was to be the 64th annual Lobster Festival. It's well orchestrated for people of all ages, a little bit of everything. The Rockland Maine Lobster Festival is located 85 miles south of Bar Harbor and 277 miles north of Hartford, CT. This is a pilgrimage that all lobster lovers have got to make at least once in your life.

Rocky, the festival mascot

As you enter the grounds the first thing you spot is (you guessed it) a gigantic lobster. The next thing you see is a sprawling mass of red, white and yellow tents set out along the rugged coast of Maine. One cannot help but wonder how this tradition all started, some six decades ago.

A little bit about the historical background on this interesting and unique event started in 1947. Shortly after the end of a long and bitter war, recent memories of Pearl Harbor, FDR dying, and rationing, left everyone a little flat. After 6 long miserable years the people of Camden, Maine yearned for a bit of the old times when things were good and wholesome. They wanted to have a summer festival with a band and parades where people could go to forget about their problems and just have a little fun. After all, who doesn't?

So it was decided to have a festival with the theme of Maine seafood, in Camden. This was borrowed from the lobster festival in Nova Scotia. If it worked for them, surely it will be a big hit here in Maine. So the Camden-Rockport Lobster Festival was formed. Maine lobster fisheries would be showcased, and Maine lobster fisherman would come into their own rite as American purveyors of this tasty crustacean.

The vice-president of the Pepsi Cola company, Mr. Talbot O. Freeman, was the master of ceremonies for the first festival in 1947. He provided soft drinks to the many volunteers working that day. Being a large fellow, he said that he "..looks forward to eating at the festival on Saturday". That statement nearly broke the festival early on.

One thing appeared in the Camden Herald that day on Thursday August 14th 1947, that would both make and break the grand idea. I imagine it was to promote the crowd that had been hunkered down for 6 long years. Whoever had that idea was initially given the keys to the city of Camden for coming up with such a brilliant thought. But a day after the festival he was probably run out of town on a rail. The front page of the Camden Herald printed:

"All the lobster you can eat for $1"

And eat, they did. When the smoke cleared from that first lobster festival they were well into the hole. The entire Camden committee quit and the festival quietley slipped from focus. Within the coming year of 1948 the festival was picked up as a pet project by the Rockland Junior Chamber of Commerce. The venue was changed to the Rockland Public Landing, a large lot overlooking the cove, where it sits today. In 1948 the festival became known as the "Maine Lobster & Seafoods Festival". The change was brought about by the Birdseye Division of General Foods, who became a large contributor to the event. One of the Birdseye donations was hundreds of pounds of ocean perch. These were cooked and added to the lobster dinners served. I'm trying to imagine how perch tasted with lobster, and I just can't bridge that gap…

Many local dealers supplied lobsters for the event and the Rockland City Band played gay tunes on Saturday afternoon. On Saturday evening they held a "coronation ball" and Ms Ruth Roberts of Rockland Maine was crowned as "Miss Maine Seafoods". If you happen to visit the Rockland Historical Society, go into the backroom where a large black & white photograh sits. It is a photograph of Ms Ruth Roberts at age 18 sewing a fishing net, and wearing a two piece bathing suit with the Rockland Festival logo on it. This photo is simply stunning. I stared at it for an hour or more, as those who see it will agree. The woman is beautiful.

By 1949 the event was a success. It was more than the Junior Chamber of Commerce could handle by themselves. They voted to form a corporation consisting of the Elks, Kiwanis Lions, Rotarty Club, American Legion and the Rockland Chamber of Commerce. It grew to a 3 day event promoting Maine's tourism, seafood, US Naval ships at berth in Rockland harbor, and the US Coast Guard Station in Rockland. The festival's recognition grew exponentially year after year. Today it is world renown. It appeared on the Food Network and is among the "Top 250" things to do in the United States. Since the time of this inaspicious local event, the venue, dates, and traditions have remained the same since 1949. They center around the selection of a Sea Goddess, a grand parade, and the sheer enjoyment of eating Maine lobster. Shuttle services run, there is a road race, and many other interesting things to see and do including an annual seafood cooking competion that caught my eye on my first trip.

Welcome to the Maine Lobster Festival

I've visited the Maine Lobster Festival several times, the first few of which were in my formative years when I looked but didn't see. I had to get back to work the next day, some 277 miles away. At first it seemed like a carnival with expensive lobster dinners. Since then I was given a blessing from the good Lord above in the form of a stroke. This slowed me down a bit at which time I enjoyed the festival more than ever before. We spent the whole weekend nosing and poking around the Rockland, Maine area and thoroughly enjoyed it. It was like I'd seen it for the very first time.

We stayed at a comfortable motel along the oceanfront near Rockland. The view was spectacular as were the surroundings. It was just about a 10-minute drive from the festival. Interestingly enough there were no lobster buoys around and I wondered why not? After all, the inlet we stayed on was perfect for setting lobster traps. I guess it must be off-limits for lobstermen, as the bay must be a breeding ground for baby lobsters. When the tide goes out, it leaves the rocks exposed.

Note the dancing lobster at the bottom left corner in the picture. I stuck my head in it for a photo taken later on.

We started our exploration of the festival by driving through the town of Rockland, not wanting to shuttle in, and seeing how close we could get. We found it to be a quaint town with friendly back streets. The festival at the Rockland Landing is not hard to get to. It's a one-way street that goes counter-clockwise past it. We found many parking spots nearby at the municipal center and walked the short distance to the festival. You can't miss it.

Walking down the side streets, we found the many jewels of the area such as the Coast Guard Station, the Rockland Historical Society, and countless restaurants of all ethnicity. This was all within walking distance and general proximity to the festival.

The big red claw was first on our stop, just outside the historical society. Walk to the end of the street and you'll get a full tour of the Coast Guard Station led by a genuine coastguardsman. Then we had a fantastic lunch at a sushi restaurant. You can spend a full day here just looking and getting the feel of the area all within walking distance.

If you go for a day, you'll miss the real meaning of this lobster fest. It is more than a plate full of expensive food. Once inside the festival, we started at the far right and swept our way to the left. After spending 2 hours standing in line at Red's Eats, the wait to tour an active US Navy vessel was well worth the wait. People as far away as Kansas and Oklahoma were standing there with us. From there we went through the "kids carnival"; yes, they have one there too. Near there was a large stage with lights and amphitheater seats set up.

There was an area for the selection of the Sea Goddess after dark. So we milled around with about 1,000 other folks until the show. It was, once again, well worth the wait. On stage each of the military branches were announced and represented by officers in the dress uniform. Each of the 12 contestants was eloquently dressed and escorted by a uniformed military member to and from the podium. The previous day each contestant was tested on the basis of skill, character, and how much each had done for the community. Also they were graded on their aspirations that ranged from lawyers to nurses to marine biologists.

The winner of the contest was indeed a talented and wonderful person, Ms. Emily Benner. She won the title of Sea Goddess 2010 and $2,000. As we walked around the festival the next day, I ran into Ms. Benner. She called for her assistants, Neptune and the Pirate (the Pirate didn't like me). These 3 figures have represented the Maine Lobster Festival since 1947 and will continue to do so until time immemorial. This will show you the depth and breadth of the coronation show that went on that evening, August 4th, 2010. It was my honor to have been there, and a true privilege to run into these folks the next day. If you are Internet connected, type this into your web browser:
http://www.youtube.com/watch?v=0bHMQHssGMM

And so we move on to the center of the festival, a well-manicured lawn cordoned off by lobster traps. Yes, lobster traps, hundreds of them. This could only lead us to one place, namely the lobster tent. All paths at the festival will funnel you toward this. It is a large open-air pavilion ready to seat hundreds of guests.

Although I've eaten more lobsters than most folks could imagine, I had to order up a triple. The price was a little high, but when you're in Maine you just have to get some lobsters!

The famous lobster cooker was said to be the largest in the world. I couldn't wait to see this and I was not disappointed. For instance, imagine steam cooking a lobster. What more does it take than a little water, heat, and a lobster? Well, it takes some imagination if you want to cook some 20,000 lbs. of lobsters within 5 days. As a matter of fact, it is a Herculean task that Neptune himself would be hard pressed to do.

The Worlds Largest Lobster Cooker

Lobsters, some 10 tons of them, are cooked in this giant cooker during the festival. They serve them at noon and throughout the days to follow.

Things go on every day during the festival including this display of hands-on touching of a lobster. You can't help but notice the very young and the very old are not afraid to step up inquisitively. They take the time to wonder about the little things that others are too busy to investigate.

The five people at the right wondered what make lobsters work. And they're not afraid to pick one up to find out.

Cooked lobster at Maine Seafood Festival

Bricks surrounding lobster cooker

The steaming lobsters continue to pour out of the cooker until the festival is over.

The bricks seen at right are chest high around the lobster cooker. They're memorialized from people that donated to the cause of lobster cookery.

All the help is voluntary and done through a signup. The festival staff is cheerful, courteous, and helpful. If you so much as look to have a question on your face, one of the staff is right there asking, "Can I help you?"

THE BEST SEAFOOD I EVER ATE

*T*he Maine Lobster Festival in Rockland Maine also held another test for me. I'd seen it done in years before and was totally entranced. Chefs from up and down the eastern seaboard labor in the one-hour cooking contest that takes place every year at this prestigious affair. They were there long before the crowds rolled in to set up their tricks, and long after the contest was over. Although the cook-off was only for an official "1 hour" of cooking and presenting, it takes a year or more of preparation. These were ranked as "amateur" chefs but by watching them they were top-rated. Those selected were by far a cut above the rest.

For starters it takes a damn good recipe, one that's unique in the entire world. First off, you must apply to a "selection committee" at least one month in advance of the contest. I'm told that there are hundreds of applicants vieing for the 5 spots available to compete. Choices will be made on some simple criteria. They are:

"..creativity, suitability of the seafood to the recipe and simplicity. The recipes can be any dish and must contain seafood found in Maine waters."

I started experimentation 2 years ahead to give myself enough time to find a recipe. Afterall, the main ingredient I know quite well and have plenty of it.

By the end of the first year I tried every combination of lobster you could imagine. I made lobster pie, lobster & beef, baked type lobster, grilled type lobster, sauteed lobster, bisque, and even a version of lobster thermadore. None of them tasted the least bit unique.

My taste-tester and biggest critic can be seen on the right. One recipe tasted so bad that she opened the slider door and threw the plateful out onto the deck. The cats wouldn't even eat it. She simply said, "Next?"

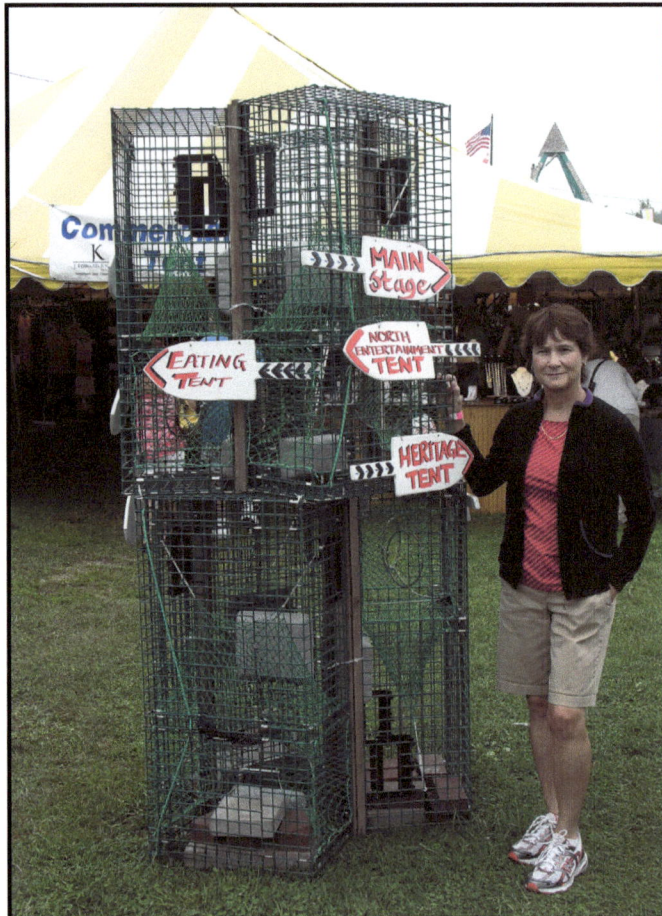

Author's wife stands near buoy pointing to North Tent, the Seafood Cooking Contest

The year that I was about to go and watch another cooking contest, God blessed me with a cerebral event called a stroke. Laying flat on the floor waiting for someone to come along and the ambulance to arrive, I recall thinking, "Well, at least I won't have to go to the dentist anymore". But I lived to eat lobster again another day, and it tasted different? Not different good or bad, just different.

After the stroke, among other things, my taste buds were swapped around. Some tastes were amplified and others were diminished. For example, beer was among my favorite things in life; the flavor was great. As a matter of fact, I had a cold Stella Artois in hand when I first felt the stroke hit me. It was like a bullet in the back to me, which also affected everything that I used to know and like. Now beer tastes like battery acid to me. I cannot take a swallow of beer without gagging. With therapy I slowly learned to talk again and my life, absent a job, had mostly come back. One thing that did not come back was taste, the way I'd learned it for nearly 60 years. It was like starting all over again as a baby would.

The spice rack had always remained a strange ornament in the kitchen. It was full of pretty bottles with colorful powder in them. Before the stroke the only spice I could taste was salt, and plenty of it. And the only other thing I could taste was butter, a little more than the salt. One day during recovery I tasted some funky reddish dust called Curry Powder. That stuff was an awakening. I could taste all the flavors that were the main ingredient in Indian type dishes. Strangely, all the spices now had meaning and taste. Ginger, dill weed, cumin, coriander, fennel, and cloves all had new flavor. Discreet tastes were awakened; ones that I'd never known or expected before. When we'd go out to dinner, it was like something I've never before experienced. Life without piling salt on every bite and frosting every thing with butter is something new to me. Suddenly the true taste of things came through loud and clear. It was an epiphany of flavor that just blew me away with every little taste at a restaurant.

With this new appreciation for food I could identify all the ingredients of a meal by taste alone. The little things that normally would be taken for granted tasted wonderful. A tiny bit too much cilantro in a meal and I could identify it immediately. I was yet to speak clearly but the tastes were divine. For rehabilitation I took several cooking classes with professional chefs. Here we learned to prepare soups, beef, lamb, poultry and pork. There was not a seafood course among them, but there was one thing I found interesting. It was the making of sauces. With one single sip I could identify the entire ingredients that made up the sauce. Conversely, I could make a sauce that paired with pork, beef, salmon, and chicken. These meats are by themselves, tasteless. Without marinade or flavoring of some kind, any one of these things is downright bland. The sauce is everything.

Then I set about making a seafood recipe that would fit the criteria to present to the Maine Lobster Festival selection committee. It may get chosen and it may not, but it would be something unique and truly unforgettable. From the audience I'd watched the "chosen five" dice, chop, mince, fry, grill, and boil seafood. They used every trick in the book to attain the title of Maine Seafood Cooking Contest Winner. Now it's my turn. I submitted an entry application 6 months ahead of time and set about finding the right combinations of seafood via my newfound taste!

I dabbled with different mixtures and finally came upon one that went well with white fish. It was a type of sauce that is called a beurre blanc. Basically, it's a reduction of white wine with some shallots diced in. You add a little butter, white pepper, sugar, lemon, cream sherry, and some heavy cream. A true beurre blanc sauce does not use the cream. A master chef will fool around for hours trying to get it right and not separate. I, on the other hand, have got one hour from the word "Go" to prepare and serve the entire meal. So I'll go with the sure thing and cheat by adding a tablespoon of heavy cream as a stabilizer. I've found that you can even bring this mixture to a boil without it separating. Separation is when the emulsion separates the butter from the wine that is being reduced.

I finally got a thumbs-up from my taste tester who is not easily impressed. This mixture was the best tasting liquid to coat lobster meat or white fish, bar none. It has a multi-layered, rich, buttery flavor. It takes only 12 to 15 minutes to make but it cannot be kept for more than a few hours. I tried to keep some of this overnight in the refrigerator but it "broke". Once separated it doesn't even remotely taste the same.

When this sauce first comes together for the first couple hours of its life, it is sheer ambrosia. Now to find something to pour it over is the next task.

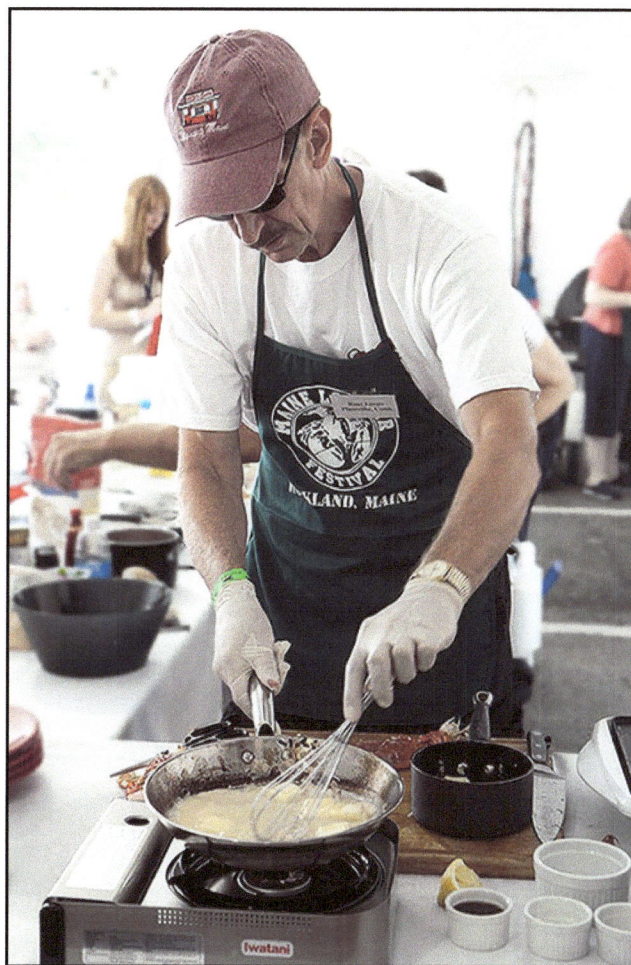

Making a sauce described as Ambrosia

My young child was a picky eater. We discovered early on that he liked large sea scallops. He liked the meaty yet light flavor of the scallop and often played with it in his plate. Steamed or braised scallops would not please him, only pan seared would do. He wasn't keen on lobster until the day I made him a "lobster castle" so that he could play with something while he ate it. Not being the kind to work at it, we had to remove the lobster from the shell and cut it into small coin shaped pieces. This vision of him playing with a lobster carapace was what I needed for my inspiration. But I needed a fancy name to set it aside from the rest, and perhaps catch the eye of the Maine Lobster Festival committee. I sent the application below and the name of: **"Pan Seared Scallops & Lobster Medallions"**

Pan Seared Sea Scallops & Lobster Medallions With Lemon Butter Sauce
Russ James, Connecticut

This fantastic Maine seafood combination is hard to beat. Can be served as an elegant appetizer or as a main entrée at your backyard picnic. It's fun to make and is easy to serve. A great way to introduce inlanders to the classic rich flavor of our New England Ocean without the mess of nutcrackers and lobster bibs!

4 Maine Lobsters, (chix) 1-¼ pounds each
1-½ pounds of large sea scallops, fresh
1 bunch of fresh broccolini (small heads of broccoli will due)
Sea salt (in a small cup for pinching) & fresh crushed black pepper in another cup
1 Tablespoon extra-virgin olive oil
½ pound of butter

Put lobsters in large covered pot. Add 2 inches of water, just enough to steam them. When steam comes out, cook for 20 minutes and remove from heat. Spill lobsters out into sink and spray with cold water, removing white yogurt looking stuff (lobster blood). Set them aside for cooling.

While lobsters are cooking, spread out a 5-sheet length of paper towels. Lay sea scallops atop the towels. Lay another 5-sheet length atop the scallops and lightly press down to dry the scallops, top and bottom. Get them as dry as possible. Dust the tops and bottoms with salt and black pepper.

Pre-heat large saucepan until the edge is too hot to touch with the side of your hand. Add olive oil and one small cube of butter until melted. One by one place scallops into pan. Do not overcrowd pan! It may take several separate pan cookings to do them all. Flip them around with tongs as they become brown. When they're done remove, set aside, and sear the next batch. You may have to add more oil and butter to the pan should it become dry.

Don't overcook the scallops! Here's how to tell when done: Make a tight fist with your left hand. Use the index finger on your right hand to poke the soft meaty part of your left hand, just below the thumb. Tap the scallops with the tong. If they feel like that soft part of your hand, THEY'RE DONE! Remember, they will continue cooking for a short time after being removed from the heat. Set all cooked scallops in a covered bowl to stay warm and moist.

In the meantime, place a small steamer pot on to boil. Cover and steam your broccolini. Lobsters will now be cool to handle. Remove claws and pull lobsters breastplate out. Pick the meat out of small legs and thoracic shell pockets. Use a spoon to scrape the tomalley (green stuff) and red roe out of lobster. Set the tomalley and roe aside in separate dish. Crack open claw and remove meat, also set this aside.

Twist the tail section from the body. Use kitchen scissors to cut along the length of the underside of tail shell, front to back. Press down on shell edges and it will crack open. Pull chunk of tail meat out and set out on cutting board. Make a shallow slice down the bottom center of tail meat. Remove and discard the dark strand, especially where it thickens at the tip of the tail. Press tail meat flat on cutting board and slice it into crosswise pieces, making thin round medallions, about ¼ of an inch thick. Use kitchen scissors to cut each of the 4 carapace shells. Trim along the edges to make a wider opening and trim the bottom so that it sits nicely upon the plate!

Intermingle scallops and lobster medallions piled high in center of plate. Crumble tomalley atop the pyramids. If you were lucky enough to have found red roe, use this as the crowning glory on each mound of succulent seafood. Place the carapace, standing, as if to be offering its bounty. Stuff one broccolini stalk into the carapace that delicately flowers out atop seafood, looking like a spray of sea kelp. Lastly, drizzle lemon butter sauce (see separate instructions) over the entire seafood medley, until it makes a golden pool of deliciousness in the plate!

I made a delicate white butter sauce from some common things found around the kitchen. It starts with white Riesling wine and shallots, and ends with cream sherry, lemon, and butter. Once you try it you'll find it easy to make, and delicious with any seafood. You'll be pleasantly surprised with the rich mellow flavor. One word of warning: This delicious topping has a "one time only" shelf life. In other words, this ambrosia cannot be refrigerated. After that, it separates and does not taste the same. While it's warm try it on cod, scallops, lobster or other white fish to add the air of eloquence to any party.

Lemon-Butter Sauce
1 cup Riesling wine
¼ cup finely chopped shallots
¼ teaspoon white pepper
1 teaspoon white sugar
¼ cup cream sherry
½ fresh lemon, squeezed and juiced
2 Tablespoons heavy cream
8 ounces (2 sticks) cold butter cut into small ¼ inch cubes

Pre-heat large saucepan and add wine, lemon juice, and shallots. Use medium heat to bring mixture to mildly bubbling simmer. Stir occasionally until mix reduces to about 75% of original liquid.

Turn heat to lowest setting available on your stove. After mix reduces, use a whisk to mix the heavy cream into the reduction. Add 4 or 5 small cubes of butter to the pan and gently "rub" them into mix with whisk. After they've slowly melted into the hot reduction, add another 4 or 5 cubes and repeat the process until all the butter is melted. The cold butter is used to flavor and cool the mix. Turn off the heat and add remaining ingredients: White pepper, sugar, and cream sherry. Gently whisk the mixture until it takes on a pure ivory white color. Let sit for 2 or 3 minutes, and then ladle the reduction atop any seafood. Serves 4

Well, if that don't catch their eye nothing would. This recipe with a beginning that read, ***"It's fun to make and is easy to serve"*** has got to catch somebody's eye. One month before the contest, I received a letter from the Maine Festival Committee. They found my recipe to be "very interesting". Accordingly, they'd like to have me make it before a panel of judges and the entire lobster loving community at the Maine Lobster Festival in Rockland, Maine. I read the letter 25 times or more before I realized it was not a rejection letter that I'd expected.

To receive a letter like that was a winner enough. After all, 4 other great seafood cooks from around the United States were selected. For this contest they were chosen from Florida, Georgia, New Jersey and Maine. As far as I'm concerned, we are all winners. But now it comes down to just one, the recipe that stands above all the rest. Whose will have the most unique flavor at the Seafood Cook-Off in Rockland, Maine? Now I've got 60 days to get ready for another challenge of a lifetime.

I started with a distinguished list of guests to try my recipe on. No one objected to an invitation of a seafood dinner served on fancy plates. My wife didn't mind because by the rules I had to physically prepare the food, serve the judges (or guests), and clean up. Then when done, you must cook a little more to serve those who haven't had any in "the crowd". Fifty times at home in practice I served people from all walks of life such people as nurses, stockbrokers, teachers, policemen, and even a lobster boat captain were served. I prepared it to guests as little as 3 and upward of 8 people at a time. As my concoction was presented time and again the presentation got more efficient. I could make pan seared scallops & lobster medallions with lemon/butter/cream sherry beurre blanc sauce, start to finish in less than 40 minutes. In the end I'd asked some 50 odd guests for honest critiques. Specifically I asked for negative opinions or what would they do differently. The answer was, to the last man and woman, always the same. "Change NOTHING! That was the best seafood I've ever eaten, especially the sauce." One lady said that she'd already eaten before she'd arrived. When she finished I noticed her wiping the last bit of sauce from an empty plate with her fingertip. So far, so good. Let's bring it to the Maine Lobster Festival and see what they think.

Serving 50 meals, over & over again

You must consider a few things before heading off to Rockland, Maine, some 280 miles from your home kitchen. First of all you don't know what cooking accouterments will be at your disposal, what type of stuff will be available including the perishables. You will not be cooking on your own little home stove. You'll be cooking on an industrial stove, set up by a crew of workers and shared among contestants.

We took a road trip to a friend's house and brought all the fixings with us. It was like meals on wheels to serve six folks in a foreign place. The things needed were cut to a minimum and the show went on the road. It went off perfectly.

There was no more left to do, or cooking challenge that hadn't been overcome. The one thing that I'd been putting off was the condition of my stroke. I couldn't speak when put under pressure, literally. I could think clearly, but there's a physiological "hole" in my brain. It's mildly noticeable to my wife and glaringly apparent to everyone else when I'm put in a situation under pressure. Similar to when stress is put on a lobster.

I was formally an eloquent speaker, but God exchanged it for some other things in life that I can enjoy for the rest of my days. Unfortunately, my public speaking is not one of them.

Chef from Atlanta Georgia made New Orleans Lobster Etouffee

My wife tried to encourage those whom I'd served to ask me lots of questions in preparation for this event. The first time I stood there, in front of a group awaiting my answers. My mind wanted to tell them an interesting story of how the sauce is melded together. Or how many years it takes a lobster to become harvestable. But all that came from me was, *"Lobster, it's good?"*

I've done many crazy things in my life, some that have scared me to death. But to stand in front of a crowd, all looking at me with a microphone to my lips saying, "Lobster, it's good?" is worse than death. I'd seen the food reporters interview the five contestant chefs. Each one was more articulate and specific than the one before him. Now, here I am, a broken machine. All I had was a recipe to show and the capability to prepare it in under 40 minutes blindfolded. But I could not speak, so I thought.

128

Interviewed by Maine Channel TV-85

Before the cooking bell started I tried to go unnoticed. I'd brought my "meals on wheels" show, including 6 prime lobsters fresh from Long Island Sound, 3-lbs. of sea scallops, a slew of spices and a portable cooking stove to complete the show.

I wore a pair of dark sunglasses and kept my head down during the set up. I hoped that there would be no interviews but it was not to be. After all, this event would showcase the prime ingredient in an industry that is world renown for the Maine lobster.

Questions were easy at first, who are you, where do you come from, tell us a little about yourself. I had all that I could do to make the words come out of my lips to say where I lived. Telling a little bit about myself was too embarrassing to mention that I had a stroke and should've died 6 months ago. Then they got a tad more in depth with questions like, "Could you tell our viewers the theme of your recipe and how you discovered it?"

Now if the dark sunglasses were removed, you'd see my eyes squinted shut trying to make the words come out. Thousands of viewers waited for me to say something. So I thought back to my speech pathologist telling me in rehabilitation, "Just take a deep breath and start out like a child". Although it was a shadow of my former self, I got through.

My wife was allowed to set up the table by the rules. She chose a simple set up of red plates, seagoing candles, Riesling wine, and a decanter of water to cleanse the palate.

That's all that she was allowed to do. After that she took her seat in the audience. There's no more that anyone else can do, except me.

Table set for judges

Introduction of Judges

The emcee was a woman by the name of Louise MacLellan. She was clearly in charge with a voice that could be heard like a bell above the rustling crowd.

She was a smart orator and introduced the judges in no particular order. The first of them was a US Navy Commander. He was in charge of the destroyer USS Mahan (DDG 72), at berth just offshore in Rockland harbor.

I'd never served a Naval Commander. I could only imagine the culinary staff at his disposal. He came ashore with an entourage of men. Hopefully, none of them were among his cooking staff. But, then again I wouldn't know if mine was truly the best if they were not there?

Ms. MacLellan went on with the introduction of the judges. Among them was a woman with a no-nonsense look on her face. She simply nodded and continued to stare at us, the five contestants. Her credentials included being the chef and owner of several seafood restaurants. My mind was spinning when Louise mentioned one thing that brought me to attention. She said, "She is also a master class chef, specializing in sauces."

Now I'm in for the fight of my life, 250 miles from home. What have I gotten myself into, here among the top seafood cooks on the eastern seaboard? My wife is sitting in the audience and the countdown begins.

The darkened sunglasses were not enough to hide my stroke-induced stress. My hands started shaking uncontrollably. They shook so much that Louise noticed. She went to my wife in the crowd and asked if I always got that nervous. When she got the answer, I'm told that she shed a tear for me. No one else but her would know.

The coveted prize

The countdown went on and the cooking began in a blur of motion. Each chef started grabbing his or her stuff from here and there. Fires were lit, things started to boil, and plates were laid out. All started dicing, chopping, and mincing while liquids were poured, here and there. There was a flurry of knives, boiling oil, and dying lobsters. In other words from my perspective, it was sheer bedlam.

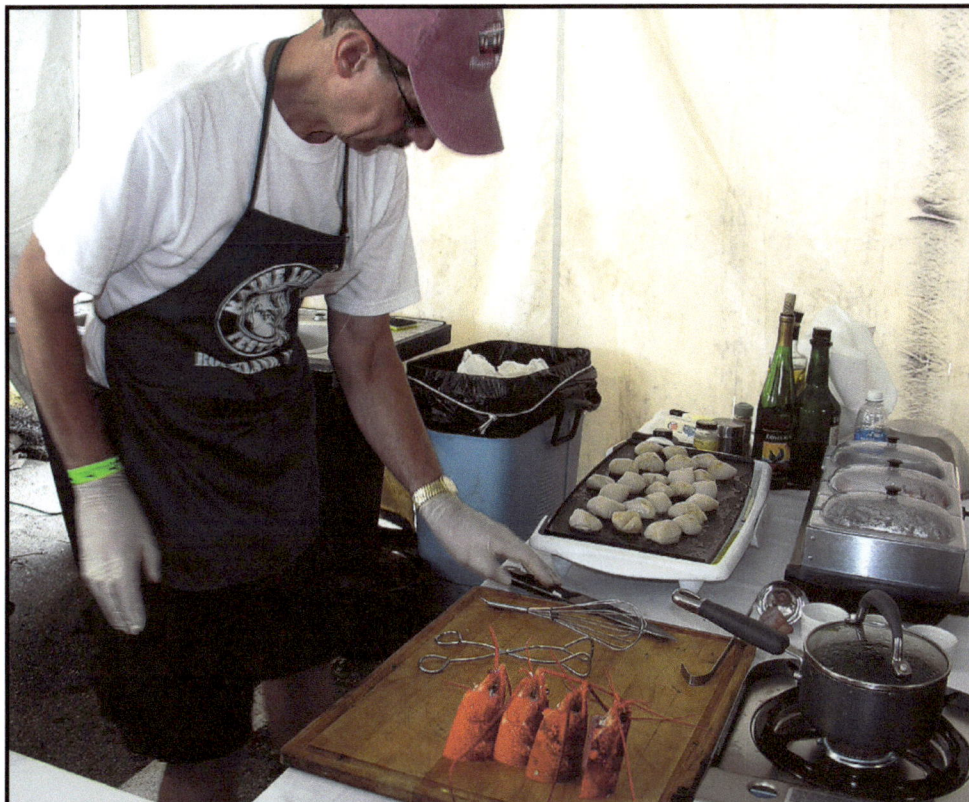

The first 10 minutes of my time were spent trying to get my gloves on. Thankfully, Louise came around to me and said, "Slow down; there's plenty of time". Thankfully, it gave me a full 50 minutes to prepare the meal that I knew could be done in 30 minutes under pressure.

Lobster castles..

Making this is really easy and all I had to do was serve only 4 people. But the news folks were encouraged to roam about, and ask whatever they wanted. One of the contestants was really chatty, with a flowery show, thank God! The newscasters and food critics were all over that one. That way I could get the job done without having to talk.

Surely that chef had won, as they poured over the display. I just wanted it to be done and go home.

We all drew a number from a bag. That would be the ordinal of who was to serve the judges first through last. The first to be served was mine! This was the moment and there was no more dilly-dallying to be had. The other four chefs seemed to labor over one thing at a time, cutting one thing until done, boiling until done, etc. I put my head down and made everything at once, like I'd done countless times before in practice.

While the scallops were pan seared, the lobsters were boiled. The sauce was reduced and blended while the carapaces where cut and trimmed. Lemons were sliced and the broccolini was steamed. When I looked up, there was a crowd around me? What in the world would anyone want to take a picture of me for?

But when I looked up, it was all done but the tasting. As I'd assembled my presentation I didn't even taste the sauce. Because I knew what it tasted like after tasting it so many times before.

Plating the seafood

The whole shebang took me only 20 minutes to prepare, start to finish. The judges were sitting at my table prepared for a long wait but I was serving them right away.

"Bon appetite," was all that I could think of to say as I plunked a plateful of seafood down in front of each judge. I wanted to watch them as they ate and the notes they took. But when I returned to my cooking station the "foodies" swamped me. Foodies are the folks who professionally write and talk about food. Especially the things they find to be unique and pleasing to the eye.

Bon Appetite

Apparently my dish appeared unique and pleasing in a Maine seafood type of way. The little spray of broccolini on the top was my wife's idea to get my kid to eat a vegetable without him knowing it. We referred to it as a "sea fern" that the lobster was eating. In this particular cooking vernacular it's called a spray, which "tops off the bounty".

The judges tasted my presentation surrounded by onlookers. Meanwhile I was asked to make a little extra for the audience. I had enough for all to taste the scallop & lobster combination, each presented with a small dollop of sauce.

The way that I was approached gave me a pretty good idea that the dish was a hit. In the hustle and bustle of the contest I answered many questions, some by the audience and some by the newscasters. I answered each person with as much patience and dignity as could be mustered from a man who'd had a stroke a few months before.

Of the many people who asked me how to prepare the stuff I'd made, there was one who was specific. The woman said that the sauce was a very complex and creative blend. She then vanished into the crowd of faces. One of the foodies quietly told me, "She's a master chef in sauces, judge number 3."

As Ms. MacLellan read the overall results, in reverse order it was final. I had won the 2011 Maine Lobster Cooking Contest. She put her arm around me and gave me a kiss on the cheek. She knew I couldn't speak a word and she spoke for me. For that I am eternally grateful. This was an achievement that I won't soon forget.

2011 Maine Lobster Festival Cooking Contest Winner

In the end, as I was cleaning up my workstation there was one more question. It seemed to be the question asked by many. Louise came over to me after the show and said, "Will you be here next year to defend your title?" All the others I gave the pat answer of "Well, I'll definitely think about it". Ms MacLellan knew of my shortcoming and didn't let on a bit throughout the contest. The least I could do is to be honest with her.

I explained that I was given a second chance in life. It was a wonderful opportunity to enjoy different things and other points of view. Things that I've never been able to see, feel, or taste. To make a meal for the Maine Lobster Festival judges was special for me, win or loose. In the end I won. I won't be returning to compete, ever again. After all, I've only got one meal to show for it. It's the 2011 Maine Lobster Festival Cooking Contest winning recipe. It's best described by the *Maine Food & Lifestyle Magazine* in saying that,

"His recipe for Pan Seared Sea Scallops & Lobster Medallions with Lemon Butter Sauce wowed judges and audience members alike with its delicious taste and artful presentation."

Pan Seared Scallops & Lobster Medallions
With Lemon Sherry Buerre Blanc

THINGS ABOUT LOBSTERS YOU ALWAYS WANTED TO KNOW BUT WERE AFRAID TO ASK

*S*ince you've read this far, you certainly have a keen interest in lobsters. With this in mind, there are a few odd lobster terms, buzzwords, physical and biological functions that may be of interest to you. For some, these will come under the category of "useless trivia". For others it can be a unique asset to draw upon for personal advantage. Imagine how impressed your friends and family will be when you use words like *ecdysis* (lobster shell molt) or *hemolymph* (lobster blood) at the next house party or business gathering? Or, you can be the life of a lobster-dinner by saying, "Hey, everybody, check out the pair of *gonopods* on this bigboy!" In a more academic application, imagine your biology teacher's jaw hitting the floor when you say, "My pet Homarus americanus engaged in a rare *intermolt* copulation last night. Man alive, you should've seen the *pleopods* fluttering!"

Let's start out with some information that is totally useless unless you're on "Who Wants to be a Millionaire" writing a term paper, or the arcane use of Latin as a speaking language. I'm talking about the scientific name and designation of the New England lobster. The American lobster's (aka: New England or Maine lobster, Atlantic lobster, True lobster) scientific name is *Homarus americanus*. Homarus is the *genus type*; lobster. Americanus is the *family type,* American. They are from the *phylum Arthropoda*, meaning to have a segmented body with jointed appendages, such as insects, spiders, and all crustaceans. The later puts them in the *subphylum* of *Crustacea*. Their *class* is *Malacostraca*, meaning "soft shell", as opposed to their hard-shelled cousins the oyster and mussel. Their *order* is *Decopada*, which means they have 10 (ten) feet. Lobsters have 8 walker legs and 2 big claws. The claws are actually highly adapted feet used as much for bodily movement and locomotion as they are for crushing things. American lobsters are in the *infraorder* of *Astacidea.* This puts them in a much more finite sub-grouping of the jointed, 10-legged creatures such as freshwater crayfish and warm water reef lobsters. And finally, they are in the *family* of *Nephropedae*, which comprises the larger clawed lobsters often revered for their edibility and fine taste. Lastly and of least importance is the man who placed our beloved American lobster in its current *binomial classification,* of *Homarus americanus*, the eminent French zoologist *Henri Milne-Edwards*, circa 1837. Now, armed with the aforementioned trivia and $1.87, you can either pull off a marginal passing grade on your first Marine Biology 101 essay or get a medium size cup of hot coffee at Dunkin Donuts, your choice.

Probably the most important thing to know about lobsters is the names of their parts and how they work. This has a practical application when sitting with a well-to-do group of diners at a lobster dinner. Point out and explain the smallest appendages of that steaming red plate-spider. The kids at the table will be first to drop their nutcrackers and stare at you with mouths agape. The adults will not look directly at you at first, out of embarrassment for NOT knowing how to tell if what they're eating is a male or a female. Eventually, they'll all be looking at you, eyebrows furrowed, with a thought-bubble over each of their heads, thinking; "How in hell does he/she know all this stuff?" I've done it so many times that my family refuses to eat lobsters at the same table with me whenever there is a "new ear" in attendance.

Let's start at the front of the lobster and work our way to the trailing end as retold from one of my dining room diatribes. The setting is this, an elegant upscale restaurant in the Hamptons near a beach on Long Island, New York. Several couples are sitting around a grand table covered in white linen, drinking Dom Perignon in suits and dresses. This was an informal meeting of some historical aviation buffs. We'd just spent a day flying mock dogfights (aerial combat) with each other in laser sighted, high-performance Italian dogfighters called Siai Marchetti SF-260's. Laser tag in the sky if you will. The conversation starts out with a toast to the 6 other contestant pilots that were not with us. They'd gotten violently sick from the high G-force jostling.

**Siai Marchetti SF-260,
a laser mounted dogfighter**

Teams of waiters whisk their way to our table and place big silver platters in front of us. In unison the big silver steam lids are removed. Before each of us sat a large 3lb. lobster on its back in a fluffy green bed of fresh chicory, split down the middle, with a white ramekin full of melted butter nestled between the claws at the head. This is dining at its finest (not so in the 1700's). I waste no time in changing the subject from the dry nuances of pulling off an aerial combat reversal using a maneuver called "the rolling scissors", to *Lobsters are more than mere food.* I much prefer talking about the latter.

My wife busily starts dissecting her lobster, head down on the plate, knowing what will most likely happen in the next few minutes. Sure enough, someone eventually comments on the size of his/her lobster's "tail" being full of meat. My wife winces, and slowly shakes her head with a sigh. "Did you say tail? Actually, what you're referring to is the lobster's *abdomen.* The *tail* is comprised of the circular flipper shells, five of them by the way, attached to the rear tip of the abdomen. If you rip off the outer tail flippers, you'll find tasty chunks of meat inside," And in the words of the inimitable Jackie Gleason, awaaaay we go from here!

"Did you know that these leathery whip-like antennae are lined with chemosensory receptors unlike any other creature on earth? It's how a lobster perceives his world" I then pick my lobster up from the plate by the antennae and reach around to pull up one of the eyes, now retracted from the effects of cooking into its shell socket. "These are a lobster's eye stalks. They have limited prismatic vision. Lobsters have amazing eyes, highly adapted to see in murky low-light conditions. Lobster eyes work by **reflection**, not **refraction** like human eyes. The light kinda' reflects down a mirrored shaft via a highly specialized optic made of straight walls and right angles. In essence they can perceive multiple focused objects at one time unlike humans who use a system of curved rod & cones to focus on a single object at a set distance. And, by the way, you may also be interested to know that the natural color of lobster eyes is bright blue!"

Lobster's eyes are a brilliant deep blue color.
They see by reflection unlike humans who see by refraction

"I'm sure that you'll all be interested to know that the US Department of Defense's Home Land Security unit has mechanically replicated a lobster eye device to see through walls for military and anti-terrorist use. It's called the "LEXID, *Lobster Eye X-ray Imaging Device*" At this point I was dreadfully close to overplaying my hand. Regardless, I pressed on with more lobster trivia.

"Did you know that if you cut out a lobster's eyes it will automatically shed its shell in a few days?" At least one person is listening and has to ask, "How come?" The answer, "Because a lobster's eye stalks secrete a powerful stabilizing protein that inhibits the molting process when they shed their shells to get bigger" I was hesitant to mention the actual name of that protein being, *methyl farnesoate* for risk of being deemed a rambling knowit-all and braggart.

"Hey? Does anybody know if you're eating a male or female lobster?" This is always a guaranteed attention-getter. Look at the bottom of the abdomen (tail). It is lined with pairs of feathery little moth-like wings. These are officially called *pleopods*, but in laymen's terms they're called *swimmerets*. Lobsters use these for several purposes. They are mainly used as mini-thrusters for locomotion. Pleopods also work extremely well as an underwater whiskbroom. Cleaning up a filthy den or blasting a hole in the sand for a new burrow is short work for these little rows of underwater conveyor-belt fans. Also they make a great tool for stationary aeration of a close-ended burrow hideout. A lobster simply perches himself up on tail and claw-tips, arches his back and then pulses water currents in and out with swimmerets for a cooling breath of fresh air.

Swimmerets being used like feather dusters to remove debris from lobster's burrow

At this point in the dinner party, all but one of the group had set down their forks and nutcrackers. They realized two things: a) what I was saying was in fact somewhat interesting and b) I was not going to shut up until finished with my speech. Only one stuffy woman, an ex US Airforce officer, kept her head down working on her lobster. I knew she was listening to me but she wanted to be thought of, as already knowing all that boring lobster stuff. She ended up getting her just desserts in the end, literally and figuratively. For now, I had a table full of interested folks, save one, looking at me and nodding up and down as if to be saying "Hm? I did not know that." Regardless, I stood a chance at losing my audience, so I went on to the next point of interest.

"Check out the swimmeret at the forward-most end of the lower abdomen, where it joins the thorax (body). If the forward-most pair of swimmerets is feathery like the others, it is a female lobster. If they are stiff like a pair of plastic prongs, these are called gonopods and the lobster you're eating is a male." (figures #1 & #2) They all looked down to see what gender the lobsters in front of them actually were.

"Now that we know how to tell a girl from a boy lobster, you may be wondering how they mate?" I tried to keep the explanation simple. I certainly could've quoted them some of the voluminous text compiled by Jelle Atema in his decades of study on the subject. However, I was afraid to push the already steaming mad Airforce retiree over the edge. She was at the breaking point and about to heave her dinner fork at me so I decided to forego the use of technical terms such as *"serial monogamy"*. This is an alternative mating procedure observed in Homarus americanus. Serial monogamy is characterized by a series of long or short-term sexually exclusive relationships, occurring consecutively. I kept the description simple.

"Female lobsters pick a boyfriend, usually the largest and most aggressive male in her path. Her would-be boyfriend at this point would love nothing better than to tear her to pieces and eat her. Obviously, the species would've gone extinct long ago if this sly female didn't have something up her sleeve, not unlike human females." I got a snicker from the men in the crowd.

"The female lobster splashes a very powerful pheromone or perfume into her boyfriend's burrow and the water all around him. He becomes instantly mesmerized and stunned senseless. The fierce male monster starts acting silly, like a playful puppy dog, not unlike human males on a date." The ladies in the crowd now laughed aloud.

"The female lobster squeezes her way into his burrow and they spend quality time, side by side. If the bigboy doesn't know what to do, the female instinctively teases him, and tries to back her way under him. She pushes so hard that his body will sometimes lift up off the ground. She will often molt out of her old shell while in the males burrow near him. While in a softened pristine state, the big male takes her into his arms underneath him. He gently rolls her over on her back with her soft claws outstretched over her head. They mate in the bottom-to-bottom position, which takes about 2 or 3 minutes, disengage, and sit quietly side by side for a while. Often they both dine on her old discarded shell like a romantic post-copulation dinner."

"She continues intoxicating her mate with small amounts of pheromone until her new shell hardens. After this time, perhaps a week, she bids her boyfriend a fond adieu and leaves him forevermore." I've witnessed this with my own eyes only once and it was absolutely amazing. In captivity however, once the pheromones ended, the male lobster obsessively hunted down his former mate, slowly cut her to pieces bit by bit and eventually killed her.

"She stores her boyfriend's semen in an internal pouch for a later time when conditions are right for her to extrude the eggs which are inside her, unfertilized at that point. Some of us eating female lobsters right now can see what lobster eggs look like, before fertilization. In a natural uncooked state, they look like dark green jello. When cooked they become bright crimson red, are fully edible, and considered a tasty treat by many lobster connoisseur." I struck a small cord of disgust in the crowd at that point. Several of them had a big ball of red unfertilized lobster eggs sitting on plates in front of them. "Don't worry; it is delicious and not poison. Feel free to scoop it out and pass any unwanted lobster roe and tomalley over here to me. All donations will be welcome!" That got a laugh and put them at ease.

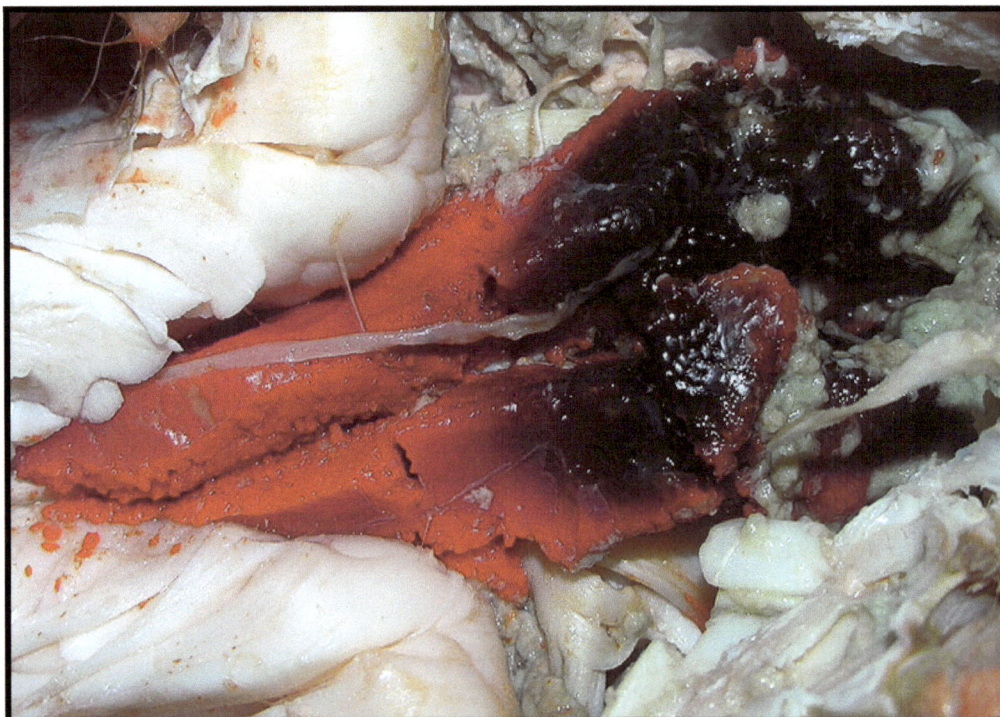

**Internal, unfertilized lobster eggs are naturally dark greenish
but turn crimson red when cooked. Many consider this to be a delicacy.**

"Once a female lobster extrudes fertilized eggs, usually in the fall months, they become attached to the underside of her abdomen (tail) with a waterproof kind of crazy-glue specifically for egg attachment. Thousands of these dark brown eggs stick to her underside in big clusters."

Extruded fertilized lobster eggs attached to a "berried" female lobster.
Only 5 of these stand a chance of growing to be a mature lobster.
Eggers must be immediately released.

"These eggs, thousands of them, take between 9 and 11 months to mature and will molt up to 35 times within their tiny egg sack. They hatch in the summer months and start out like tiny mosquitoes, free-floating near the top of the water, at the whim of the tide. The few who survive to the final larval stage are called super-lobster because for a short time they are able to move in a forward position. These little guys look like Superman flying headfirst through the water. This stage lasts about 2 weeks as the super-lobster flies his way to the ocean floor for the first time since hatching. He hides among the rocks and bottom substrate and remains there for the rest of his life."

"Every living thing that the tiny lobster encounters wants to kill and eat him, so he learns quickly to only come out at night. The few that survive the first 5 or 6 years, molting about 25 times a year get ever larger in size. Eventually they grow to slightly over one pound, big enough to be caught and kept by lobstermen. Fewer yet escape the vast dragnet of lobster traps and grow to the size of the ones in our plates right now. Bon appetite~"

They all looked at the amazing 20-year-old creatures on their dinner plates with a new appreciation. I was sure that at least one of them could comprehend the unique metamorphosis that this creature has gone through in order to get to their plate. We all dug in to the wonderful meal without another word being said before the melted butter got cold.

As I was squirting fresh lemon juice across the length of my lobster I looked down to the other end of our large banquet sized dinner table. Madame Airforce retiree was working on the tail-meat and shaking her head in silent protest at my informational lecture. A cartoon like thought-bubble appeared over her head saying, "That man is an overzealous, pompous blowhard!" As luck would have it, she'd plucked out the very last tidbit of tail-meat and dunked it in the melted butter ramekin in front of her. I waited until the forkful of meat was headed for her mouth before speaking. The timing would have to be perfect. I quickly reached in to the split tail section of my lobster and pulled out a dark strand of intestine buried deeply in the aft section of the meat.

"Oh, by the way, I hope everyone has removed this portion? You really shouldn't eat this part." (Actually I've eaten it thousands of times.) I held the dangling black-tipped intestinal strand high in the air. Everyone looked at me, including the sour-faced woman who was chewing on the piece of lobster intestine that I was now holding aloft. "This is the lobster's anus," She spat the mouthful out into her serviette, gagged, and quickly left the room.

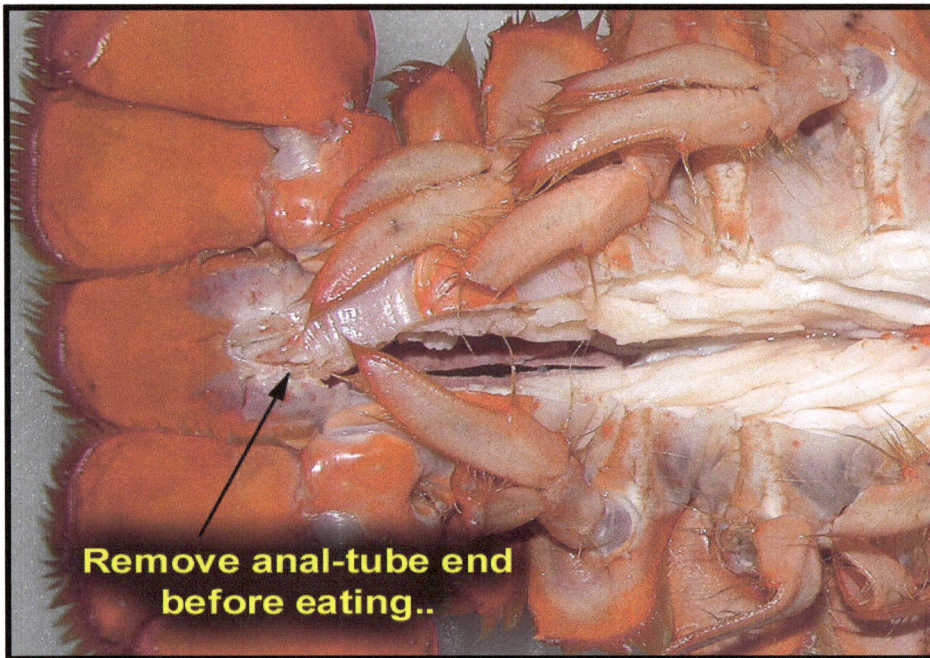

Remove anal-tube end before eating..

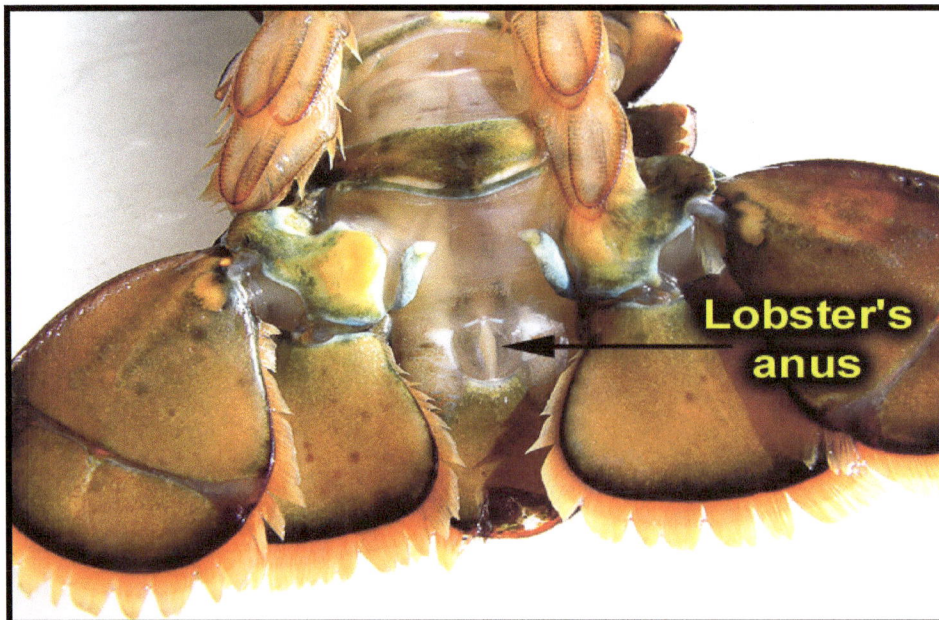

Lobster's anus

HERE TODAY GONE TOMALLEY
THE PERFECT STORM OF 1999

*I*n 1614 the Dutch navigator Adriaen Block sailed through a narrow passage of water running between two islands, now called Manhattan Island & Long Island. This narrow waterway was later named the East River of New York. Block eventually exited the East River at its northern most end, entering an open straight of ocean. Protected from the open ocean by a long spit of land, this beautiful stretch of sheltered water was called Long Island Sound.

The Long Island Sound is a body of seawater that is enclosed on three sides. It is an estuary of the Atlantic Ocean bordered on the north by the length of Connecticut's entire south shoreline. The Sound's south border is the north-most shoreline of Long Island, New York, extending to Orient Point and across the water to Fisher's Island, New York. The eastern-most end of Long Island Sound abuts the open ocean waters of Block Island Sound, named after Captain Block. This wide body of sheltered ocean contains many rocky reefs, sandy shoals, salt-marsh inlets, and tributary runoffs. It was an absolutely perfect haven and breeding ground for shellfish and lobsters. The key word, unfortunately, in the previous sentence being "was".

In the years preceding 1999, the Long Island Sound lobster fishery was booming. Catch logs reported to the Department of Environmental Protection reached nearly 3 million pounds of New England lobster per year. The overall revenue to fishermen, restaurants, markets, and tourism generated from this vibrant industry was reported to be around $100 million a year. Every boy with a rowboat on the Connecticut shore was tending a few lobster traps for dinner fare or to make a few dollars in spending money. It was taken for granted that this endless natural resource would be self-sustaining and last forever. But, as my father always said, "There's only one thing for certain about mother nature. She loves change and not always for the better."

Being an old Connecticut Yankee, I've lived long enough to see some of the slow but sure changes that Mother Nature has taken. From this point of view, watching things evolve over the decades, you can start to make sense of the natural order all around you. You don't need a degree in the marine sciences to tell you that something is going dreadfully wrong, or why it's happening. You pretty much know why and with a little research you can quickly find documented data to substantiate your observations and beliefs as I did. The following is an example.

As a young boy I loved going out fishing in the sound with my uncle Milt. He was a World-War II combat veteran with a crumbling pain-racked body. He fished the eastern part of the Long Island sound every single day of the week for years after his return from Europe. He'd miraculously survived a direct hit from a German 88mm artillery round, ambushes that killed his entire squad, and a march across Europe. Ironically, he was nearly killed in a mess hall accident when 50-gallons of scalding hot coffee fell on him at the CC Camp in Voluntown, Connecticut.

We'd leave the docks at Groton and make our way out to the eastern tip of Fisher's Island, picking our way through a veritable solid wall of lobster buoys. He brought a pair of big wooden peach baskets covered with a wet burlap bag. On the way out to sea, the baskets contained one salami grinder sandwich, one six-pack of Narragansett beer, one small bottle of Old Mr. Boston brandy, and a small snuff tin containing 2 painkiller pills. He lived in pain every hour of the day with shrapnel-shredded, burned legs. We'd fish the Catumb reef area out to the deep waters off the southeastern side of Fisher's Island, NY. We rarely saw another fishing boat out there, and we'd catch fish nonstop from the first drop to the last. He had one motto that always made me laugh, even today, as far as the upkeep of his battered 24-foot cabin cruiser, "The hell with the boat; get the lines overboard!"

One day we were catching tautog near the tip of Fisher's Island, just off the beach near a summer cottage. These togs were huge, in the 12~18lb. class. Uncle Milt was reeling a big one in when his stiff boat-rod fishing pole went down onto the rail with a loud WHACK! Then it went loose as he reeled a dead weight up from the bottom. On the hook was the head of a massive blackfish. It'd been bitten and severed in half just behind the gills. The head alone was as big as a basketball. Milt quipped, "Damn shark", baited up a new rig and got the line back overboard ASAP. A little while later we saw a man on the beach playing with his dog, a large red Irish setter. The man threw a stick out into the surf and the dog playfully splashed into the water to retrieve it. The dog spotted our anchored boat and decided to swim out past the surf break to us. It was like a scene from the movie, "Jaws". A big dark blue dorsal fin was making a beeline for that silly setter doing a slow doggie paddle to our boat. Uncle Milt, a true dog lover, fired up the engine and went full-throttle towards the dog, dragging the anchor behind the boat. He reached over and grabbed that sopping wet Irish setter and hauled it inboard. The owner was traumatized as we brought the dog ashore.

We caught big codfish on sea-clams in uncle Milt's "Secret Spot" in the deep waters just southeast of Fisher's Island. It was a spot on his nautical chart that had a big red outline around it. There was no GPS or Loran electronics back then and he'd locate the spot by lining up church steeples with water towers on Fisher's. He put us on target using a pair of German officer's field binoculars that he'd liberated after a battle in the Vosges Mountains of France.

One day Milt's rod started peeling off line like I'd never seen before. He never cared for fishing in freshwater and had another famous saying, "I love fishing in saltwater because you can never tell what you might catch." The thing on the end of his line was unstoppable, but the 150lb. test cloth braid line would not break. The tail end of the boat starting turning towards the giant fish, many feet below us. Eventually, the line broke and he reeled in slack. The gigantic nose of a United States Nuclear submarine breached the surface about 300 yards away, in an explosion of white foamy seawater. He flew from his seat and we sped away at wide-open throttle back into Napatree Point passage. He'd been fishing in a highly restricted area allocated to the military for submarine sea trials after repairs at the Groton Electric Boat shipyard.

We always came in with overflowing fish-filled peach baskets. It looked like Poseidon's cornucopia: cod fish, large tautog the size of small hogs, porgies the size of car hubcaps and big summer flounder (fluke). In the wintertime when his boat was dry-docked, Milt fished in a saltwater tributary off the Barn Island railroad trestle. He'd drop a sandworm on a hook down through the railroad ties and pull up a burlap bag full of winter flounder, sea robins, and tasty little "tomcod" or "frost fish". He fished the trestle every single day of the winter. Not one of his fish ever went to waste. After a day at sea he'd drive around delivering fresh fish to the poor families in our town and he'd even clean & fillet the fish for the old folks and widows.

Circa 1966, Codfish caught by author inshore near Fisher's Island NY. They disappeared from these waters in the 1970's

First, among other things that slowly faded away over the years, was the codfish. There are absolutely none in any of the inshore regions where we used to catch them. Today, you must travel miles offshore to areas like the Stellwagen Banks to catch a codfish. The next to go extinct in the sound was the little tomcod, "Frost Fish". They just disappeared around the early 70's and have never been seen again in our waters. The winter flounder, "Flats", are now hard to find in the eastern sound as well.

There was no official open or closed season for these fast disappearing fish. Now the open seasons are all regulated to a mere few weeks on certain species. Summer flounder, "Fluke", populations are becoming so thin that the Federal marine regulatory commissions have set stringent quota and size limits on this dwindling stock. The "open season" and minimum size limit are relegated to a handful. The same critical limitations are also being placed on tautog, porgies, and black sea bass that we caught so regularly that they were considered a junk fish.

Lastly, the two other things that you don't see anymore are large pelagic sharks in the Sound and nuclear submarines breaching the surface in dramatic Hollywood fashion. The big sharks have no regular food supply to draw them in close to shore anymore, and the submarines must traverse the Sound at orderly topwater cruise speeds, to and from the open ocean. Subs are now surrounded by a bevy of US Coast Guard gunboats as the subs come and go like the one below. I've often wondered if some sailor thought it as funny as I did when he found my uncle Milt's cod rig and 300' of braid fishing line tangled in the periscope.

One species of fish was glaringly absent in the 60's and 70's and rarely seen or heard of within the Long Island Sound It was the Atlantic Striped Bass (*Morone saxatilis*). Milt would often talk about this mysterious, highly sought after game fish, but I cannot ever recall him actually catching one in his daily trips out to sea. It is well known that striped bass, also called "Rock Bass" actively hunt and eat lobsters. There were no stripers in any great numbers in the Long Island Sound back then. Throughout the years, stripers experienced a history of rise and fall as did the lobsters. Their numbers seem to have a direct affect on lobster populations, and vice versa in an endless balancing act of nature. For instance, simplistically speaking, without stripers, lobster populations grow and overcrowd the reef community. The following year stripers swoop in, eat the lobsters, then reproduce in great numbers, and lobster numbers shrink. Lobsters become scarce and striper numbers go down. Stripers become scarce and lobster numbers increase and on and on. Of course, hundreds of other sub-groups of undersea creatures are also affected by this seesawing of striper / lobster populations. Nature's balance is perfect without the hand of man interfering.

In 1639 the Massachusetts Bay Colony passed one of the earliest environmental protection laws on record. The new law stated that striped bass and codfish could no longer be used for fertilizer, a popular method of raising crops back then among shoreline farmers. In 1776 the states of New York and Massachusetts prohibited the sales of cod and stripers during winter months.

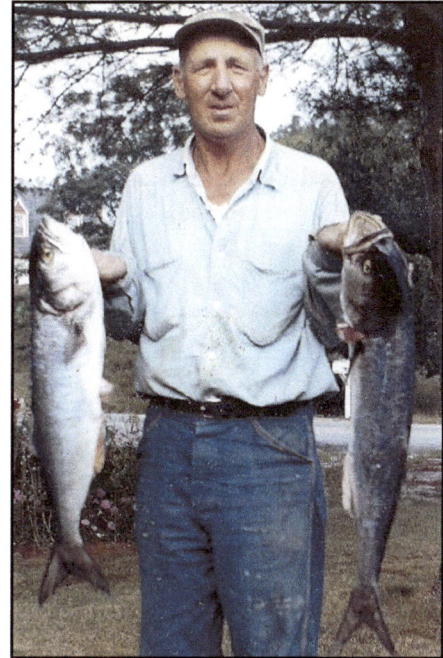

Uncle Milt Lockwood
Purple Heart recipient WWII

A US Nuclear Submarine popping up in Long Island Sound nowadays

There was no pollution or industries dumping waste directly into the runoff streams and tributaries back then so the conservation acts had a direct impact on the species, unlike today. The continuous harvesting of striped bass lead to a severe decline of the species in the 1970's according to the Rhode Island Sea-Grant fact sheet #P-1413. The rapid deterioration of the striped bass fisheries lead to serious regulatory meetings at state and federal levels. In 1984 the US Congress passed the "Striped Bass Conservation Act". This empowered the Atlantic States Marine Fisheries Commission (ASMFC) to regulate striper fishing throughout all eastern seaboard states. These shoreline states were then bound to comply with some of the strictest fishing regulations on record. Among these were size limits, seasonal closures, daily bag limits and commercial quota limits that become highly unpopular among sportsmen and commercial fishermen alike. Along with these regulatory measures, efforts were also made to control water pollution, artificial stocking, and even the use of hormonal stimulation on female stripers to promote ovulation.

Author's son caught this Atlantic Striped Bass as big as him
This female cow could easily suck down a 2-lb. lobster

As you can see, great effort was made to "Save the Striper". This was the first of many innocuous appearing actions that would start the domino effect leading to the ultimate demise of the booming lobster population in the Sound. Nowadays, Long Island Sound is teaming with highly regulated and protected striped bass. Every spring they pour into the Long Island Sound basin and they are extremely hungry, bad news for lobsters. I'm sure that more than a few Long Island Sound lobstermen of the mid 1970's applauded this gallant effort. Afterall, wouldn't it be nice to bring home a big striped bass to grill for dinner after a long day of hauling in traps filled with lobsters? They had no idea that the signing of the Striped Bass Conservation Act was the opening death knell to their entire industry. In 1995 the Atlantic Striped Bass was officially declared to be a "restored stock". This was the first cloud of a gathering storm on the horizon; a future perfect storm that would see the sun set on all Long Island Sound lobster fisheries.

In 1997 a rise in water temperatures within the Sound was noted. The National Oceanic and Atmospheric Administration (NOAA) reported *that the global mean temperature for June through August 1999, was well above the long-term average* based on preliminary data. In fact, for nearly every month in the past 10 years, the global mean land temperature has been above the long-term averages of 1880-1998.

LIS Bottom Water Temperatures August-October

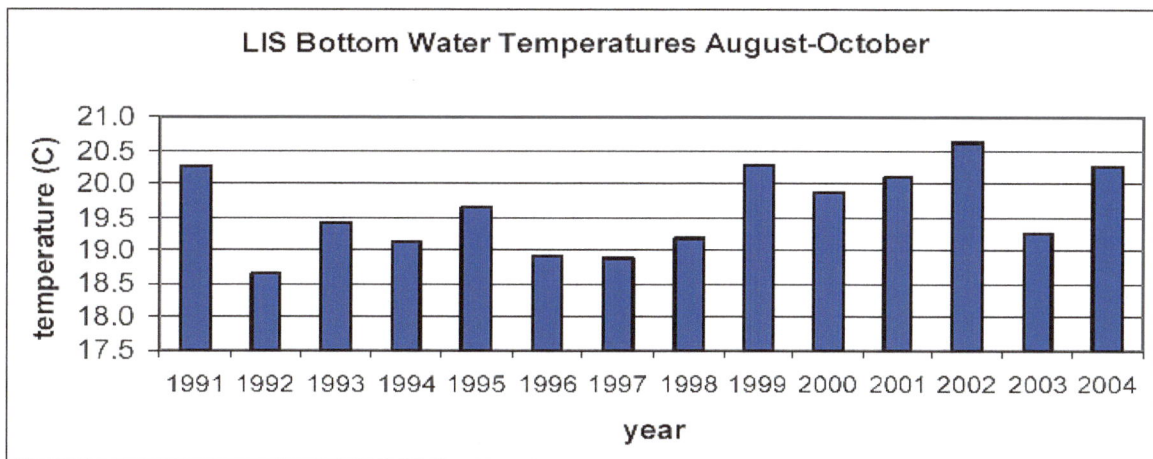

**Long Island Sound chart showing pattern of rising temps over 14-year period.
Note spikes in '99 & '02.**
Source: US Dept of Commerce National Atmospheric & Oceanic Administration
National Fisheries & Marine Service

Lobster fisheries were still reporting yearly catch totals near 4 million pounds, so there was no great concern over the slow rise in water temperature. Perhaps this was due to random seasonal anomalies or perhaps it was due to the early effects of global warming. Regardless, the water temperature in Long Island Sound was on the rise, being another dark cloud in the gathering storm.

Long Island Sound (LIS) lobstermen continued to mortgage their homes for new boats and equipment, and life was good. Few of them took historical notice of the facts that since the first US Census in 1790, the New York City metropolitan area was, has been, and remains the single most densely populated area in the entire United States. The East River is a narrow channel that separates Manhattan and Long Island and connects the New York Harbor with the Western Long Island Sound (WLIS). It is the most heavily populated estuarine system in the entire United States. The East River / WLIS receives treated sewage from 18 (yes, eighteen!) wastewater treatment plants in New York and southern Connecticut in addition to industrial discharges and miscellaneous sewer overflows. A marine pollution bulletin (#48) appearing in an Elsevier Academic Journal put this into laymen's perspective. They stated that the combined discharge of these plants (flowing into the East River and WLIS) is enough to fill Yankee Stadium to the top, every 4 hours, every day of the year. They went on to state that the sediments of the East River are some of the most toxic in the entire Raritan-Hudson basin. Also that high levels of toxic metals in bottom sediments and hypoxia are causing problems with bottom dwelling fish, clams, and crustaceans. One sobering statement in the Elsevier report pretty much said it all, "Western Long Island Sound sediment ranks among the 10 most contaminated among coastal locations around the United States and copper concentrations in many species of bivalves (the lobster's primary food source) approach or exceed toxic levels.." The report went on in great scientific detail, all bad stuff for LIS lobsters.

In 1999 the western hemisphere saw the first case of the West Nile Virus, a mosquito borne disease that had been proven fatal to human beings. It was confirmed that some folks in New York City, New Jersey and Connecticut had contracted this frightening new disease. The Center for Disease Control (CDC) was doing its best to contend with the outbreak of West Nile, which caused illness in humans and sometimes leading to fatalities in humans and livestock. Some of the unpleasant symptoms include: headache, high fever, neck stiffness, stupor, disorientation, coma, tremors, convulsions, muscle weakness, and paralysis.

The spring and summer of 1999 were one of the wettest and warmest on record in southern New England, ideal breeding conditions for mosquitoes. People were understandably worried about this parasite driven pox now upon them. A frightening new word was heard on the news; a word that brought fear to parents, young, and old alike. The word was *"Pandemic"*. People were afraid to go outside after dark. They were advised to wear clothing akin to a full biohazard body-condom suit whenever leaving the house. Children's clothes were continuously drenched in bug spray and a chemical called *"Deet"*, the active ingredient in pesticides. After the immediate threat had passed, a television news account reported that the overuse of Deet caused more short-term illness in humans trying to avoid the West Nile virus than the virus itself.

Although we really had nothing to fear but fear itself, we pressured our leaders for some immediate action in protecting us from the perceived imminent scourge about to befall us. The quickest and most powerful response to this threat is in our hardware and technology. Massive aerial aerosol larvacidal spraying programs were started throughout the 5 boroughs of New York City, Long Island, and Connecticut areas. They used a pesticide called *"Malathion"* in the aerial assault, which continued on a grand scale up until the hot fall of 1999.

This seemingly unrelated entomological episode would later be blamed for the ecological disaster now only days away in Long Island Sound. It was surmised that since the malathion spraying was mainly being done around the inland regions and no great rainfalls had been noted, the odds of contamination by tributary runoff was minimal. According to NOAA the average total precipitation for the contiguous U.S. for the period June through August 1999 was well below the long-term average, and falling below the long-term average for the first time in 8 years. Ergo, little or no rainfall, thus far, during the malathion spraying was a good thing.

In the first week of September 1999, all helicopter pesticide distribution flights were cancelled and participating aircraft were sent to secure areas inland. The final nail in the coffin of lobster fisheries in Long Island Sound could be seen far out to sea in the form of a massive swirling cloud. It was a black juggernaut of destruction hurtling towards the mainland at over 120 mph.

Floyd was a massive category-4 hurricane when it made landfall on September 15th, 1999. It had sustained winds of nearly 100 mph and gusts up to 122 mph. It created a storm surge of around 10ft. and produced extreme rainfall totals as high as 15 to 20 inches. The intense rainfall caused mudslides and flooding in southern New England closing roads for nearly a week. It swept over Long Island, NY like a tsunami.

The rain, wind, and overall ferocity of Hurricane Floyd caused everything bad to flow into Long Island Sound. Not only did every bit of the West Nile pesticide (malathion, etc) wash into the Sound, so did overflowing sewers, agricultural fertilizer, paints, and just about any other thing that a 100 mph wind blast could dislodge or become uprooted from a biblical class flood.

Satellite view of Hurricane Floyd, September 15th 1999

Eventually the floodwaters of hurricane Floyd receded and the sun came back out. Southern New Englanders, a hearty breed, are used to being battered by winter storms, summer droughts, and fall hurricanes. We cleared our roads, restrung our downed power lines, and patched up our battered lobster boats; some found far inland lying in cornfields. Within a few days LIS lobstermen headed back out into the Sound to tend their traps, business as usual. The mortgage payments don't stop because of a windy day. As they motored out to process their lobster trap trawls, life as they knew it would change, literally overnight.

The first lobster traps to break the surface of Long Island Sound after hurricane Floyd, were as they'd always been, pretty much full of lobsters and crabs. But the faces of Long Island Sound lobstermen paled to white when they reached in to pull their catch out. The lobsters were dead. They'd crawled into the traps, taken a few nibbles on the bait bags, and dropped dead in their tracks. Dying and dead lobsters were pulled up from the bottom of the Sound in trap after trap. The remaining live lobsters that came to the surface were described as being "limp" and dying, thousands and thousands of them. In a 24-hour period the Long Island Sound lobster fisheries collapsed. It was officially declared to be a federal ecological disaster. There were 1,200 commercial lobstermen at the time, all supporting families, local businesses, restaurants and tourism. I'll put this in proportional perspective from the viewpoint of a commercial lobsterman. During previous years decreases in lobster catch were around 3~5% in a bad year. The families were forced to live without many daily necessities and simply "make do" until the following year. In the late fall of 1999 it was reported that lobsters in the Western Long Island Sound area were 99% gone. This was clearly not just a mere temporary shortfall in lobsters; it was called a *"mass extinction event."*

Rare photo of dead lobsters & crabs pulled from traps in fall of 1999. University of CT Sea Grant report CTSG-06-02 Photo credit to CT DEEP

There have been countless studies done on the world renowned 1999 LIS lobster dieoff event. Millions of dollars in grant funding have been poured into scientific research and analysis. Theories and hypotheses galore have been written. Some theories come from marine scientists and geniuses. Some theories come from the lunatic fringe saying that this event heralds the last days of man and that Armageddon is nigh!

The collective best and brightest marine scientists on earth were given unlimited resources to work on this puzzling conundrum for many years. We, the lobster loving public, watched the price of lobsters skyrocket to an all-time high as we waited for scientists to announce the single cause of this horrible debacle. The conclusive answer never came. The possible causes came in dribs and drabs with complete uncertainty. Each of us with a vested personal interest plucked tidbits of possible causation to use for our own best interest. For example, the LIS commercial lobstermen, now all in financial ruin, sued the Cheminova chemical company claiming that the pesticide runoff was the culprit. The pesticide company cited the results of extensive scientific tests performed on lobsters using malathion. The reports stated that indeed malathion did adversely affect lobsters, but not fatally so in laboratory testing using high and low dosages.

One researcher, Christopher Perkins the associate director of the University of Connecticut's Environmental Research Institute, was closely involved with lobster testing. Perkins and his team were hell bent to find the cause of the 1999 lobster dieoff. He was called upon to voice some of the results found in his laboratories. He said "..testing of lobsters this year did not reveal detectable levels of pesticides sprayed to control mosquitoes during the West Nile outbreak."

Mr. Perkins surely left the crowd flat when he could not produce the magic bullet that killed the LIS lobsters. He said, "I don't think there is anybody who likes to get up and say, 'I couldn't find anything'". But, that's what he said, and that said it all. Several Long Island Lobster Health Symposiums were held after the 1999 event. They were attended by some of the top scientists, researchers, lobstermen, ecologists, marine scholars and fisheries' experts from around the world. Transcript reports of these symposiums present some very interesting reading and can be obtained online. If you are ever having a sleepless night and want to get drowsy really quickly, I suggest reading some of the scientific diatribe presented at one of these symposiums. That being said, I'll paraphrase some of the information gleaned from my research of the symposium transcripts on an introspective level.

Researchers initially concluded that record high seasonal water temperatures and pesticides were the root cause. They tested and dissected hundreds of lobsters in their laboratories simply looking for scientific numbers to document the foregone initial conclusions. Starving lobstermen were screaming for that final report. They were desperate to get on with their lawsuits and attempts to recoup financial losses through governmental subsidies once the scientific facts were in hand. Time passed and the lobster test results became a bit muddy. The numbers being found did not clearly substantiate the initial assumptions. We, the lobster loving public, assumed that the scientist were merely dragging their feet with the final report so they could use up every bit of the $7.9 million dollars in grant funding ($6.9 million from the federal government and $1 million from the state of Connecticut) before stating the single cause.

The researchers soon had to do a complete objective about-face as the unadulterated scientific indications were pointing to something other than mere warm water temps and chemical pollutants. Each of the sampled dead lobsters that were dissected postmortem had a strange parameoba parasite in its system. This parasite had attacked the lobster's nervous system and was eventually proven to be the ultimate cause of death in nearly all the LIS lobsters. Mr. Perkins' statement that there simply is no smoking gun that fired a single magic bullet to kill the Long Island Sound lobsters seems to be, in the end, absolutely true.

Diane Cowen, executive director of the Lobster Conservancy, called female LIS lobsters "stay at home Moms" due to the fact that they don't ever leave Long Island Sound. Thus the gene pool produces weaker and weaker lobster spawn with each passing season. Eventually it all came to a head in the fall of 1999.

Now that you've read enough mumbo jumbo jargon, numbers, and statistics to be completely stymied, let me put it to you simply. The lobsters in and around the Long Island Sound are becoming extinct. It started in the 1999 die-off because of a combination of 7 things, on a grand scale:

1) *Mosquito spraying near riverine estuary*
2) *The water temperature getting warmer*
3) *Pollutants from nearby sources*
4) *A cataclysmic hurricane*
5) *Lobster over population*
6) *Parameoba parasites*
7) *Closed genetic pool*

Due to these seven things, the long history and heritage of a booming lobster industry in Long Island Sound collapsed. All the best laid plans for bigger boats and more traps came to an abrupt halt on September 15th, 1999. The lobsters are no more in the great numbers that existed before then. They are dwindling in a downward spiral even now. Too many proud Long Island Sound lobsterman went broke and are now welders at Electric Boat or clerks at Home Depot. In the words of the inimitable Forrest Gump to the old lady sitting on the bench at the bus station:

"And just like that, my lobstering days was over"

STRESS & SHELL DISEASE

*A*ny one of the above would in itself be manageable to the hearty New England lobster, but all six sent stress levels through the roof. "Stress" in a lobster can be like the amount of electricity left in a battery. Suppose you have a flashlight that runs on a 9-volt battery. It has an automatic re-charger that charges it up every night, but it takes all night to do so. Lobsters have a finite amount of "energy" by which to do their business, like a 9-volt battery in a flashlight. When they move, or fight, or raise claws they use a little bit of the battery power available. When they're injured, the battery power required to send blood to a missing appendage for clotting or regeneration of a missing part uses up to 4 times the amount of remaining energy. Sometimes after a long battle, multiple injuries, or extreme shell-disease, lobsters just run out of battery power and will die because of it. When this begins to happen, they become, what is called "stressed" and they shutdown.

Stressed lobster

Stressed lobsters fold their antennae tightly back against their carapace. They appear listless and the only way you can tell if they're still alive is by the one single small antennule whisker that may be slightly flicking up and down. This is its last single line of alert to incoming danger while all other sensory systems have shut down. The flicking of this single nose feather takes the least amount of energy to operate while the lobster's battery is undergoing recharge and repair.

The lobster on the left is saying, "I may be stressed, but I dare you to so much as touch the whisker on my nose!"

Have you ever noticed when purchasing lobsters in the market how some lobsters appeared more active than others do? For instance, you order 3 lobsters. The first one pulled out half-heartedly raises a claw. The second lobster raises both claws and walker legs are moving quickly. The third one is wildly swinging the claws, its tail flapping a spray of water, and its swimmerets are flailing rapidly. These animals all have different energy states due to being stressed by recent environmental occurrences. Some of these stresses may be not being fed, being handled too many times, or fighting with other lobsters.

The one on the right is growing a new claw. This process puts a large stressor on its system. To do so it must disregard other system damage control, like *EPIZOOTIC SHELL DISEASE.*

Epimorphic regeneration of a new claw!
Similar to stem cells in humans.

Among the many other things that wrack a lobster's system, you may add the stress of chitinolytic bacteria, aka, **SHELL DISEASE**. Some say it comes from disposing of plastic in the water, while others say that it is a bacterial infection or "common cold", that was always present but never noticed because their strong lobster bodies could easily fight it off. As time went on, more and more stresses were added to the list. Kind of like when we add a new payment for that shiny car or a bigger house. Eventually we go into a negative spiral out of control with payments outweighing the income. One of several things has got to give for the lobster, and one of those things is shell disease.

We pulled our first traps after taking a 25-year hiatus from SCUBA diving. It was refreshing to see lobsters once again caught in the wild, but there was something different. Something I hadn't ever seen before and knew nothing about. It looked as though someone had splashed battery acid over the top of the lobster?

Shell diseased lobster

At first I thought it was an anomaly but later found it to be routine. The insidious little bacterium is technically called *epizootic shell disease*. This, among countless other things, has been a study to find out why it's happening now to New England lobsters another blight to contend with for Homarus americanus. Add this to the mounting stack of stressors. I wrote to Dr. Rick Cawthorn, PhD, Professor of Parasitology at AVC Lobster Science Center, the University of Prince Edward Island, Canada. He was interested in many of the images that I captured. After communicating with Dr. Cawthorn for some time, one thing became apparent. All the kings horses and all the kings men (a lot smarter than I) know not why shell disease runs rampant. One thing is for sure. In the long run, it is not a good sign for the lobster.

I hadn't seen this affliction during my SCUBA diving days back in the early 1970's. But back in 1937 a man named Hess noted something called "impoundment shell disease". He found this in samplings of lobsters impounded in Yarmouth, Nova Scotia, Canada. This was the first sign of a microorganism collected from as far north as the Canadian waters some 80 years ago. Hess' note was merely a footnote to some marine journal back then. It made an interesting notation, but nothing serious. After all, who cares about a couple of odd-looking lobsters among thousands of healthy ones? Well, here we are some 80 years in the future and the shell disease has spread to an epic and growing proportion.

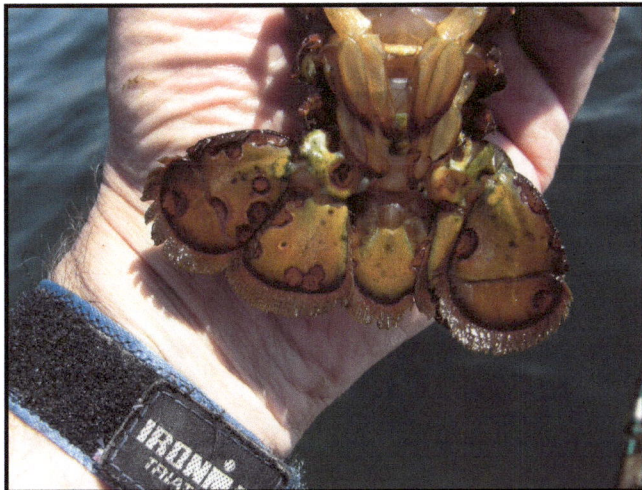

Stage-2 shell disease on lobster tail bottom

This disease (SD) is not spread through contact, as was initially thought when calling it "impoundment shell disease." I found out for myself that an afflicted lobster would not infect the others in a tank full of lobsters in close quarters. Hess noted in 1937 that "lobsters held in impoundments at high densities..." cause severe shell disease, but those found in native populations are "relatively rare."

Acting as a backyard marine biologist, I tried to make sense of SD as each stricken lobster was caught. I carefully logged each catch: date caught, the state of the SD found, the gender, and so on. Several things soon became apparent to me as I found shell diseased lobsters in my traps one after another.

Initially, I'd thought that the disease appeared to have fallen on the lobster, from the top down, like acid rain falls onto the ground. I knew I was wrong when I turned over a SD lobster and saw the undeniable round marks under the flipper (as can be seen above). SD occurs in the water all around the lobster. It is not particular to any one place on the shell.

Shell disease, eaten completely through to the organs

The SD chooses a host at random, be it male or female. It seems to prefer female lobsters, as they are egg bearing. Most female lobsters protectively guard their extruded eggs and will not molt until the release of eggs (hatch). Failure to do so often ends up in death for these diseased animals.

However, a lobster with shell disease can be eaten by a human with no effect. I've eaten many of them. Once you get past the looks, they're as good as the rest!

As a matter of fact, have you ever stopped for a lobster-roll along the highway? You're likely to have enjoyed the taste of a shell-diseased lobster and you never even knew it.

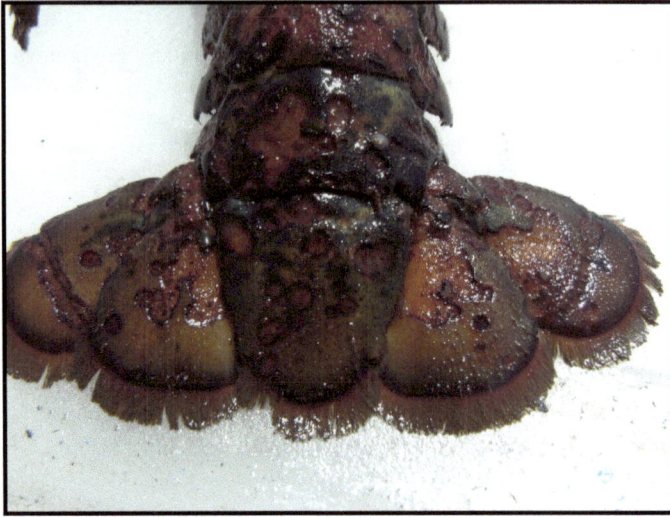

Here's how it works. The microbial bacteria will eat into the chitin of a lobster exoskeleton at will. It starts out as little round whitish circles found on the claws or carapace.

It will progress to a series of pits or dents in the shell, eventually linking together, making a small swath of what appears to be missing "skin".

When you see a lobster in this, the 2nd stage of SD, you think how it must hurt! Actually it doesn't hurt at all. It's business as usual with the daily routine, just a bit constrictive in shell movement.

There are four distinct stages of the disease, depending on the percentage of SD that consumes the overall shell. The 1st stage is barely noticeable and the spots are often unseen as they mix right in with the lobsters' natural camouflage. Look at the lobster below. It's healthy and has a shiny new hard shell, but can you spot the shell disease?

You wouldn't even notice the small avulsion on the 2nd to last walker leg would you? That tiny spot heralds an upcoming year of misery for this lobster.

Let's jump ahead and get to the real nitty gritty of stage #4 shell disease. It's described as being over 90% of the shell eaten away. In reality it is a "non survivable event"; the lobster will die. I can only imagine the kinds of death available to a lobster. You've got your being eaten by a large fish or crushed by another lobster. Then you've got your 1999 event where you crawl into a trap and die of exhaustion. Maybe if you're lucky, you'll be boiled and eaten by human beings. All these, and many more consist of death in a second. Having a great life, in good health and good times and, POOF! You're gone before you know it.

Now let's look at stage #4. It's put a drain on the lobster's system, building as time goes on. At the point of stage #3, the lobster had one final chance to escape by molting into a new shell. Carrying fertilized eggs makes it almost impossible. You'll find most SD lobsters to be female and carrying eggs. The egg-bearing female is trapped within her own body and will protect her eggs until she dies.

The lesions have connected and have nowhere else to go. The bacteria has eaten all there is to eat of the shell. The lobster has a decreased energy, every day, to go about things that a lobster usually does. Day after day the lobster attempts to slog along, often finding that it no longer can flip its tail. It can barely support its own weight in water. The shell disease has completely fused the carapace joint to the tail. Resembling extreme arthritis in a very old person, this poor lobster was only 5 years old. At this point it could not molt; therefore, it is the walking dead.

I've caught several of these sad souls. At first I thought it was just another pile of goo to be cleaned out of the trap. On closer examination I found a lobster, still alive. It was unable to walk or move and the only thing that discerned it from the dead was its eyes. They looked at me as my hand moved above it, begging for death. How it was able to walk into the trap is beyond me. Nothing else moved.

As I picked it up, (it can only be described as "it",) the appendages all hung down, rotted and lifeless. The antennae that once inquisitively whipped their way around, lay listless, waiting to rot off. Its nose structure had slowly been eaten away by the bacteria and her entire face drooped. Barnacles were growing on what was left of a one time shiny, hard carapace, now paper-thin. The once clean and proud animal was now something barely recognizable. Yet, the eyes followed me, as those were the only things that weren't fused together. This lobster would only live a few more hours, which must have seemed like an eternity.

I gently laid the animal down on my bait board, its legs crumbled under it. The lobster was of legal size to keep or do as I please and I did so. It looked at me for a minute and I granted its last wish with one fell swoop of the knife. I returned the once proud creature to the ocean, right then and there.

They're a hearty species as you've already seen. They can take a kick in the pants and get back up there to fight another day. But, they are going to need a little respite to revitalize the stock in Long Island Sound and parts north to Buzzards Bay, Massachusetts and beyond. I've been to several informational lobster meetings throughout. They always end up in a shouting match between the lobstermen and the government presenter. Statistical numbers show a need for outright closure on lobstering. Lobstermen say that the statistics are skewed.

In my humble opinion, the American lobster, in one form or another, will be around long after we are gone. They were here 511 million years ago, found in limestone deposits in Shropshire, England, then preceding the Cambrian era. They may not look or act the same in coming days due to natural adaption, but they will survive. As a matter of fact, the lobster will probably be the last to go when the ocean dissolves and the sun goes supernova 5 billion years from now. That would be something, wouldn't it? All this conjecture and planning to have the last living thing on earth be a lobster.

NOOFIE

*A*s her mother dragged the little girl away from the store lobster tank, the big lobster watched her go out of sight. He lumbered back to his corner, swinging around sharply before tucking his antennae over his shoulders. The wide elastic claw-bands had been there for a while as they'd dug deeply into his shell. Smaller lobsters slowly marched atop him. Soon all that could be seen of him was his massive claw tips, now covered in smaller lobsters. He appeared to be stressed as he'd been in the tank for very long time. Lobsters can live for quite a while without food, but this one was at the end. He was apparently too big for the lobster-eating consumer with the old belief that "big lobsters are tough to chew." In reality, and lucky for him, that is a total fallacy.

I purchased that big male lobster and transported him home via a large marine cooler with oxygenated salt-water. He was immediately placed in one of my large salt-water environmental tanks at home. His claws, legs, and pleopods hung listlessly as I quickly transferred him. I've never been able to revive a lobster that was this far-gone, but I was determined to try. I gave this specimen a 100% rehabilitation effort using every trick known to me.

He responded well to heavy oxygenation and started eating within a week. Within a month, he was moving around the tank bottom and began "burrowing" into the substrate, a favorite pastime of lobsters. His claw bands indicated that he was from Newfoundland, and he was given the name of "Noofie." It was now late December and too cold for inshore boat release so Noofie hunkered in with us for the winter. As the tank water temps dipped to a chilly 38'ish degrees, he went into what appeared to be a hibernatic slowdown. In other words he slept a lot.

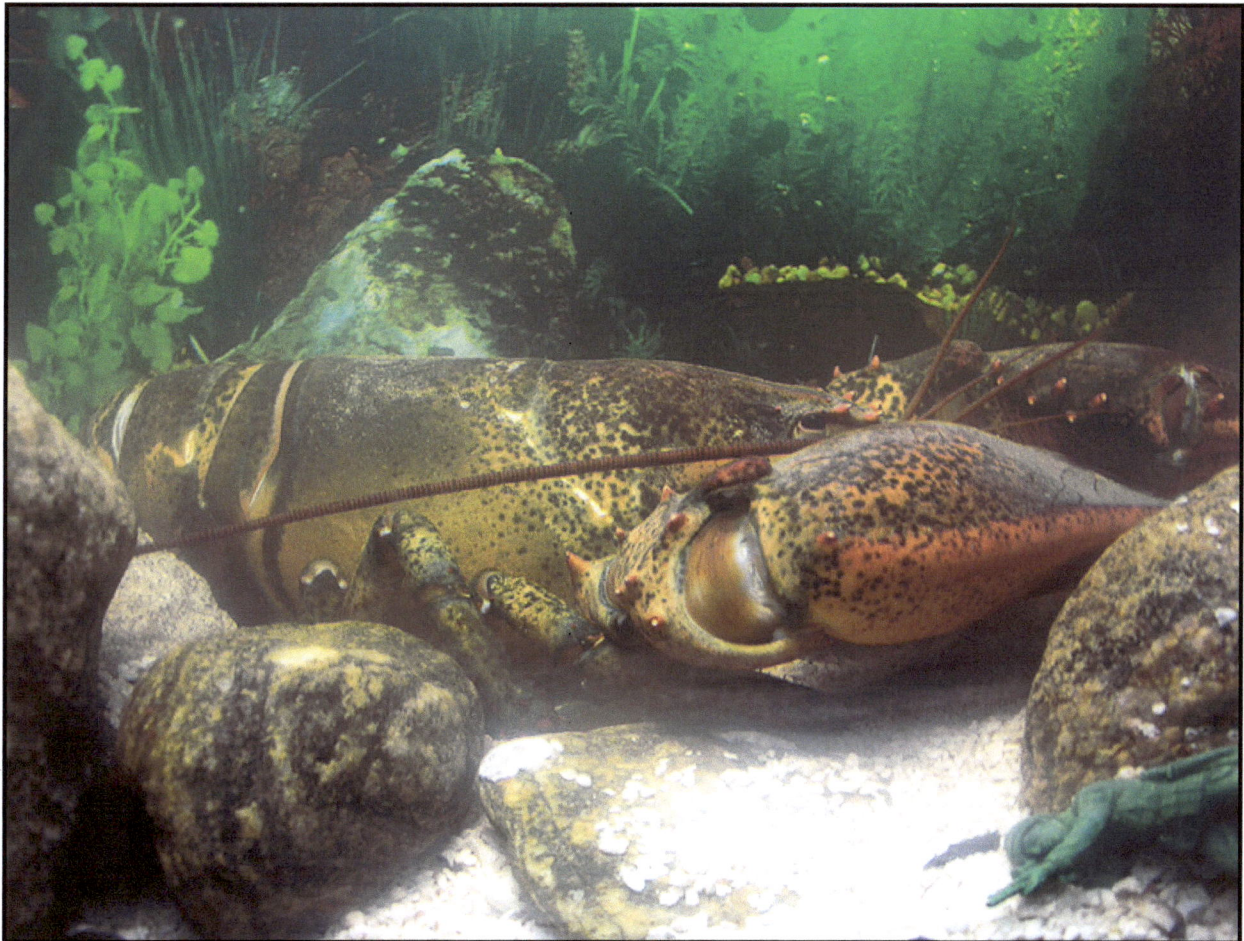

Note the green toy army soldier in the foreground. Lobsters quickly get bored in captivity and will destroy the filtration units, aeration hoses, etc., unless you give them something to play with. He loved marching that army-man around the tank bottom. He eventually crushed it into green pieces.

By January, 2010, he was fully rehabilitated and full of vigor. I reached in the tank to remove his claw bands, and he kicked up a storm of dust with his big tail. This was the first time he'd been touched by a human hand in several months. As I was trying to remove the last band, the water was very cloudy, and I felt a very light touch around my left wrist. I looked to see his massive crusher claw fully encircling my wrist up to the claw's hinge joint!

He was capable of and certainly could have crushed or severed my left hand completely off with no effort at all. Instead, Noofie allowed me to slowly pull my hand out and away from the water. It was a miracle. This has never happened to me in 50 years of handling lobsters. He looked at me from the tank bottom with his big pincher claw gaping wide and raised above his head. He said to me, in no uncertain terms, "Now, we are even. Don't touch me ever again or I won't be so kind." I thanked him and heeded his warning. I cautioned my family (who often fed him) to be extremely careful around Noofie. His pincher claw was *LIGHTNING QUICK,* faster than the eye could see. It made a metallic sounding *SNICK!* when it snapped shut. Amazingly, I've never seen a lobster with this type of claw response. This once fragile dying creature was no longer a toothless heel-hound. He was a fully charged, un-banded, highly dangerous, wild animal. This is how it should be. My job was almost done.

We made meticulous plans the days before his repatriation (release) in May 2010. I wanted the release to be perfect. This lobster was to have the absolute best chances of survival after his return to the sea. Noofie was given a "Last Supper" with humans, a large fresh quahog clam, his favorite. You don't want to feed them immediately before the release process as the post-digestion period makes them somewhat lethargic, almost mildly stressed.

We watched him devour the entire clam, and when he was done, he did something odd. Something that he never did after eating. He turned to face us through the tank glass, cocked his body around, and raised his big pincher claw up, as high as he could reach. It was as if he was giving us a last "salute" of thanks. Of course, he often used the tank temperature-meter as a punching bag, which also may have been the reason for this little display (see photo on previous page). We prefer to believe that it was his way of saying "Good bye, humans".

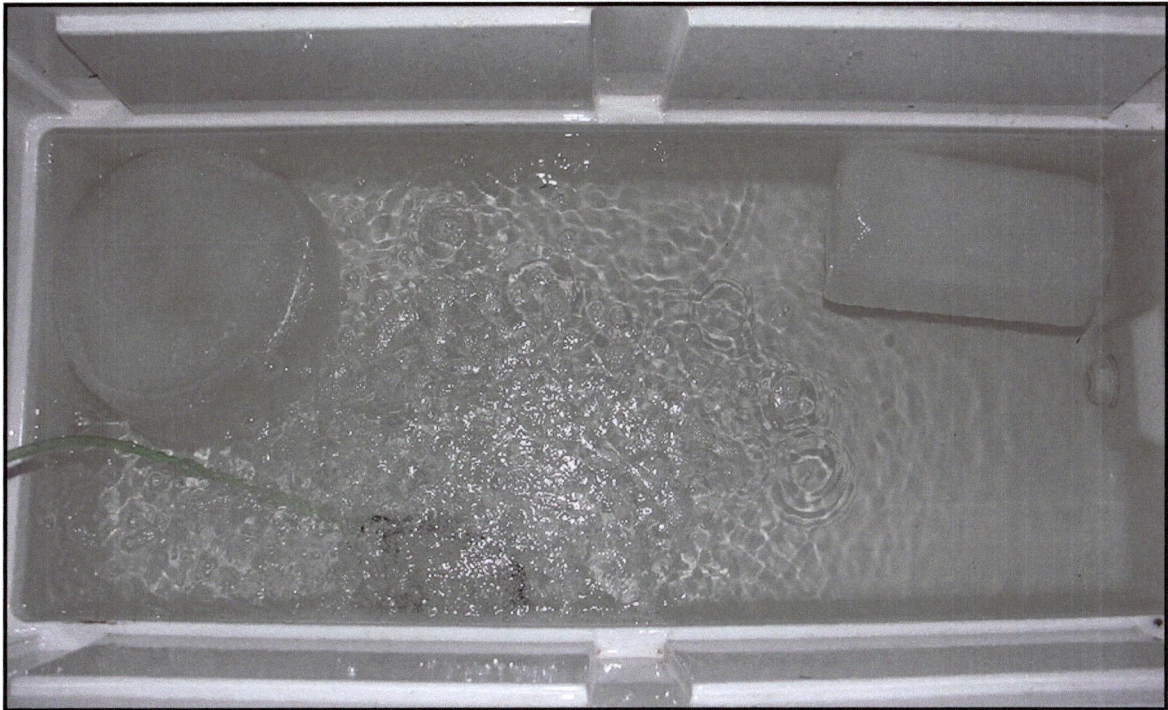

A large 100-qt. marine cooler was filled with fresh filtered seawater. Blocks of frozen ocean water were placed in the cooler to lower the water temp to 40~45° deg f, the optimal best temp for Homarus americanus. Most importantly, the water was hyper-oxygenated overnight with an aeration bubbler.

The transport cooler was secured in the front of my boat. I used large plastic bags crimped under the cooler lid to reduce some of the "slosh" movement when motoring out to the drop point in rough water. This decreases another point of "stress" in the release process.

Noofie saw the sun for the first time in nearly a year. He was scared at first, understandably. If you look at the photo at the left, you'll note his claws pinched shut, tail curled under, and both antennae pinned back over his shoulders. All are classic signs of fear and uncertainty in a lobster.

I chose a release point that is treacherous to boat traffic and SCUBA divers, a place that is strewn with jagged boulders and rip currents that would challenge the most seasoned diver. Getting in there was a real test of boat handling. I lost some paint on the trip in and out. The lobster I was about to release is far too big to be threatened by inshore fish or other lobsters. His crusher claw alone will not fit into the entry-ring of any standard inshore lobster trap, recreational or commercial fisheries of this entire region. If by some wild chance he is captured by SCUBA diver, it is illegal to bring him ashore as his carapace size is too large. Any such animal must be returned to the water.

I cautiously lifted him out of the cooler and slowly lowered him into the sea. I held his tail so it wouldn't "dry-clap" and injure himself. I prayed that his pair of lightning fast claws wouldn't leave me with a hospitalization parting gift. This was the 2nd time that a human hand had touched him in a year, and he'd already warned me about touching him.

By all odds and logical assessment, he will be the apex predator and unchallenged ruler of his new domain. This 35-year-old lobster will be returned to live a full and natural life, to fulfill his destiny. He will survive many, many years from now and die of natural causes.

The few I've told this have always asked me, "Why?" They say it doesn't matter; there are thousands in pens waiting to be eaten. My answer is in telling a story of a father and young daughter walking along the beach after a storm. There were countless starfish washed up on the sand about to die. The little girl picked one up. After a great deal of trouble, the girl managed to throw 1 starfish of thousands out into the surf. They walked along for a while holding hands. Finally, her father asked, "Why did you throw one starfish back? There are thousands of them. It doesn't matter to them?" The girl looked up at her father and said, "But it did matter, to him."

Slowly, surely, he stood on my supporting gloved hands. His antennae whipped up to touch my arms, one last time, and he stepped off me into the sea. I expected him to merely drop into the sea like a dead weight. Instead, he fell away a few inches, started snapping his massive tail, and literally flew away like a small torpedo, down, and out of sight into the deep green ocean. He's back home now; this is my gift to him.

It's an infraction to release Noofie, or any other "alien" fish into the waters. Now for the first time in my life, I violated a lobster law. I'd welcome a chance to tell a judge the story of this lobster, which lived. But I doubt they'll throw up any roadblocks trying to catch an old man like me for this one-time faux pas.

As for Noofie, I'm sure he hit the sea floor with his feet running. Later that night we celebrated this with a glass of wine. My wife commented, "God help the unwary SCUBA diver, or striped bass that swims past him," recalling his quick claws. Now, a few years later, I wonder what he's doing or if he still lives? There certainly have been no articles in the shoreline newspaper that a monstrous lobster has been caught. The likes of Noofie would have been cause for many news articles if he'd been taken.

I wonder how many girl friends he has had and how life is going for him? He's a giant in a world of peons that none can challenge. For one with the instincts to fight must sadden him having no one to spar with. Even a relatively large lobster for this area would only be the size of one of his claws. I can't help but wonder if in his brain, the little sack behind his eyes, he thinks about his time with humans? Perhaps it's all a fantasy for him. He lives the lobster life of Forest Gump, always thinking, "What's next?"

THE END OF A LOBSTER TALE..

*N*ow you know my story and a little bit about the American lobster. I don't expect you to have pity for the lobster or stop eating them. But I hope that the next time you have a lobster for dinner you'll look at the thing you're about to consume with several thoughts. Think about all the strange places that this animal has been in the 6 or 7 years from birth to your plate. Imagine what he's been through and the miraculous metamorphosis to get there.

Long Island Sound lobsters will never be taken anywhere near the numbers caught in the pre-1999 days. We are getting too good at taking them, technologically, and we will take as many as the law permits. The water temperatures are slowly climbing year after year. The onslaught of disease will eventually make its way around the corner of Buzzards Bay on its way north and there'll be hell to pay. There have been and always will be lobsters, they will adapt and survive. They're very good at this. But the price of a lobster will soon be far more than the mortal man or woman can afford. I hope I'm wrong, but it looks to be this way in the next couple thousand years or so.

And so if you don't, or can't eat lobster, stop in front of the lobster tank at your local grocery store. Pick out the biggest lobster there and watch him closely. Go over and tap your finger on the tank. As crazy at it may seem, whisper "hello" to him. If he finds you interesting enough, he may keep an eye on you. And if he thinks you're worth the effort, he just might strut from the herd and tap his antennae on the glass, and say, "Hello human."

Noofie & the author, May 10th, 2010

OTHER READINGS, REFERANCES & WEBSITES

Some references used in this book and readings about the American lobster can be found in such writings as the ones below. Any one of the following can lead you to a lifetime of research, or at the very least cause you to say, "Humph? I did not know that?" From here, the sky is the limit..

Lab 257, by Michael C. Carroll
Lobsters, by Martha E. H. Rustad
Lobster at Home, by Jasper White
The Lobster Coast, by Collin Woodard
The Lobster Chronicles, by Linda Greenlaw
The Great Lobster War, Ronald P. Formisano
The Secret Life of Lobsters, by Trevor Corson
Lobster: A Global History, by Elisabeth Townsend
I, Lobster: A Crustacean Odyssey, by Nancy Frazier
A Shore Diving Guide to New England, by Jerry Shine
Natural History of the American Lobster, by Francis H. Herrick
Biology of the Lobster: Homarus americanus, by Jan Robert Factor
How to Catch a Lobster in Down East Maine, by Christina LeMieux Orag
Red's Eats: World's Best Lobster Shack, by Virginia Wright & Debbie Cronk
Lobsters: Biology, Management, Aquaculture & Fisheries, by Bruce F. Phillips
Lobstering Off Cape Ann: A Lifetime Lobsterman Remembers, by Peter K. Prybot
Lobster Shacks: A Road Guide to New England's Best Lobster Joints, by Mike Urban
The North American Lobster in the Classroom, by George Smith, George Smith Publishing
CRC Handbook of Mariculture: Crustacean Aquaculture, Volume 1, edited by James P MacVey
The Florida Spiny Lobster: How to Catch It, Its Biology, a Crawfish Cookbook, by John Kappes
Connecticut Wildlife: Biodiversity, Natural History, and Conservation, by Geoffrey A. Hammerson
Robbing the Lobster Cradle, published New York Times, March 5th 2006, by Dr. Diane Cowan PhD
Transportation of Lobsters to California – 1874, by The Fisherman's Voice, July 2011 vol 16, number 7
United States Fish Commission, Volume XV for 1895, 54 Congress 1st Session, Harvard College Library
A Humane End for Lobsters, published by New Zealand Science Monthly, by Gregory, Neville, & Lowe
Biennial Report Secretary of State California July 1st 1877, Journal: Appendix.Vol 1 by Cal. Legislature
Guide to the aquarium of the Zoological station at Naples, by Stazione zoologica di Napoli, Princeton Univ
SHELL DISEASE IN LOBSTERS: A SYNTHESIS, by J. Stanley Cobb and Kathleen M. Castro May 2006
Homarid Lobster Hatcheries: Their History & Role in Research Management & Aquaculture, by F. Nicosia
The Providence & Rhode Island Cookbook: Big recipes from the smallest state, page 96. By Linda Beaulieu

And some very interesting stuff used in making this book can be found at these websites:

http://www.lobsters.org/
http://www.mainelobsterfestival.com/
http://penbay.org/cof/COF_1879_XVI.pdf
http://www.asmfc.org/americanLobster.htm
http://penbay.org/cof/cof_1873-1875_xiv.pdf
http://umaine.edu/lobsterinstitute/publications/
http://www.youtube.com/watch?v=E5tDe-XPWvo
https://www.facebook.com/#!/mainelobsterfestival
http://www.youtube.com/watch?v=0bHMQHssGMM
http://www.lobster.um.maine.edu/media/vol14_1188.pdf
http://www.ifoce.com/contests.php?action=detail&eventID=47
http://blog.mainefoodandlifestyle.com/2011/08/finalist-russ-james.html
http://news.nationalgeographic.com/news/2001/07/0719_crustacean.html
http://www.fishermensvoice.com/archives/0711TransportationOfLobstersToCalifornia1874.html
http://www.gloucestertimes.com/local/x645267450/Divers-vs-Lobstermen-Ongoing-feud-runs-deep
http://bangordailynews.com/2011/08/11/living/recipes/maine-lobster-festival-cooking-contest-winners-announced-recipes-shared/

ABOUT THE AUTHOR

Russ James lives at home with his wife and his only son, Adam. He is a retired policeman, where he worked as a sergeant for over 32 years. Among his accomplishments are that he holds a 2nd degree black belt in Japanese style karate, a PADI certified SCUBA diver, and a licensed airplane pilot. He also became well known in the field of combat handgunnery. Using all of these skills he was the first officer in his department to teach defensive tactics, a police search & rescue diver, an aerial photographer, weapons armorer and firearms instructor.

Early on in his police career, he accepted an over-time position as the "Animal Control" officer. This proved to be the most challenging of all. With the help of his wife, they managed to place countless unwanted pets in homes of need. Most friends and neighbors were reluctant to open their doors. But once they got in, an unwanted pet and sometimes two, became a family member.

Competing around the world in countries such as Venezuela, Australia, and South Africa, in the mid 1980's he scored among the top competitors in the shooting field of IPSC (International Practical Shooting Confederation). He was designated to be the United States Team Captain among an All-Star list of shooting notables in the USPSA (United States Practical Shooting Confederation). Some of those included Rob Leatham, Doug Koenig, and Jerry Barnhardt, and Mike Plaxco, all National & World Champions. **http://www.vtxpress.com/instructor.htm**

His wife, Ms. Deborah James, and he were married in 1978. They became friends in 1974, when they first fell in love with the undersea world, and each other. Ms. James went on to become a champion in her own right. She captured four USPSA/IPSC National Championship titles in a row. Along the way she also won two World IPSC Championship titles. She retired in 1992 a champion, never losing a match. She is a retired teacher and keeps busy in the yard, plays tennis, and golfs with friends.

Russ is an NRA instructor who teaches that, "Shooting can be fun". He currently competes in the sport of *"Cowboy Action Shooting"* and spends most of his time at the cabin with family and friends. He goes to the seashore and fishes now and again, but does not keep his catch. He no longer SCUBA dives or traps lobsters.

A SPECIAL THANKS...

     Finishing this book is another check-off on my bucket list of life's things to do. Thinking back on the people, places, and things that made life so rewarding to me, and they are many, two people stick out loud and clear. My personal thanks to Maureen Wilhelm. A special person, who carefully read my manuscript from end to end and corrected my punctuation meticulously. Without her oversight this project would be nothing more than a memory.

     Lastly, is a person who is best described as my "brother from another mother." He is the kind of person that you grew up with, fought with, and mostly laughed with all of your life together. The things that were funny in 6th grade remain funny to this very day. From discovering lobsters as children, to the day he drove my 16-foot open boat, trying to pick up lobster traps in a hurricane, he remains my one true friend. It goes without saying "thanks" to Clarence "Beany" Macomber.

Clarence "Beany" Macomber

Maureen Wilhelm (left)

www.ingramcontent.com/pod-product-compliance
Lightning Source LLC
Chambersburg PA
CBHW060812270326
41929CB00002B/13